Philosophy
of
Religion

Philosophy
of
Religion

Julius R. Weinberg
Keith E. Yandell
University of Wisconsin

Problems In Philosophical Inquiry
Volume IV

HOLT, RINEHART AND WINSTON, INC.
New York   Chicago   San Francisco   Atlanta
Dallas   Montreal   Toronto   London   Sydney

For
ILSE
and
SHARON

Library of Congress Catalog Card Number: 73–148058

SBN: 03–085665–5

Printed in the United States of America

1 2 3 4   0 3 8   9 8 7 6 5 4 3 2 1

This volume is Part IV of the four-part volume
Problems in Philosophical Inquiry

Preface

In planning Problems in Philosophical Inquiry, our desire was to gather a representative collection of essays, each complete in itself, which would provide the beginning student with a fair sampling of the problems, solutions, and techniques of argument and appraisal with which philosophers have been concerned for more than two millennia. The essays are arranged into sections, each deals with one central issue, most are arranged so that an essay presents a solution to a problem and is then criticized by the essay or essays that follow. The introductions trace the thread of one argument through the essays they introduce, and thus make no pretense of raising all the issues that the essays themselves raise.

It is perhaps easier to "do" philosophy than to define it. The same probably holds for science and (if we replace "do" by "believe") for religion. Rather than attempt a general definition of philosophy, which might produce a feeling of edification but not much actual illumination, it undoubtedly will be more helpful at the introductory level to discuss the philosophy of religion as one of the fields of philosophy, noting the problems dealt with in that field and clarifying why these are problems for which people have sought solutions in the past and present.

What relation has Jerusalem (religious faith) to Athens (philosophical inquiry)? The answers have varied. Some philosophical systems are also ways of salvation. This is true of Plato's and Spinoza's answers. Other philosophical frameworks provided their originators with a way to reinterpret radically (or was it contradict?) religion, as did Kant's or Hegel's. But relationship by competition or reinterpretation is not the most frequent manner in which philosophy and religion have had concourse.

Philosophers who were themselves religious believers have, not surprisingly, used the tools of philosophical argument and reflection to support their beliefs. In particular, arguments offered for the existence of God and the immortality of the human soul were most often regarded as having premises which could be known independent of divine revelation, either because they were self-evident or because they were evident to the senses. There is no necessity that an argument for the existence of God should follow this format, but in fact most have done so. It should not be thought that all religious believers accepted these arguments. The monk Gaunilon was not much impressed, for example, with Anselm's argument, and many believers—both among the ordinary and among the intellectually gifted—do not suppose that any argument has succeeded in establishing the divine existence.

Philosophers who were themselves unbelievers have, also not surprisingly, used the tools of philosophical argument and reflection to support their unbelief. It is fair to say that the problem of evil—the issue of whether one can both consistently and reasonably believe in an all-powerful, all-good creative Providence while accepting the fact that evil exists—has been the greatest source of tension for believers in the Judeo-Christian tradition and of polemics against faith for critics of that tradition. More recently, though very much with roots in past philosophy, the practice of arguing that religious beliefs are in fact not *beliefs* at all, but at most *feelings,* has gained wide approval among both philosophers and theologians. The argument is that religious language is unintelligible or meaningless in the way that "triangles devour elephants" is unintelligible or meaningless. But meaningless language cannot express beliefs. The core of the charge of meaninglessness is that religious language cannot provide sentences which possess truth value (are *either* true *or* false). Religious belief cannot, the charge is, attain even to the dignity of falsehood. It may serve to express one's own emotions, such as "Ouch" does, or to elicit the emotions of others; but religious beliefs cannot be true or false either. In any case, the verification principle—roughly, the thesis that a sentence is meaningful only if it is either true or false by definition or if there is some conceivable empirical, sensory observation which would render it false—has fallen into disrepute of late. Its major defect, it would seem, is expressed in the title of a journal article: "Indirectly Verifiable: Everything or Nothing."

We have noted some of the uses that have been made of philosophical arguments to establish religious beliefs and others to refute religious beliefs. Until recently, the fashion was to eschew offering proofs of God's existence but to discuss the issue of meaningfulness or lack thereof. Recently, new versions of the proof have been offered and with the demise of the verification principle there seems to be a bit less discussion of meaningfulness, though neither issue is likely to cease to concern philosophers of religion. But it is time to note that another sort of concourse between philosophy and religion is possible. While it, too, may fall short of complete neutrality, it offers an important alternative or supplement to those mentioned.

Such terms as *conceptual clarification, analysis of meaning* (use), *the unpacking of concepts, the "logic" of a concept or proposition* have been heard frequently in the past few decades. They reflect the use of philosophical techniques to understand more clearly what is being said by a particular religious community, scientific hypothesis or theory, metaphysical system, and so on. It was Augustine's and Anselm's view that one should believe in order to understand. The consensus of opinion by one school of philosophy may be summarized by saying that by the careful study of the interrelationships between concepts within a religious tradition one can understand what that tradition maintains, whether one believes it or not. The same sort of descriptive pose is taken by those phenomenologists who purport to discern the structure of religious experience by techniques somewhat different from those used by more analytical philosophers. It is thus possible that philosophy can clarify and illuminate religious beliefs for those who have them or are interested in them. But it is easy for description to become evaluation and analysis to become appraisal, and for these to shade off into one another at various points.

It is sometimes supposed that religious belief is somehow trivialized by talk about "religious language." (Not that there is "religious language" in the sense that there is a French language; what is meant is the use to which a religious community puts language.) It is also sometimes supposed that the problems philosophers of religion now deal with and the techniques they use are different in kind from those they considered and used before the so-called revolution in philosophy. These views seem to reinforce one another, so that if one believes that philosophers are not dealing as of old with religion, it may also be supposed that they have trivialized religion too. No doubt one can find cases which give point to these suspicions, but the student should read carefully in both the traditional and contemporary sources to see if continuity is not at least as evident as discontinuity, if concern for religious truth (the truth of one's religious beliefs) is not as evident in many contemporaries as was the case in the past. Then he must make up his own mind.

Madison, Wisconsin
January 1971

K. E. Y.

Contents

Philosophy
of
Religion

he philosophy of religion consists in the attempt to answer certain questions. Among these questions are the following: (1) Can it be proved that God exists, or proved that He does not? (2) Are "God exists" and "There is evil" logically incompatible in the sense that anyone who holds that both statements are true contradicts himself? (3) Do we directly experience God so that we know that He exists not by inferring that He does but by encountering Him? (4) Does man survive his death? (5) Are such claims as "God loves us" meaningful at all—that is, do they succeed in communicating something either true or false, as opposed to being simply and only a way of expressing our own feelings or evoking feelings in others? Selections elaborating these questions are included here.

There are, of course, still other questions that are relevant to the philosophy of religion: How, if at all, are religion and morality related? Is there an essence of religion—a core of belief, acceptance of which is essential to every religion? Does religious experience provide any evidence of the truth of religious belief? And there are others as well.

The approach to these questions, insofar as it is purely philosophical, will appeal to reasons and arguments that do not depend on the authority of a divine revelation. Traditionally theology has been concerned with the explication and systematization of the statements contained in a sacred text. A philosopher, as philosopher, has no such text. He is allowed appeal only to what he can defend as true, on some other ground than that the claim in question was revealed by God, or to what hopefully is so clearly true as not to need defense. Issues concerning logical consistency, proof, evidence, and intelligibility or meaningfulness loom large here as elsewhere in philosophy. The role of such issues in attempts to answer questions in the philosophy of religion is illustrated rather fully in the essays that follow.

K. E. Y.

Can the Existence of God Be Proved?

The Ontological Argument

*I*f *the denial* of a statement is contradictory, clearly the statement being denied is necessarily true. If "God does not exist" is contradictory, "God exists" is necessarily true.

St. Anselm endeavored to show that by reflecting on the meaning of the word "God," we can see that the statement "God exists" is true in just this way. His argument can be stated in this manner. The word "God" means "the being than whom no greater can be conceived." So "God exists" is identical to "The being than whom no greater can be conceived exists." Now suppose someone denies that there is such a being. He will be maintaining that this statement is true: "The being than whom no greater can be conceived does not exist." But anyone who maintains that the being than whom no greater can be conceived does not exist cannot be right. For suppose that no such being exists. The man who denies that God exists understands what the phrase "the being than whom no greater can be conceived" means, for he denies that there is any such being. Let us say, then, that when one understands what such a phrase as "the being than whom no greater, etc." means, that being exists in his understanding. Roughly, this means that he has an *idea* of this being, where an idea is conceived as a mental phenomenon. Let us say that a being exists "in reality" if it exists independently of whether anyone has an idea of it or not. Now, Anselm asserts, to exist in the understanding *and* in reality is greater than to exist in the understanding alone. If we suppose that the being than whom no greater can be conceived exists in the understanding alone, then we can in fact conceive of a greater being—one existing *both* in the understanding and in reality. So if we take (1) the being than whom no greater can be conceived does not exist (in reality) as true, we admit that (2) the being than whom no greater can be conceived exists (only) in the understanding. Since (3) it is greater to exist both in understanding and reality than to exist in the understanding alone, it follows that (4) a being can be conceived which is greater than the being than whom no greater can be conceived—namely, a being like the one described in (2) but one that exists also in reality. But (4) is contradictory. Since (1), (2), and (3) entail (4), at least one of these statements must be false. Since (2) is entailed by (1)—plus the claim that what we understand exists in the understanding—we can eliminate (2) and consider only (1) and (3). But (3) is obviously true. So (1) must be false. Hence a being than whom no greater can be conceived exists (in reality).

Put this way, Anselm's argument relies on two crucial doctrines in addition to his analysis of the word "God." These doctrines are:

(1′) When one understands the word "God," there exists something in his understanding (some mental phenomenon) in virtue of which he understands that word.

(3) To exist in the understanding and reality is greater than to exist in the understanding alone.

It is (1′) that Gregory of Rimini attacks, making these two criticisms. First, consider the phrase "the round square." We understand the phrase well enough to know that it does not, and cannot, designate any actual entity (anything which exists "in reality"). But any idea adequate to this phrase would also have to be both round and square—which is impossible. The point is not that an idea must be both round and square, for ideas are not extended entities. The point is rather that if an idea *I* is to represent an object *O*, *I* must correspond to *O*. But no idea could correspond to an entity whose description is contradictory, as ideas represent only what *can be*. So (1′) is not, as it stands, true. What concerns Gregory is how we can be sure that (1′) is true. We can be sure that (1′) is true if we can discover some general and true, principle from which (1′) follows. One such principle might be: (P_1) When one understands *any* word, there is something in his understanding (some mental phenomenon) in virtue of which he understands that word. And presumably this "something" must be such that the word in question applies to it. But there is *nothing* to which "the round square" does, or could, apply. But all that this shows is that some *other* principle than (P_1) must be used to justify (1′).

Here is such a principle: (P_2) Whenever one understands a word *W*, where it is logically possible that there is something to which W applies, there is something in his understanding (some mental phenomenon) in virtue of which he understands what W means (and, presumably, to which W applies).

Here, however, Gregory's second criticism is relevant. Consider the phrase "the number one higher than that number ever specifically thought of by any human being." Suppose the highest number that anyone has ever specifically thought of is four trillion. Then two things become evident. First, the phrase *does* designate; it designates what "four trillion and one" designates. Second, since no one has thought of this number, there is nothing (no mental phenomenon) to which this phrase applies in virtue of which one understands that phrase. So this principle (P_2) is false. So we have no reason to accept $(1')$ or (3) and hence no reason to accept Anselm's argument.

Some philosophers have suggested that we read Anselm in a quite different way. Anselm, it is suggested, was wrong to put his insights in terms of an *argument*. Accepting the view expressed in $(1')$, Nicholas Malebranche argued that since God is infinite, He cannot be represented by any idea, because any idea is finite. Since we know what the word "God" means, and since $(1')$ is true, we must be directly aware of God Himself. We do not *infer* that God exists, but rather we *encounter* Him. It looks, however, as if we *infer* that we encounter Him, and our confidence concerning the truth of this conclusion depends on the premises from which it is inferred. Among these premises, in addition to $(1')$, are these: (P_3) If an idea I represents a being B, then idea I must contain as much ideal reality (that is, capacity to represent reality external to our minds) as the being has nonideal reality, and (P_4) no idea can have an infinite amount of ideal reality. Such premises are enormously hard to state clearly enough to make appraisal of them possible.

Among the philosophers who believe that Anselm's argument misleadingly states a genuine insight, not all have held to premises such as $(1')$, (P_3) and (P_4). Rather, in the case of W. E. Hocking, the claim is made that in becoming aware of our own limitations and finitude, we also become aware of a being without limitation and so infinite. But while Hocking does not appeal to $(1')$, (P_3) or (P_4), it is quite plain that he has his own system of claims, in terms of which he interprets his experience. He thus illustrates nicely that an appeal to religious experience is also an appeal to a particular way of interpreting one's experience and is not merely a report of one's experience in purely descriptive and indisputable terms.

It Is Self-Contradictory to Deny That God Exists

ANSELM

*L*ord, who gives understanding to faith give to me as much as you deem suitable, that I may understand that You are as we believe You to be, and that

You are what we believe You to be. Now we believe that You are something than which nothing greater can be thought. But perhaps there is no such

FROM: *Prosologian,* Chapters 2 and 3; J. R. Weinberg, trans. (originally published c. 1077).

nature since 'the fool hath said in his heart: There is no God?' But surely this very same fool, when he hears what I say: 'something than which nothing greater can be thought,' understands what he hears, and what he understands is in his mind, even if he does not understand that it exists. For it is one thing for a thing to be in the mind, but something else to understand that a thing exists. For when a painter pre-thinks what is about to be made, he has it in mind but he does not yet understand that it exists because he has not yet made it. But when he has already painted it, he both has it in his mind and also understands that it exists because he has already made it. Hence, even the fool is convinced that something exists in the mind than which nothing greater can be thought, because when he hears this he understands and whatever is understood is in the mind. But surely that than which a greater cannot be thought cannot exist merely in the mind. For if it exists merely in the mind, it can be thought to exist also in reality which is greater. So if that than which a greater cannot be thought exists merely in the mind, that very same thing than which a greater cannot be thought is something than which a greater can be thought. But surely this cannot be. Hence, without doubt, something than which a greater cannot be thought exists both in the mind and in reality.

Indeed, it exists so truly that it cannot be thought not to be. For something can be thought to exist which cannot be thought not to exist, which is greater than what can be thought not to exist. So, if that than which a greater cannot be thought can be thought not to exist, that very thing than which a greater cannot be thought, is not that than which a greater cannot be thought; which is impossible. So there exists so truly something than which a greater cannot be thought that it cannot be thought not to exist.

You are that very thing, Lord our God.

A Critique of Anselm
GREGORY OF RIMINI

When it is argued: "By following natural reason it must be stated that there is really something than which a greater cannot be thought, hence something of infinite intensive power must be posited," I reply that the antecedent can be understood in two different ways. First, the word "greater" can be understood to precede the phrase "can be thought," second, it can be understood to come after the phrase "can be thought." That the second clearly differs from the first is obvious from an example. Let us suppose that it is impossible for there to be an ant bigger than an elephant. Then "no ant bigger than an elephant can be thought" is true, because its denial "some ant bigger than an elephant can be thought" is false. For there is no true singular statement from "Some ant bigger than an elephant can be thought." Indeed, any singular statement of the kind is false because it has a false implication on the point of the subject,[1] whether an existing or merely imagined ant is indicated. Nevertheless, if "bigger" is put after "can be thought," as in "no ant can be thought [to be] greater than an elephant," the statement

[1] I.e., that there is an ant bigger than an elephant.

FROM: *Questions on the First Book of the Sentences* Distinctions 42–44, ed. of 1522, folio. 70ff.; J. R. Weinberg, trans.

is false, because there is nothing to prevent anyone from supposing that some or any ant is bigger than an elephant.[2]

So if the antecedent of the main argument is taken in the first way, then Aristotle or anyone else who maintains that something perfect exists which is not an infinitely powerful being could concede that antecedent, and yet deny what is supposed to follow from it. For he could say that ". . . a greater than anything of finite power can be thought" is false, although he could allow that "something can be thought to be greater than anything of finite power" but the implication [that something greater than anything of finite power exists] would not be proved thereby.

When he [Anselm] says that something than which a greater cannot be thought is in the intellect, but not merely in the intellect but also in reality, it is clear that if it is to serve for a proof, the word "greater" must be understood to come after "can be thought." And

[2] Thus "some ant is bigger than an elephant" can be thought as true. This will, of course, be a false thought, but that false thoughts occur is certainly the case.

taken in this sense, the antecedent could be denied.

Thus "the expression 'what does not exist' exists, so what does not exist exists" is an invalid implication, for here the antecedent is true, but the consequent implies a contradiction if its subject-term stands for an object.

For, just as it does not follow from "The expression 'what cannot be thought' can be thought," that "what cannot be thought can be thought," (since anyone hearing me say "what cannot be thought" thinks what he hears and what he thinks is thought, but the consequent implies a contradiction if its subject-term is taken to stand for an object), so also, anyone hearing the expression "a greater than that than which a greater cannot be thought" understands what he hears, yet it is not valid to infer from "the expression 'a greater than that than which a greater cannot be thought' is understood" that "a greater than that than which a greater can be thought is understood." For the antecedent of this inference is true, but the consequent is false, if its subject-term is taken to stand for an object even according to Anselm.

A Brief Comment on Gregory's Critique
J. R. WEINBERG

Gregory of Rimini's critique of the argument of Anselm is almost unique in medieval philosophical criticism. Instead of directly challenging the assumption that there is no proper concept of God on the basis of an Aristotelian theory of the sensory origin of all concepts, Gregory asks whether the assumption "If I understand a statement, something exists in my mind [that] corresponds to the grammatical subject of the statement" is generally correct. It had been assumed (for example by Aristotle and Augustine) that there are verbal elements of consciousness to which the subject-terms of sentences refer. That there are and must be exceptions to such a generalization is the point made in the selection just offered. Perhaps a modern example will make the point clearer.

It can be proved that there is no prime number whose square root equals the quotient of two integers. The proof follows: Suppose there is a prime number p whose square root equals m/n, that is, $\sqrt{p} = m/n$.

$$\text{Then } p = m^2/n^2 \text{ , or}$$
$$n^2p = m^2.$$

Now it is known that (1) every whole number has a unique set of primes as its ultimate factors, and (2) the square of any whole number will contain an even number of prime factors. Hence m^2 and n^2 each have an even number of prime factors. But pn^2 has an odd number of prime factors. So $pn^2=m^2$ is a self-contradictory formula. Hence our supposition "There is a prime number p whose square root equals m/n" is also logically false, and its denial, "There is no prime number whose square root equals m/n," is logically true. But this means that, although we understood the statement "There is a prime number whose square root equals the quotient m/n," nothing in or outside of consciousness could possibly correspond to the subject "prime whose square root equals m/n." That is, we can understand the sentence as a whole without supposing that there is anything in the mind to which the grammatical subject refers.

Hence Anselm has not established his main initial point, namely, that if I understand the expression "that than which nothing greater can be thought exists," there must be something in my mind that corresponds to "that than which nothing greater can be thought." Gregory's several examples bring out this point very nicely.

We Can Be Directly Aware of God
NICHOLAS MALEBRANCHE

THE EXISTENCE OF GOD
WE SEE ALL THINGS IN GOD,
AND NOTHING FINITE IS CAPABLE
OF REPRESENTING HIM—
THUS IT IS SUFFICIENT TO THINK
OF HIM TO KNOW THAT HE EXISTS.

THEODORE. Well, Aristes, what do you think of that intelligible world into which I led you yesterday? Does it still startle your imagination? Does your mind advance firmly and steadily in the land of meditative spirits, in this region inaccessible to those who listen only to their senses?

ARISTES. What a beautiful spectacle is this archetype of the universe, Theodore! I have been contemplating it with much satisfaction. What an agreeable surprise it is for the soul to find itself without suffering death transported into this land of truth, where it discovers an abundance of nourishment. I am not yet, it is true, accustomed to this celestial manna, to this nourishment which is all spiritual. At certain moments it seems quite hollow and slight. But when I partake of it with proper attention I find so much savour and solidity therein that I can no longer think of feeding with the brutes in a material world.

THEODORE. Oh, my dear Aristes, what are you telling me? Are you speaking seriously?

ARISTES. Quite seriously. I wish no

FROM: *Dialogues on Metaphysics and on Religion*, Dialogue Two, Morris Ginsberg (London: George Allen & Unwin, Ltd., 1921), pp. 86–98. Reprinted by permission of George Allen & Unwin, Ltd. Originally published in 1688.

longer to listen to my senses. I wish always to enter into the innermost core of my being and to live on the abundance which I find there. My senses are adapted for leading my body to the ordinary pastures. I am willing that it should follow them. But that I should follow them, I myself! That I shall never do again. I wish to follow Reason alone, and to step by the aid of my attention into the land of truth, where I may find delicious repasts, repasts which alone are fit nourishment for intelligent beings.

THEODORE. You have, then, surely forgotten that you have a body. But you will not be long without thinking of it, or rather without thinking with reference to it. This body which you neglect now will force you soon to obtain food for it and to occupy yourself with its wants. For as yet the mind cannot free itself so readily from matter. Yet now that your mind is firm, tell me, pray, what you have discovered in this land of ideas. Do you understand, now, what this Reason is, of which we speak in the material and terrestrial world and of which we know so little? I promised you yesterday to lead you beyond all created things to the very presence of the Creator. Have you not flown there by yourself and without thinking of Theodore?

ARISTES. I confess I did think that, without lacking in the respect which I owe to you, I could go myself along the road which you had shown me. I have followed it, and I have, it seems to me, recognised clearly what you told me yesterday, namely, that the universal Reason is eternal and that it has its being in God alone. I will indicate the steps of the argument in a few words. Judge, then, and tell me if I have gone astray.

After you left me I remained for some time in hesitation and suspense. But, driven by a secret enthusiasm, I seemed to be saying to myself, I do not know how: "Reason belongs to me in common with Theodore; why then can I not consult it and follow it?" and it has led me, unless I am mistaken, up to Him who possesses it as His own, and by the necessity of His being; for it seems

to lead there quite naturally. Here, then, is the argument in simple and non-figurative language:

Infinite intelligible extension is not a modification of my mind. It is immutable, eternal, necessary. I cannot doubt its reality or immensity. But nothing that is immutable, eternal, necessary, and, above all, infinite is a created thing, nor can it belong to a created thing. Hence it belongs to the Creator and can be only in God. Hence there is a God, and a Reason, a God in whom there is the archetype which I contemplate of the created world which I inhabit—a God in whom there is that Reason which illumines me by means of the purely intellectual ideas which it furnishes in abundance to my mind and to the minds of all men. For I am sure that all men are united with the same Reason as I am, and since I am certain that they see or can see what I see when I enter into myself and when I discover therein the truth or necessary relations which are contained in the intelligible substance of the universal Reason which dwells in me, or rather in which all intelligences dwell.

THEODORE. You have not been led astray, my dear Aristes. You have followed reason, and it has led you to Him who engendered it out of His own substance and who possesses it throughout all eternity. But do not imagine that it has disclosed to you the nature of that supreme Being to whom it has led you. When you contemplate intelligible extension you only see as yet the archetype of the material world which we inhabit and that of an infinity of other possible worlds. You do in truth see the divine Substance, for it alone is visible, it alone can illumine the mind. Yet you do not see it in itself or as it really is. You only see it in its relation to material creations, you only see it so far as they participate in it, or in so far as it is representative of them. Consequently it is not, strictly speaking, God Himself that you see, but only the matter which He can produce.

You certainly see, by means of the infinite intelligible extension, *that* God is. For He alone can possess all that you see, since nothing finite can contain an infinite reality. But you do not see *what* God is. For there is no limit to the Divine perfections, and that which you see when you think of immense spaces is lacking in an infinity of perfections. I say "that which you see," not the substance which represents to you what you see. For this substance, which you do not see in itself, has infinite perfections.

Assuredly, the substance which contains this intelligible extension is all-powerful. It is infinitely wise. It includes an infinity of perfections and realities. It includes, for example, an infinity of intelligible numbers. But the intelligible extension has nothing in common with all these things. There is no wisdom, power or unity in all this extension which you contemplate. For you know that all numbers are commensurable among themselves, since they have unity for a common measure. If, then, the parts of extension divided and subdivided by the mind can be reduced to unity, they will always be commensurable amongst themselves by this unity, which as you know is certainly not the case. Thus the divine Substance in that simplicity to which we cannot attain contains an infinity of quite different intelligible perfections by means of which God illumines us without allowing Himself to be seen as He is, or in His individual and absolute reality, but merely in His reality which is general and relative to possible created beings. Nevertheless, try to follow me. I will try to lead you as near as possible to the Divine.

The infinite intelligible extension is only the archetype of an infinity of possible worlds similar to our own. By means of it I only see certain determinate beings—material things. When I think of this extension I do not see the divine Substance, except in so far as it is representative of bodies and is participated in by them. But now, when I think of Being, and not of determinate beings, when I think of *the* Infinite, and not of such and such an infinite, it is certain,

in the first place, that I do not see such a vast reality in the modifications of my mind. For if I cannot find in these modifications sufficient reality to enable me to represent to myself an infinity in extension, a fortiori I cannot find in it sufficient reality for representing to myself what is infinite in every way. Thus, it is only God, the Infinite, the Unlimited, it is only the Infinite infinitely infinite who can comprise the infinitely infinite reality which I see when I think of Being, and not of such and such beings or of such and such infinities.

In the second place, it is certain that the idea of Being, of reality, of unlimited perfection, or of the infinite in every way, is not the divine substance in so far as it is representative of such and such a created thing or is participated in by such and such a created thing. For every created thing is necessarily a definite being. It is a contradiction that God should make or create a Being in general or one Infinite in every way which should not be God Himself, or should not be equal to His own principle. The Son or the Holy Spirit do not merely share in the divine Being. They receive Him in His entirety, or, to speak of things more within the reach of our minds, it is clear that our idea of a circle in general is only the idea of intelligible extension in so far as it represents a certain circle or is shared in by a certain circle. For the idea of a circle in general, or of the essence of a circle, represents infinite circles, is adapted to infinite circles. This idea comprises the idea of the infinite. For to think of a circle in general is to think of an infinite number of circles as a single circle. I do not know whether you follow what I wish to make you understand. Here it is in two words. The idea of Being without restrictions, of the infinite, of the general, is not the idea of created things, or of the essences of created things, but the idea which represents the Divine or the essence of the Divine. All particular beings participate in Being, but no particular being can equal it. Being comprises all things, but all beings created or possible, in all their manifold variety, cannot exhaust the immense extension of Being.

ARISTES. It seems to me, I can see your meaning. You define God as He defined Himself in speaking to Moses, "God is that which is."[1] Intelligible extension is the idea or archetype of bodies. But the being without restrictions, in a word, Being, is the idea of God; it is that which represents Him to our minds as we see Him in this life.

THEODORE. Very good. But above all you must note that God or the Infinite is not visible by an idea representative of Him. The Infinite is its own idea. It has no Archetype. It can be known, but it cannot be constructed. Only created things, only determinate beings, can be constructed, or can be visible through ideas which represent them even before they are produced. We can see a circle, a house, a sun, though they may not actually exist. For all that is finite can be seen in the Infinite, which comprises all intelligible ideas of the finite. The Infinite, on the other hand, can be seen only in itself, for nothing finite can represent the Infinite. If we think of God, it follows that He exists. A finite being, though known, may not exist. We can see its essence without its existence, its idea without itself. But we cannot see the essence of the Infinite without its existence, or the idea of Being without Being. For Being can have no idea representative of it. There is no archetype which could comprise all its intelligible reality. The Infinite is its own archetype, and contains within itself the archetype of all beings.

Thus, you see that the proposition, "there is a God," is in itself the clearest of all existential propositions, and that it is even as certain as the proposition, "I think, therefore I am." You see, moreover, what is meant by God, for God, Being, and the Infinite, are one and the same.

But, once more, make no mistake about this matter. You see only con-

fusedly and as from a distance what God is. You do not see Him as He is, because, though you see the Infinite or Being without restriction, you only see it in a very imperfect manner. You do not see it as a single being. You see a multiplicity of created things in the infinity of uncreated Being, but you do not see its unity distinctly. For you cannot see it so much in its absolute reality as in the reality which attaches to it in its relation to possible created things, the number of which it could increase indefinitely without their ever equalling the reality which represents them. You see it as the universal Reason which illumines all intelligences according to the measure of light necessary for their guidance, and for revealing as much of His perfections as can be shared in by limited beings. But you do not discover the property which is essential to the Infinite, that, namely, of being at the same time one and many; composed, so to speak, of an infinity of different perfections, and yet so simple that in it each perfection comprises all the others without any real distinction.[2]

God does not communicate His substance to any of His creatures; He only communicates to them His perfections; not as they are in His substance, but in so far as His substance is representative of them, and in accordance with the limitations bound up with the nature of created things. Intelligible extension, for instance, represents bodies; it is their archetype or their idea. But, although this extension occupies no place, bodies are and must be locally extended because of the limitations essential to all finite created things, and because no finite created thing can have this property or character, incomprehensible to the human mind, of being at the same time one thing and all things, of being at the same time perfectly simple and yet in possession of all sorts of perfections.

Thus, intelligible extension represents infinite spaces, but it does not fill

[1] Exod. iii. 14.

[2] Cf. *Première lettre touchant la Défense de M. Arnauld*, Note 18.

any; and although it fills, so to speak, all minds and discloses itself to them, it follows in no way that our mind is spatial. If our mind could only see infinite spaces through local conjunction with locally extended spaces, then, in order to see infinite spaces, it would itself have to be infinitely extended.[3]

The divine Substance is everywhere, without being extended locally. It has no limits. It is not contained in the universe. But it is not this Substance as expanded everywhere that we see when we think of spaces. For were this the case our mind, being finite, would never be able to think of infinite spaces.[4] Yet the intelligible extension, which we see in the divine Substance which comprises it, is this Substance only in so far as it is representative of material beings and participated in by them. This is all I can tell you. But observe, that this Being without restriction, or the Infinite in every way which we think of, is not merely the divine Substance in so far as it is representative of all possible beings; for, though we have no detailed ideas of all these beings, we are yet assured that they cannot equal or exhaust the intelligible reality of the Infinite. In a sense, then, it is the divine Substance of God that we see. But in this life we only see it in a way so confused and distant, that we see rather *that* it is than *what* it is; we see rather that it is the source and archetype of all being than its own nature or its perfections in themselves.

ARISTES. Is there not a contradiction in what you are saying? If nothing finite can have enough reality to represent the Infinite (and this appears evident), does it not necessarily follow that we see the divine Substance in itself?

THEODORE. I do not deny that we see the divine Substance in itself. We see it in itself in this sense that we do not see it through any finite thing representing it. But we do *not* see it in itself in the sense that we can reach its simplicity or discover its perfections.

[3] *Ibid.*, second and eleven following notes.

[4] *Ibid.*, and Dialogue VIII.

Since you agree that nothing finite can represent the Infinite, it is clear that if you see the Infinite you can only see it in itself. But it is certain that you do see it; for otherwise when you ask me whether there is a God or an Infinite Being, you would be asking a ridiculous question, by means of a proposition the terms of which you do not understand. It would be just as if you were to ask me whether there is a Blictri,[5] that is to say, a particular thing without knowing what thing.

Assuredly, all men have the idea of God or are thinking of the Infinite when they ask whether He exists. But they believe they could think of Him though He did not really exist, for they do not realise that nothing finite can represent Him. As they can think of several things which do not exist because created things can be seen though they do not exist, since they are not seen in themselves, but in the ideas which represent them, they imagine that it is the same in the case of the Infinite, and that He could be thought of though He does not exist. This is the reason which makes them seek, without recognising Him whom they encounter at all moments, and whom they would recognise soon enough if they entered into themselves and reflected on their ideas.

ARISTES. You convince me, Theodore, but there still remains some doubt. It seems to me that the idea which I have of Being in general or of the Infinite is an idea of my own workmanship. It seems to me that the mind can make general ideas out of several particular ideas. When one has seen several trees, an apple-tree, a pear-tree, a plum-tree, etc., one gets the general idea of a tree. In the same way, when one has seen several beings, one forms the general idea of Being. Hence this general idea of Being is only a confused assemblage of all the others. Thus I have been taught and thus I have always understood the matter.

THEODORE. Your mind, Aristes, is

[5] A nonsense word.

a marvellous worker. It can extract the Infinite from the finite, the idea of Being without restriction from the ideas of particular beings. Perhaps it finds in the wealth of its own supply sufficient reality to give to finite ideas that which they want in order to be infinite. I do not know whether this is what you have been taught, but I believe I do know that you have never comprehended it.

ARISTES. If our ideas were infinite, assuredly they would not be products of our work nor modifications of our mind. That cannot be disputed. But perhaps they are finite, though through them we can think of the Infinite. Or perhaps the Infinite which we see is not really infinite. It may be, as I have just said, a confused conglomeration of several finite things. The general idea of Being is perhaps only a confused mass of particular beings. I have some difficulty in ridding my mind of this thought.

THEODORE. Yes, Aristes, our ideas are finite, if by our ideas you understand our perceptions or the modifications of our minds. But if you understand by the idea of the Infinite that which the mind sees when it thinks of it, or that which is then the immediate object of the mind, assuredly that is infinite, for it is seen as such. Note, I say it is seen as such. The impression which the Infinite makes on the mind is finite. There is even more perception in the mind, and the idea makes a greater impression, in a word, there is more thought, when we know a small object clearly and distinctly, than when we think confusedly of a big object or even of the Infinite. But, though the mind is nearly always more affected, penetrated, modified by a finite idea than by an infinite one, there is nevertheless more reality in the infinite idea than in the finite one, more reality in Being without restriction than in any finite being you could mention.

You cannot rid your mind of the thought that general ideas are no more than a confused collection of certain particular ideas, or at least of the thought that you have the power to form them

out of this collective whole. Let us see how much truth and how much falsehood there is in this thought for which you show so strong a bias. You think, Aristes, now of a circle with a diameter of one foot, then of one whose diameter is two feet, three feet, four feet, etc., and finally you do not determine the length of the diameter at all, and you think of a circle in general. The idea of this circle in general, you would say, is the confused collection of the circles of which you have thought. This conclusion is certainly false. For the idea of a circle in general represents infinite circles and is applicable to them all, and you have only thought of a finite number of circles. What happens must rather be that you have discovered the secret of forming the idea of a circle in general out of five or six circles that you have seen, and this is true in one sense and false in another. It is false if you mean that there is enough reality in the idea of five or six circles to form the idea of a circle in general. But it is true in the sense that after having recognised that the magnitude of the circles does not change their properties, you have perhaps ceased to consider them one after another as having a determinate magnitude in order to consider in general only an indeterminate magnitude. Thus you have, so to speak, formed the idea of a circle in general by spreading the idea of generality over the confused ideas of the circles which you have imagined. Yet I submit to you that you can form general ideas at all only because you find in the idea of Infinity enough reality to give generality to your ideas. You can think of an indeterminate diameter only because you see the infinite in extension and because you can increase or diminish it *ad infinitum*. I submit to you that you could never think of the abstract forms of genera and species, if the idea of the Infinite which is inseparable from your mind did not naturally become united with the particular idea of which you are aware. You could think of a definite circle, but not of a circle in general. You could become aware of a certain definite equality between radii but not of a general equality between indeterminate radii.

The reason is that no finite and determinate idea can ever represent anything infinite or indeterminate. The mind, however, without any reflection adds to its finite ideas the idea of generality which it finds in the Infinite. For just as the mind spreads over the idea of a definite extension, though it be divisible *ad infinitum,* the idea of indivisible unity, so it spreads over certain particular ideas the general idea of perfect equality. And it is this which leads the mind into an infinite number of errors. For all the falsity of our ideas has its source in the fact that we confuse them one with another and further with our own mental modifications. But of this we shall speak on another occasion.

ARISTES. What you say is all very well, Theodore. But, are you not looking upon ideas as entirely distinct from our perceptions? It seems to me that the idea of a circle in general is only a confused perception of several circles of varied size, in other words, a collection of diverse, rather indistinct mental modifications, each of which is the idea or the perception of a certain circle.

THEODORE. Yes, without doubt,[6] I think there is a good deal of difference between our ideas and our perceptions, between ourselves who are aware and that of which we are aware. For I know that the finite cannot find within itself that whereby to represent the Infinite. I know that I do not possess within myself any intelligible reality, and that so far from finding in my own substance the idea of all things I cannot even find therein the idea of my own being. For I am entirely unintelligible to myself, and I can never see what I am except when it pleases God to disclose to me the idea or archetype of minds which is comprised in the universal Reason. But of this we shall speak on another occasion.[7]

[6] Cf. *Réponse au livre des Vraies et des Fausses Idées.*

[7] Cf. *Recherche,* Bk. III, Pt. II, Ch. VII.

Assuredly, Aristes, if your ideas were only modifications of your mind, the confused collection of thousands upon thousands of ideas would only yield a confused complex, incapable of any generality. Take twenty colours, mix them together so as to excite in you a sensation of a colour in general. At the same time produce within yourself several different feelings or sensations so as to form a sensation or feeling in general. You will soon see that this is impossible. For in mixing diverse colours you turn green, grey, blue into what is after all always some particular colour. Dizziness is but a confused agglomeration of sensations or modifications of the soul; yet it is after all a particular feeling or sensation. This is so because every modification of a particular being and of our mind cannot but be particular. It can never rise to the generality which ideas possess. It is true you can think of pain in general, but your mind could never be modified except by a particular pain. And if you can think of pain in general, it is because you can add generality to all things. But, now, you could not obtain this idea of generality from the resources of your own mind. It has too much reality. It follows, therefore, that the Infinite Mind must furnish you with it out of its own abundance.

ARISTES. I have nothing to say in reply. All that you are telling me seems to be evident, but I am surprised that these general ideas, which have infinitely more reality than particular ideas, should affect or touch me less than these latter, and should appear to me to have much less solidity.

THEODORE. That is so because they make themselves felt in a less degree, or rather because they do not make themselves felt at all. Do not judge, Aristes, of the reality of ideas in the way children judge of the reality of bodies. Children think that the space between the earth and the sky is not real because it does not make itself felt. And there are few people who discern that there is just as much matter in a cubic foot of air as in a cubic foot of lead, because lead is harder, heavier, in a word, more capable of affecting the senses than air. Do not follow their example. Judge the reality of ideas not by the feelings which you have of them, which indicate their action upon you in a confused manner, but by the light of intelligence which reveals their nature to you. Otherwise you will think that the ideas which are sensed and those which affect you, as, for example, the idea which you have of the floor which you press with your foot, have more reality than the purely intelligible ideas, though at bottom there is no difference.

ARISTES. No *difference*, Theodore? Do you mean to assert that the idea of extension of which I think is not different from the idea of the extension which I see, which I press with my foot, which offers resistance?

THEODORE. No, Aristes, there are not two kinds of extension, nor two kinds of ideas representative of them. And if this extension of which you think were to touch you or to modify your soul affectively, intelligible though it be, it would appear to you sensible. It would appear to you hard, cold, coloured, and perhaps painful, for you would perhaps attribute to it all the feelings which you would have. Once more, we must not judge of things by the feelings which we have of them. We must not think that ice has more reality than water because it exhibits a greater resistance.

If you believed that fire had more force or efficiency than earth, your mistake would have some justification. For there is some reason for judging of the magnitude of forces by that of their effects. But to believe that the idea of extension which affects you through some feeling is of another nature, or has more reality, than the extension of which you think, without having a sensible impression of it, is to take the absolute for the relative, or to judge of the nature of things as they are in themselves

through the relation in which they stand to us. Along that line we should ascribe more reality to the point of a thorn than to all the rest of the universe, or even to the infinite Being. When you get accustomed to distinguishing your feelings from your ideas, you will recognise that the same idea of extension can be known, imagined, felt, according to the various ways in which the divine Substance which comprises it applies it to your mind. Do not believe then that the Infinite, or Being in general, has less reality than the idea of a definite object which is affecting you at the moment in a very vivid and sensible fashion. Judge of things by the ideas which represent them, and do not attribute to them anything that resembles the feelings that affect you. Later you will understand more clearly what at present I am merely indicating in outline.

ARISTES. All that you have just told me, Theodore, is fearfully abstract, and I have difficulty in keeping a firm hold upon it. My mind is strangely overstrained; a little repose, if you please. I must think over all these great and sublime truths at my leisure. I will endeavour to make myself familiar with them by the difficult effort of pure attention. But at present I am not capable of such an effort. I must have rest in order to recoup my strength.

THEODORE. I knew quite well, Aristes that you could not keep your mind clear for long. Go, lead your body to the pasture ground. Refresh your imagination with a variety of reassuring and pleasing things. But try nevertheless to retain some taste for truth, and as soon as you feel yourself capable of nourishing yourself with it and of meditating upon it, leave all else for its sake. Forget even what you are as much as possible. Your needs must attend to the wants of the body, but it is a great mistake to occupy yourself with its pleasures.

The Ontological Argument Reinterpreted
WILLIAM HOCKING

Nature appears to men as their most general bond of community. Nature also appears as existence *par excellence*. When we lose sight of God, Nature becomes our standard of reality. If we have a God we should like to make his existence as sure as *that!* Hence it is that most attempts at proof of God have begun with Nature, and have tried to make his existence secure by showing him in some valid connection with this world, such as that of cause to the world as effect. God as cause of the world would be real even as the world is real. The so-called cosmological argument follows this line of connection, and finds that the world has a single conscious cause, itself uncaused, who is God.

If we wish to be assured that this cause is not only a voluntary cause but a benevolent one as well, we make a premise of the *good* which as experienced in the world is our natural type of goodness; and we find that the intender of this is good even as the result is good.

But by these means we do not find God. If we could prove a first and conscious cause, still we could prove only such cause as is equivalent to his effect; we could prove only such goodness as is equivalent to this mixture of goodness and evil that we here find. A very limited Being would this be, a God who is only as great as his world, only as good, and finally *only as real.*

By such ways we can only reach a being in whom the qualities of experience are refunded, without change or heightening. But in such case, we may as well believe in the world as we find it; and proceed with our work of mastering it, without reference to God.

Such proofs are not wholly true to the spirit of religion; for historically men have lifted their minds to God rather because the world is unsatisfactory, than because it satisfies. We wish a God who is greater than the world, also better than the world as found, and also more real.

And such more perfect being is what these proofs have in spirit sought: for in referring the world to a conscious Will, they have meant to imply that Will is greater than Nature; and in making the world dependent upon a divine Purpose they have intended to show that the Good is more real than the evil, and will vindicate itself. But clearly no such results can be gained by taking Nature as a standard and moving toward God by relations of causality or purpose: these relations can rise no higher than their source. It is the denial of that assumed starting-point that is the intellectual heart of religion.

On the other hand, we cannot dispense with the world as a point of beginning for the reasons given. What other way, then, can be found of relating this world to God? Follow the history of religion. Observe the Mind dissatisfied with its world. Note the criticism which it makes of Nature, as less than self-sufficient, less than all-good, less than real. And note that of a sudden it has claimed to possess the self-sufficient, the good, the real. What has occurred to the mind of man?

It may seem as though that with which man had been criticizing his experience, namely, his idea of a better and more real, had in a moment taken on objective shape to him. His dissatisfaction with his world has implied a conception of a world not thus defective, and this conception has been set up as sub-

FROM: *The Meaning of God in Human Experience*, William Hocking. (New Haven, Conn.: Yale University Press, 1912), pp. 304–316. Reprinted by permission of Yale University Press.

stantial fact, in his idea of God. He has turned his idea into a reality; or he has instinctively assigned a reality to his idea, yet without blurring the features of his actual world. It is *some leap from idea to reality* that constitutes the essential historic movement of the mind to God.

Now it is just this leap from idea to reality that distinguishes an ancient proof of God's existence; a proof which has become known as the "ontological argument," the argument which assigns a real or ontological value to an idea. I have an idea of God: therefore God exists.

In general, the circumstance that I have an idea of an object is the emptiest of reasons for supposing that object to exist. Whatever force such reasoning can have must depend on some peculiarities of the idea of God, not found in ideas or ideals generally. It must be shown, as we tried to show of the idea of Other Mind, that this idea has something unique about it which forbids the supposition that it is a "mere idea." This, with various degrees of success, have the thinkers who resort to the ontological argument—from Augustine and Anselm to Hegel and Royce—tried to do. It is always with some incredulity that we meet the assertion that any idea of ours carries with it its own guarantee of reality. Yet this same ontological argument is the only one which is wholly faithful to the history, the anthropology, of religion. It is the only proof of God.

Although an idea which should carry on its face an assurance of reality must have something unique about it, we are not without analogies which may help to interpret this extraordinary type of argument. The idea of God is not the only one of our ideas which seems to convey an assurance of objectivity. My idea of *space*, for example, I incline to regard as real. Of my idea of *causality*, I can hardly think that it is an idea only, a form of relating events without an objective counterpart. So also with the beauty of things, or their goodness; I know that these are ideas of mine,

and yet as I regard these qualities valid for other viewers of the same objects, I attribute these qualities to the objects. Instinctively also we project beyond ourselves, or repudiate in some way as not our own, whatever in idea is new, whatever is sublime and holy, whatever is obligatory, whatever strikes me with a consciousness of my self as a lesser thing. Even self-consciousness seems to come, at times, as a revelation from beyond myself. It is not without precedent, then, that an idea should convey with itself some apparent title to reality: it is not impossible that some idea, as perchance the idea of God, should be able to make this title good.

Let us examine this movement of thought more nearly. Nature must early have appeared to man as somewhat less than real—else those early speculations with regard to a creator or maker would hardly have occurred to him. At the root of all these awkward conceptions regarding clay-shaping or egg-laying or spewing or magic-word-pronouncing deities lies an uneasy persuasion that the things of physical existence are subject to something; and to something of the quality of human spirit. If Nature ever wore to early man that aspect which seems primary to us—the aspect of *self-sufficiency*, it must have gone hand in hand with a quite contrary aspect—that of being *illusory*, also possible to us, though with some effort.

We may find that illusory aspect by such considerations as these: The appearance of self-sufficiency belongs not more to Nature as a whole than to each thing in Nature. By that same view which shows us Nature as *there* in its own right, is also each thing there in its own right. But with regard to the several things in Nature we know that this appearance is not true. The apparent self-sufficiency of single things if real would make the World an aggregate in which every thing went its own way without regard to another: self-sufficiency of the parts is equivalent to *accidentality*. Each thing is in reality infinitely dependent on all the rest. But with the banishment of self-sufficiency in the parts, there is no retaining of it in the Whole: there is nothing in which this infinite dependence of part on part comes to rest, unless I conceive the whole thing as *dependent on my Self*, dream-fashion,—deriving its reality, so to speak, from the center outward, rather than from inaccessible infinitely distant world-borders and beginnings inward. The world is real I now say simply *as my experience*—a not-unheard-of point of view. The self-sufficient world of Nature has suddenly become an *illusion*.

Yet I cannot rest here; because I know that I am not the source of the reality of Nature. True, if I am not real, nothing is real: something in my conception of reality starts from me; and all my objects become real, as by infection from that. But true it is, likewise, that unless Nature is real, nothing is real: something in my conception of reality is borne in upon me from beyond. I am real, in part, by virtue of what is not-myself. The real must partake of the qualities of myself and of Nature; and must be other than either.

Through this experience of cognitive restlessness (or "dialectic") early man, to whom the illusory side of Nature was more familiar probably than to us, may have passed in his own readier way; he finds as his resting place the real as Creative Spirit. Nature settles into its third stage of regard: it is neither self-sufficient nor illusory; it has *derivative reality*. As over against me, it is real; as over against the Creative Spirit, it is not real. But how is this conception hit upon? May it be that this thought of Nature as dependent on Spirit is some quick embodiment of an elusive but genuine experience? This idea of a creator does indeed quickly float away from any experience it may have sprung from; becoming promptly materialized and set in the sky as part of the world-created—removed from that World, yet all too much involved in it. Yet may it be that *this idea* is one which must have reality?

Must it not be so? For one thing I cannot by any means escape: namely,

that reality itself is present to me in experience; and all of this process of judging this and that thing to be unreal or less than real is made possible simply by the grasp of that reality which at any moment I have. My negations are made possible by my one secure position; and as my hold on reality is variable, so my ability to see through the various pretenders-to-reality to reality itself will vary. Nature can only appear to me as illusory in some moment of unusual clearness of perception; for ordinarily the pretence of nature to be self-sufficient is a harmless and even useful simplification of my view. So if my own existence is recognized by me in some moment as partial and dependent existence, that recognition is a moment of "illumination," which the relation of my self to what is beyond my self becomes presently distinct: and in grasping this relation, I am catching some fleeting glimpse of the *terms* between which the relation exists. I am experiencing that which is beyond myself in no wise differently than in that moment I am experiencing myself: and my judgment of dependence is made possible by a positive and present knowledge of that upon which I depend.

If, then, I discover that my world of nature and self, taken severally or together, falls short of reality, this discovery is due to what I know of reality —not abstractly, but in experience. If I judge this system of nature-and-self to be non-self-sufficient, it is by a knowledge of the self-sufficient; if I condemn, it is by virtue of something in my possession not subject to condemnation; if I criticize and correct, it is by comparison with or reference to some present object not subject to criticism and correction. When I perceive myself in this curious relation to the world of physical facts— superior and not superior, creative and unable to create—that play of unrest is due to, and is defining, a simultaneous perception of the object to which this unrest does not apply. The positive content which I give to that absolute object is a report of experience; whatever idea I make of it is an idea derived nowhere but from that experience. If I am able to frame a tenable conception of nature in dependence upon a creative spirit not myself, that conception is true; for my idea can set me outside of nature only as in experience I have already broken away from the spell of the natural world. In whatever sense, then, I am able to conceive nature as dependent upon spirit, in that sense nature is dependent upon spirit. This idea carries its reality with it.

It is impossible that my idea should be a "mere" idea, for it is only possible for me to take this standpoint, external to nature and myself, in idea in so far as I do at the same time take it in experience also. And that this experience of a more valid reality than that of nature is truly described as an experience of other mind, we have in our previous chapter sufficiently dwelt upon. The ontological argument may be regarded as a logical epitome of what we there, in our own independent research, came upon. The ontological argument, in its true form, is a report of experience.

If we wished, in briefest compass, to state the antithesis between the ontological argument and other arguments for the existence of a God, we might put the situation thus:

These other arguments reason that *because the world is God is.* The ontological argument reasons that *because the world is not, God is.* It is not from the world as a stable premise that we can proceed to God as a conclusion: it is rather when the world ceases to satisfy us as a premise, and appears as a conclusion from something more substantial, that we find God—proceeding then from the world as a conclusion to God as a premise. We have no other premise to begin with: no proof of God can be deductive. It is because neither my world nor myself can serve as a foundation for thought and action that I must grope for a deeper foundation. And what I learn in this groping is, that my consciousness of those defects will reveal, though in faintest degree, the positive object which is free therefrom. It is because we cannot infer from nature to

God along causal or other natural lines, and only because of this, that the idea of God implies existence.

It is not every historical form of the ontological argument that has expressed this experience: and not every form of it appears to me valid. It does not seem to me that any abstract idea of an "all-perfect being" must necessarily be real. Nor does it seem to me that we are justified in inferring from any idea to its reality unless that reality can be present to the idea in experience. No form of the argument can be valid which finds God at the level of thought only, and not at the level of sensation. We are only justified in attributing reality to an idea if reality is already present in the discovery of the idea. When in our search for reality we fix attention upon Nature, it is because we already know that whatever reality is, it cannot be out of connection with that world of Nature-experience: and when we judge Nature unreal, it is only as we discover at the same time in concrete way how Nature is related to the Real. I can infer from that idea by which I criticize Nature to the reality of that idea only because I know Nature (and Self) to contain some characters of reality that cannot be omitted, or left behind. My real must already be given, in order that my idea may be found real. The true idea of God is not one which can leave out either Nature or myself; if my idea of God is real, it is real in experience. Hence I have preferred to state the argument not thus: I have an idea of God, therefore God exists. But rather thus: I have an idea of God, therefore I have an experience of God.

Reality can only be proved by the ontological argument; and conversely, the ontological argument can only be applied to reality. But in so far as reality dwells in Self, or Other Mind, or Nature, an ontological argument may be stated in proof of their existence. Thus, the Cartesian certitude may with greater validity be put into this form:

I think myself, therefore I exist; or
I have an idea of Self, Self exists.

For in thinking myself I find myself in experience and thus in living relation to that reality which experience presents. So may it be with Nature:

I have an idea of physical Nature, Nature exists.

That is, in whatever sense I conceive Nature, in that sense physical nature is real. Idealism has wavered much in its judgment regarding the reality of Nature, and of "material substance." (It has said that we have no idea of matter; and again it has said that matter does not exist, which implies that we have an idea of it.) Some meaning, however, we do attribute to the word matter; and without enquiring what that definable meaning may be, we may say in advance that whatever idea is framable corresponds to reality as experienced. We need not fear that this realism of Nature will detach Nature from God; though if we could think it so detached it would doubtless so exist. For of independence also, in whatever sense I can think the independence of beings, in that sense independence obtains between them. That which is most independent of me, namely the Other Mind, has been the first object of our ontological findings. The object of certain knowledge has this threefold structure, Self, Nature, and Other Mind; and God, the appropriate object of ontological proof, includes these three.

And is not, after all, this same ancient ontological argument the great and timely necessity for man in all his thinking? That which permanently threatens all our thinking is the damning commentary, "mere thought"—our own commentary on our own work, especially upon our own religion. Escape from illusion is what we require, whether in dealing with God or man or nature; escape from phantasmal intercourse, from subjective prisons from whose walls words and prayers rebound without outer effect. *Idea* we must have if we think; but an adequate realism for our idea we must also have. We shall never be too fully assured that our idea has reached beyond ourself, and has its ground in that which is not ourself.

Any reflection that can infallibly break the walls of the Self, opens up at once an infinite World-field. Set a second to my One, and I have given all the numbers. A single point outside the circle of "*Bewusstseins-immanenz*," and I am free to open myself to all reality and to all men. It is this point that the ontological argument aims to put into our possession; the reflection which this argument embodies is the only, and wholly simple, defence against our besetting subjectivity. "Bethink thyself of the ground whereon thou standest. *By what idea* hast thou judged thy thought to be illusion, and mere subjectivity? Is it not by an idea of something wholly actual and immediate? Is not that Reality thy own present possession?"

This present actuality of experience, "pure experience," finds me in living relation with that which is most utterly not-myself. Here, in the immediate, is my absolute escape from immediacy. Here in the given present is my escape from myself, my window opening upon infinity, my exit into God. Religion thus becomes the concrete bond between men; for he who has consciously found his way to God, has found his way to man also.

Thus it is that idea may give back the reality of which idea is forever robbing us; for while idea is the greatest enemy of the actual, it is only through idea that idea can be held firmly to its compelling and controlling object, the real as found in experience.

the existing God can found in our experience.

The
Cosmological
and Teleological
Arguments

S *t. Thomas Aquinas* believed that there are true statements—statements
that it would be altogether unreasonable to doubt—which rationally justify
the belief that God exists. Thus he offered "Five Ways" of proving that God
exists. Each of these arguments is intended to prove something different about
God. Other considerations were taken to show that the five conclusions were
indeed true of *one* being, not five different beings. The first argument can be
put in this fashion: (1) Some things are in motion; (2) nothing can move
itself; (3) there cannot be an infinite series of things moved by other things.
So (4) there must be a First Mover.

Several points must be made in order to understand this argument. First,
being "in motion" is simply to *change*, not only in place but in any other way.
Second, (1) is intended to be "evident to the senses." But (1), in the sense
intended by Aquinas, can be true only if something persists or remains the
same throughout perceived alterations. Critics have made it clear that this
claim involves an analysis of perceptual experience and is no mere report

of what is open to sensory observation. Third, there is a subproof for (2). Aquinas is not denying that one can, on one's own, walk across the room or wave one's hand. His claim is made somewhat clearer by the defense he offers of (2). Let *X* and *Y* be things capable of changing, and let *Q* be any quality. Aquinas argues: (2a) To move is to go from potentiality to actuality with respect to some quality—or, conversely, from actuality to potentiality (a thing is an actuality with respect to a quality *Q* if it has *Q*, and in potentiality with respect to *Q* if it could have *Q* but does not have *Q*). (2b) *X* can move *Y* from potentiality to actuality with respect to a quality *Q* only if *X* has *Q*. (2c) In order for *X* to change itself with respect to *Q*, *X* would have to *have Q*. (2d) In order for *X* to change itself with respect to *Q*, *X* would have to be able to *become Q*, and so *not* have *Q*. Hence (2e) in order for *X* to change itself with respect to any quality *Q*, *X* must at the same time both have and not have *Q*. But since this is impossible, *X* cannot change itself with respect to any quality. The crucial premise in this subproof is (2b). Many changes occur that *seem* to be counterexamples to (2b). Paint that turns a board red when applied to it must itself be red, but must a steak that satisfies my hunger have its own hunger satisfied (whatever that might be like)? I may cause surprise in someone by giving him an unexpected present, but I and my present need not have the feeling of surprise in order to cause it in the recipient. If (2b) does not apply to such cases, *why* not? And if it does, perhaps things can—contrary to (2)—change (move) themselves. Or if these cases (and many others) are not really counterexamples to (2b), this has to be shown; and it is not easy to see how this will be done. In reaction to such problems, the scope of (2) is sometimes restricted to coming into existence and ceasing to exist. Restating the argument with this restriction on (2)—and also on (3)—is left as an exercise for the interested reader.

Fourth, premise (3) requires some comment. Aquinas admits that it is in no way impossible that there has been an infinite past series of causes and effects. His denial that the world has always existed is based upon his belief that the book of *Genesis* denies this, not on any philosophical argument. How, then, can he hold (3) to be true? Because it is not a *past* infinite series that he has in mind. Basically Aquinas' view is this: In order for us to have an adequate explanation at any given time *T* that a contingent being (that is, a being that *could* fail to exist) exists at *T*, there must exist a necessary being (that is, a being that could *not* fail to exist) which also exists at *T*. Whether at *T* only two beings or a billion beings exist, *one* necessary being must exist at *T* or there is no sufficient explanation of the fact that something rather than nothing exists at *T*. And since this is true of *any* time you please, it is true at *all* times. Thus Aquinas' point is not that there must have been a temporally first member of a temporal series going back a while into the past. It is that if *right now* something exists that *could* fail to exist now, there must be something existing that could *not* fail to exist (now or any other time). And this undercuts the criticism that even if Aquinas proved that there was a First Cause, this would not prove that this First Cause still exists.

Finally, there is also a subproof for (3). It goes like this: (3a) If everything is moved by something other than itself, then there is no First Mover; (3b) if there is no First Mover, there is no subsequent mover; (3c) if there is no subsequent mover, there is no motion now; but (3d) there is motion now, so (3e) there are subsequent movers; hence (3f) there must be a First Mover. Premise (3b), however, is ambiguous. If a "subsequent mover" is simply "a mover that follows the First Mover," (3b) is true by definition, but we are left quite uninformed as to why (3c) is true. One could not, on pain of begging the question, appeal to (3) in defending (3c), for (3c) is supposedly going to provide some support for (3).

Or "subsequent mover" can be defined simply as "a mover that follows some other mover (whether First or not)." Then (3b) is not true by definition, so we must ask why it is to be accepted. On this reading, it says that nothing can move unless there is a First Mover. Why? Well, there would seem to be only one reason—that an infinite series of beings, all of which are moved by something else, is impossible. But once again this is (3), and whereas (3b) was supposed to provide support for (3), it looks as if (3) is needed if we are to have any basis for asserting (3b). The subproof, then, seems singularly unhelpful.

Substantially similar remarks can, I believe, be made about the Second Way. The Third Way, then, goes as follows: (1) There are contingent beings (that is, things that *do* exist but that could have failed to exist); (2) whatever is contingent will at some time cease to exist; (3) if everything is contingent, then at some time nothing will exist; (4) if at some past time nothing existed, since nothing can come into existence save through something that exists, there would be nothing existing now; (5) since something exists now, it is false that there was a past time when nothing existed; so (6) it is also false that everything that exists is contingent; that is, some being is necessary (noncontingent).

Once again, the argument requires interpretation due to the compressed form in which it appears. There is an obvious gap between premises (3) and (4). The time mentioned in (3) is not specified to be past; it might just as well be future. Now Aquinas is here allowing (for the sake of argument) that past time may indeed be infinite. If past time *were* infinite, then every possible occurrence would have occurred. One such possibility, if everything is contingent, is that nothing existed at some past time. And then (4) fits nicely into place. On the other hand, if past time is viewed as finite, there is no clear connection between (3) and (4).

There is evidently an inference in Aquinas' reasoning from (2) to (3); he reasons that since every contingent thing can cease to exist, at some time no contingent things will exist. The inference is plainly fallacious. (2) is analogous to (2′) every swan will die; and (3) is analogous to (3′) at some time no swan will exist. But so long as new swans are born, there will continue to be swans; (2′) does not by itself entail (3′). Nor does (2) by itself entail (3). Further, it is hardly clear that (2) is true; that something (say, the moon) *can* cease to exist does not entail that it *will* cease to exist.

In spite of the apparent temporal reference of its premises, the argument can be read in an atemporal manner. Part at any rate of the thesis of the Third Way would seem to be this: that a contingent being exists at time T (no matter whether T is past, present, or future) entails that a noncontingent being (a necessary being) exists. Otherwise there could be no contingent beings at all. In his critique of this kind of argumentation, David Hume focuses his attention on the concepts of contingency and necessity and the theses to which Aquinas appeals which make use of these notions. C. J. Ducasse, a contemporary philosopher, criticizes this argument and the first two arguments as well.

Hume's powerful critique is briefly stated. His challenge can be summarized in this manner: (a) to claim a being is *necessary* is to claim that something exists whose nonexistence is not conceivable; but "whatever we conceive as existent, we can conceive as nonexistent"; (b) waiving (a), if there is a necessary being, why can't it simply be the universe? (c) if a series of events is genuinely conceived as infinite (toward the past), then *necessarily* it has no first cause; (d) the *whole* series cannot be said to have a cause that the members taken singly do not have—to explain the existence of a causal series is not to explain the existence of its members and *also* to explain the existence of the series itself. I think that (a) is best conceived as offering this challenge: the clearest notion of necessity that we have is "logically necessary," but no being is necessary in this sense, for that would mean that its nonexistence was inconceivable; so what sense of "necessary" (if any) can be provided in which a being can be necessary in such a way as to provide explanation for the existence of other beings but itself need no explanation? And (b) is best considered as a challenge to a defender of Aquinas to show that God exists "necessarily" in a way in which the universe could not also be said to do so.

The challenges Hume makes in (a) and (b) raise absolutely central issues, and any one who wishes to defend Aquinas must meet them successfully. Ducasse raises objections similar to (c) and (d), and we will discuss these shortly.

Ducasse offers quite representative criticisms of the cosmological and teleological arguments. With respect to the cosmological argument, he objects that: (a) if there must always be, for anything we name, a further cause, then God must also have a cause; whereas if not everything need have a further cause, nothing is wrong with an infinite regress of causes; (b) there is no contradiction in the notion of an infinite series of past events—compare Hume's objection (c); (c) the phrase *causa sui* (cause of itself) is contradictory, since something would have to not exist to be caused to exist, but also would have to exist in order to cause anything; (d) if anything is either a First Cause or a Self-caused Being, the universe itself is as good a candidate as any; just because each part of the universe is contingent (that is, could fail to exist), it does not follow that the universe as a whole (that is, every part of it) could fail to exist—compare Hume's objection (d).

It is clear that (b) and (c) do not touch Aquinas' formulation of the argument. Regarding (b), Aquinas agrees that it is not contradictory to say that there has been an infinite past series. Regarding (c), nothing in his argument commits him to saying that God is self-caused. God, as First Mover, causes all motion (change) but is Himself not caused to change at all, by Himself or by something else.

But Ducasse's (a) and (d) are relevant to Aquinas' claims. Objection (d) is in effect an answer to a possible reply to objection (a). Part of what (a) says is that if there must be a First Mover, to say that the universe is that mover is as plausible as to say that God is. A possible reply is that since every part of the universe is contingent, the universe itself must be contingent. And (d) replies that: (d1) Every part of the universe is contingent, does not entail (d2) the universe itself is contingent. Of course, the fact that every part of a whole has a property does not, in general, entail that the whole has that property; that every piece of a picture puzzle is square-shaped does not entail that the puzzle as a whole is square-shaped. But sometimes the inference can be made. That every part of a machine is made only of iron entails that the machine as a whole is made only of iron. What inferences can be made from part to whole depend on the property in question. But it is hard to see exactly what principle will sort out cases like the puzzle example from cases like the iron example, and it is not easy to see on which side the inference from (d1) to (d2) falls. Still, it does seem possible (conceivable) that there be no universe at all. If so, (d2) is true whether it follows or does not follow from (d1). The important objection, then, is (a). It includes two criticisms: (a1) Why must everything have a cause? (a2) *if* everything must have a cause, how can we except God? Even if one replies to (a2) by saying that "If God exists, then He is not caused" is necessarily true, the question expressed in (a1) remains. Since "Everything must have a cause" is not true by definition, and since it cannot be shown by experiment to be true, its truth value is not easy to decide upon. The defender of Aquinas must find a way of showing it to be true.

The Fourth Way is a version of the moral argument with which the following section is concerned. The Fifth Way, however, is a version of the teleological argument, or argument from design. A teleological explanation is an explanation in terms of the activity of a purposive agent. Such explanations abound in everyday life. "She went to the store in order to buy a dress," "He bought the brush so he could paint his house," and "People bring presents to other people to show affection" are all teleological explanations. Now sometimes objects that are not purposive agents act, so to speak, *as if* they were purposive agents. Machines work as if it were their conscious goal to produce a particular product; acorns grow into oak trees as if this result were something they had intended. Machines were designed to work as they do; so, for Aquinas (and, indeed for any orthodox Christian or Jew or Moslem), were acorns.

We are now in a position to state the Fifth Way. (1) Things which are not purposive agents "act for an end, and this is evident from their acting always, or almost always, in the same way, so as to obtain the best result"; (2) that which acts without knowledge "cannot move toward an end unless it be directed" by a purposive agent; so: (3) some purposive agent exists "by whom all natural things are directed to their end," namely, God.

It is quite clear that (3) does not follow from (1) and (2) alone. That every moving arrow (to use Aquinas' example) is shot by some bowman does not show that some *one* bowman shoots every arrow that is shot. An appeal to parsimony (roughly, the explanation that postulates the least number of entities and still explains the data is best) is also necessary (and debatable). But even if one accepts the appeal to parsimony, problems arise.

Let us say that when an object, whether an artifact or a natural object, goes through an apparently purposive process, it manifests "designedness."

Since it is at least logically possible that something, so to speak, acts as if it were designed even though it was not designed by anyone (and proponents of the teleological argument admit this), the sentence "*X* manifests designedness" does not by itself entail "*X* was designed by a purposive agent." "Designedness" is in this respect a neutral concept. The teleological argument is successful only if the best explanation of the fact that natural objects manifest designedness is that they were designed by a purposive agent. Historically a severe blow was dealt to the teleological argument by the Darwinian claim that natural selection (a process involving no purposive activity) could account for the existent forms of life. The selection from F. R. Tennant offers a formulation of the teleological argument made with full awareness of Darwin's work. It appeals more to the general order and intelligibility of the world and its suitability as a human moral environment than to particular examples of objects (for example, the eye) that manifest designedness.

Concerning the teleological argument, or argument from design, Ducasse argues that (a) if the existence of designedness in the universe requires explanation, so does the existence of someone with the capacity to produce that designedness; (b) there is (as Hume noted) no reason to postulate a *perfect* Designer or only *one* designer, even if some designer or other must be postulated: (c) again as Hume noted, designedness often does not, in human experience, result from human design: (d) we could explain the designedness of, for example, an eye, in terms of "an automatic objectification of an obscure craving or felt need to see," and this explanation is no more problematic than one requiring that a designer can, without hands or tools, design and produce an eye.

Neither (b) nor (c) require extensive commentary. It is true that the argument shows, at best, that there is (or was) a powerful and very intelligent Designer, not an absolutely all-knowing, all-powerful one. (The qualification *"or was"* shows how important it is that the First Way and the Fifth be true of the same being—the designer must be a necessary being.) This much seems indisputable; if the existence of a designer *is* proved, he *may* be (but the argument gives no reason to suppose him to be) a perfect being.

It is also true that objects of ordinary experience manifest designedness but were designed by no human agent. But it is just these objects that provide the evidence to which the teleological argument appeals. In this connection Hume also appeals to explanations of designedness other than by reference to a purposive agent, as does Ducasse in (d). It remains, then, to discuss Ducasse's (a) and (d).

It seems clear that (a) is true unless it is true that (a1), the data one appeals to in making a teleological explanation, do not themselves require explanation. And (a1) will have to be true even though (at least for the purposes of the teleological argument) it is true that (a2), states of affairs manifesting designedness, always require teleological explanation. Now (a), (a1), and (a2) raise two distinct but related questions: (1) When is it appropriate to require an explanation? and (2) is any one sort of explanation, in some sense which can be made clear, more ultimate than another sort? Is, for example, teleological explanation somehow more ultimate than causal explanation which is nonteleological? Or are both equally ultimate? Or does ultimacy, in some clear sense of the term, belong to causal explanation which is nonteleological? Again, is the datum one appeals to in formulating teleological explanation—namely, the activity of a purposive being—somehow not in need of further explanation? A defender of Aquinas or Tennant would, it seems, have to hold this view; he would have to defend (a1). It is just this view that Ducasse challenges in (a).

In offering objection (d), Ducasse raises another issue. Suppose one grants (a1). He can then suggest that (a3), the data referred to in offering explanations in terms of objectifications of felt needs, are in need of no further explanation. Further, if one explains states of affairs that manifest designedness in terms of objectifications of felt needs, one offers a nonteleological explanation. So even if (a1) is true, (a3) may also be true, in which case we need some reason for preferring teleological explanations to objectification-of-felt-need explanations. This is a further point upon which the teleological arguer is, it would seem, required to offer cogent defense.

Five Arguments for God's Existence
THOMAS AQUINAS

WHETHER IT CAN BE
DEMONSTRATED
THAT GOD EXISTS?

*W*e proceed thus to the Second Article:—
OBJECTION 1. It seems that the existence of God cannot be demonstrated. For it is an article of faith that God exists. But what is of faith cannot be demonstrated, because a demonstration produces scientific knowledge, whereas faith is of the unseen, as is clear from the Apostle (*Heb.* xi. 1). Therefore it cannot be demonstrated that God exists.

OBJ. 2. Further, essence is the middle term of demonstration. But we cannot know in what God's essence consists, but solely in what it does not consist, as Damascene says.[1] Therefore we cannot demonstrate that God exists.

OBJ. 3. Further, if the existence of God were demonstrated, this could only

[1] *De Fide Orth.*, I, 4 (PG 94, 800).

be from His effects. But His effects are not proportioned to Him, since He is infinite and His effects are finite, and between the finite and infinite there is no proportion. Therefore, since a cause cannot be demonstrated by an effect not proportioned to it, it seems that the existence of God cannot be demonstrated.

On the contrary, The Apostle says: *The invisible things of Him are clearly seen, being understood by the things that are made* (*Rom.* i. 20). But this would not be unless the existence of God could be demonstrated through the things that are made; for the first thing we must know of anything is, whether it exists.

I answer that, Demonstration can be made in two ways: One is through the cause, and is called *propter quid,* and this is to argue from what is prior absolutely. The other is through the effect, and is called a demonstration *quia;* this is to argue from what is prior relatively only to us. When an effect is better known to us than its cause, from the

FROM: *Summa Theologica,* Part I, Question 2, Articles 2, 3, in *Basic Writings of St. Thomas Aquinas,* Anton C. Pegis, ed. (New York: Random House, Inc., 1948). Reprinted by permission of Random House and Burns and Oates, Ltd.

effect we proceed to the knowledge of the cause. And from every effect the existence of its proper cause can be demonstrated, so long as its effects are better known to us; because, since every effect depends upon its cause, if the effect exists, the cause must pre-exist. Hence the existence of God, in so far as it is not self-evident to us, can be demonstrated from those of His effects which are known to us.

REPLY OBJ. 1. The existence of God and other like truths about God, which can be known by natural reason, are not articles of faith, but are preambles to the articles; for faith presupposes natural knowledge, even as grace presupposes nature and perfection the perfectible. Nevertheless, there is nothing to prevent a man, who cannot grasp a proof, from accepting, as a matter of faith, something which in itself is capable of being scientifically known and demonstrated.

REPLY OBJ. 2. When the existence of a cause is demonstrated from an effect, this effect takes the place of the definition of the cause in proving the cause's existence. This is especially the case in regard to God, because, in order to prove the existence of anything, it is necessary to accept as a middle term the meaning of the name, and not its essence, for the question of its essence follows on the question of its existence. Now the names given to God are derived from His effects, as will be later shown.[2] Consequently, in demonstrating the existence of God from His effects, we may take for the middle term the meaning of the name *God*.

REPLY OBJ. 3. From effects not proportioned to the cause no perfect knowledge of that cause can be obtained. Yet from every effect the existence of the cause can be clearly demonstrated, and so we can demonstrate the existence of God from His effects; though from them we cannot know God perfectly as He is in His essence.

[2] Q. 13, a. 1.

THIRD ARTICLE

WHETHER GOD EXISTS?

We proceed thus to the Third Article:—

OBJECTION 1. It seems that God does not exist; because if one of two contraries be infinite, the other would be altogether destroyed. But the name *God* means that He is infinite goodness. If therefore, God existed, there would be no evil discoverable; but there is evil in the world. Therefore God does not exist.

OBJ. 2. Further, it is superfluous to suppose that what can be accounted for by a few principles has been produced by many. But it seems that everything we see in the world can be accounted for by other principles, supposing God did not exist. For all natural things can be reduced to one principle, which is nature; and all voluntary things can be reduced to one principle, which is human reason, or will. Therefore there is no need to suppose God's existence.

On the contrary, It is said in the person of God: *I am Who am* (*Exod.* iii. 14).

I answer that, The existence of God can be proved in five ways.

The first and more manifest way is the argument from motion. It is certain, and evident to our senses, that in the world some things are in motion. Now whatever is moved is moved by another, for nothing can be moved except it is in potentiality to that towards which it is moved; whereas a thing moves inasmuch as it is in act. For motion is nothing else than the reduction of something from potentiality to actuality. But nothing can be reduced from potentiality to actuality, except by something in a state of actuality. Thus that which is actually hot, as fire, makes wood, which is potentially hot, to be actually hot, and thereby moves and changes it. Now it is not possible that the same thing should be at once in actuality and potentiality in the same respect, but only in different respects. For what is actually hot cannot simultaneously be potentially hot; but it is simultaneously potentially cold.

It is therefore impossible that in the same respect and in the same way a thing should be both mover and moved, *i.e.*, that it should move itself. Therefore, whatever is moved must be moved by another. If that by which it is moved be itself moved, then this also must needs be moved by another, and that by another again. But this cannot go on to infinity, because then there would be no first mover, and, consequently, no other mover, seeing that subsequent movers move only inasmuch as they are moved by the first mover; as the staff moves only because it is moved by the hand. Therefore it is necessary to arrive at a first mover, moved by no other; and this everyone understands to be God.

The second way is from the nature of efficient cause. In the world of sensible things we find there is an order of efficient causes. There is no case known (neither is it, indeed, possible) in which a thing is found to be the efficient cause of itself; for so it would be prior to itself, which is impossible. Now in efficient causes it is not possible to go on to infinity, because in all efficient causes following in order, the first is the cause of the intermediate cause, and the intermediate is the cause of the ultimate cause, whether the intermediate cause be several, or one only. Now to take away the cause is to take away the effect. Therefore, if there be no first cause among efficient causes, there will be no ultimate, nor any intermediate, cause. But if in efficient causes it is possible to go on to infinity, there will be no first efficient cause, neither will there be an ultimate effect, nor any intermediate efficient causes; all of which is plainly false. Therefore it is necessary to admit a first efficient cause, to which everyone gives the name of God.

The third way is taken from possibility and necessity, and runs thus. We find in nature things that are possible to be and not to be, since they are found to be generated, and to be corrupted, and consequently, it is possible for them to be and not to be. But it is impossible for these always to exist, for

that which can not-be at some time is not. Therefore, if everything can not-be, then at one time there was nothing in existence. Now if this were true, even now there would be nothing in existence, because that which does not exist begins to exist only through something already existing. Therefore, if at one time nothing was in existence, it would have been impossible for anything to have begun to exist; and thus even now nothing would be in existence—which is absurd. Therefore, not all beings are merely possible, but there must exist something the existence of which is necessary. But every necessary thing either has its necessity caused by another, or not. Now it is impossible to go on to infinity in necessary things which have their necessity caused by another, as has been already proved in regard to efficient causes. Therefore we cannot but admit the existence of some being having of itself its own necessity, and not receiving it from another, but rather causing in others their necessity. This all men speak of as God.

The fourth way is taken from the gradation to be found in things. Among beings there are some more and some less good, true, noble, and the like. But *more* and *less* are predicted of different things according as they resemble in their different ways something which is the maximum, as a thing is said to be hotter according as it more nearly resembles that which is hottest; so that there is something which is truest, something best, something noblest, and, consequently, something which is most being, for those things that are greatest in truth are greatest in being, as it is written in *Metaph.* ii.[3] Now the maximum in any genus is the cause of all in that genus, as fire, which is the maximum of heat, is the cause of all hot things, as is said in the same book.[4] Therefore there must also be something which is to all beings the cause of their being, goodness, and every other perfection; and this we call God.

[3] *Metaph.* Ia, 1 (993b 30).

[4] *Ibid.* (993b 25).

The fifth way is taken from the governance of the world. We see that things which lack knowledge, such as natural bodies, act for an end, and this is evident from their acting always, or nearly always, in the same way, so as to obtain the best result. Hence it is plain that they achieve their end, not fortuitously, but designedly. Now whatever lacks knowledge cannot move towards an end, unless it be directed by some being endowed with knowledge and intelligence; as the arrow is directed by the archer. Therefore some intelligent being exists by whom all natural things are directed to their end; and this being we call God.

REPLY OBJ. 1. As Augustine says: *Since God is the highest good, He would not allow any evil to exist in His works,* unless *His omnipotence and goodness were such as to bring good even out of evil.*[5] This is part of the infinite goodness of God, that He should allow evil to exist, and out of it produce good.

REPLY OBJ. 2. Since nature works for a determinate end under the direction of a higher agent, whatever is done by nature must be traced back to God as to its first cause. So likewise whatever is done voluntarily must be traced back to some higher cause other than human reason and will, since these can change and fail; for all things that are changeable and capable of defect must be traced back to an immovable and self-necessary first principle, as has been shown.

[5] *Enchir.,* XI (PL 40, 236).

The Cosmological Argument Is Not Cogent
DAVID HUME

*B*ut if so many difficulties attend the argument *a posteriori,* said Demea, had we not better adhere to that simple and sublime argument *a priori* which, by offering to us infallible demonstration, cuts off at once all doubt and difficulty? By this argument, too, we may prove the *infinity* of the Divine attributes, which, I am afraid, can never be ascertained with certainty from any other topic. For how can an effect which either is finite or, for aught we know, may be so—how can such an effect, I say, prove an infinite cause? The unity, too, of the Divine Nature it is very difficult, if not absolutely impossible, to deduce merely from contemplating the works of nature; nor will the uniformity alone of the plan, even were it allowed, give us any assurance of that attribute. Whereas the argument *a priori* . . .

You seem to reason, Demea, interposed Cleanthes, as if those advantages and conveniences in the abstract argument were full proofs of its solidity. But it is first proper, in my opinion, to determine what argument of this nature you choose to insist on; and we shall afterwards, from itself, better than from its *useful* consequences, endeavour to determine what value we ought to put upon it.

The argument, replied Demea, which I would insist on is the common one. Whatever exists must have a cause or reason of its existence, it being absolutely impossible for anything to produce itself or be the cause of its own existence. In mounting up, therefore, from effects to causes, we must either go on in tracing an infinite succession, without any ultimate cause at all, or must at least have recourse to some ultimate cause that is *necessarily* existent. Now that the first supposition is absurd may be thus proved. In the infinite chain or

FROM: *Dialogues Concerning Natural Religion,* David Hume. Part 9 (originally published in 1779).

succession of causes and effects, each single effect is determined to exist by the power and efficacy of that cause which immediately preceded; but the whole eternal chain or succession, taken together, is not determined or caused by anything, and yet it is evident that it requires a cause or reason, as much as any particular object which begins to exist in time. The question is still reasonable why this particular succession of causes existed from eternity, and not any other succession or no succession at all. If there be no necessarily existent being, any supposition which can be formed is equally possible; nor is there any more absurdity in nothing's having existed from eternity than there is in that succession of causes which constitutes the universe. What was it, then, which determined *something* to exist rather than *nothing*, and bestowed being on a particular possibility, exclusive of the rest? *External causes*, there are supposed to be none. *Chance* is a word without a meaning. Was it *nothing*? But that can never produce anything. We must, therefore, have recourse to a necessarily existent Being who carries the *reason* of his existence in himself, and who cannot be supposed not to exist, without an express contradiction. There is, consequently, such a Being—that is, there is a Deity.

I shall not leave it to Philo, said Cleanthes, though I know that the starting objections is his chief delight, to point out the weakness of this metaphysical reasoning. It seems to me so obviously ill-grounded, and at the same time of so little consequence to the cause of true piety and religion, that I shall myself venture to show the fallacy of it.

I shall begin with observing that there is an evident absurdity in pretending to demonstrate a matter of fact, or to prove it by any arguments *a priori*. Nothing is demonstrable unless the contrary implies a contradiction. Nothing that is distinctly conceivable implies a contradiction. Whatever we conceive as existent, we can also conceive as non-existent. There is no being, therefore, whose non-existence implies a contradic-

tion. Consequently there is no being whose existence is demonstrable. I propose this argument as entirely decisive, and am willing to rest the whole controversy upon it.

It is pretended that the Deity is a necessarily existent being; and this necessity of his existence is attempted to be explained by asserting that, if we knew his whole essence or nature, we should perceive it to be as impossible for him not to exist, as for twice two not to be four. But it is evident that this can never happen, while our faculties remain the same as at present. It will still be possible for us, at any time, to conceive the non-existence of what we formerly conceived to exist; nor can the mind ever lie under a necessity of supposing any object to remain always in being; in the same manner as we lie under a necessity of always conceiving twice two to be four. The words, therefore, *necessary existence* have no meaning or, which is the same thing, none that is consistent.

But further, why may not the material universe be the necessarily existent Being, according to this pretended explication of necessity? We dare not affirm that we know all the qualities of matter; and, for aught we can determine, it may contain some qualities which, were they known, would make its non-existence appear as great a contradiction as that twice two is five. I find only one argument employed to prove that the material world is not the necessarily existent Being; and this argument is derived from the contingency both of the matter and form of the world. "Any particle of matter," it is said, "may be *conceived* to be annihilated, and any form may be *conceived* to be altered. Such an annihilation or alteration, therefore, is not impossible."[1] But it seems a great partiality not to perceive that the same argument extends equally to the Deity, so far as we have any conception of him, and that the mind can at least imagine him to be non-existent or his attributes to be altered. It must be some unknown, inconceivable

[1] Dr. Clarke.

qualities which can make his non-existence appear impossible or his attributes
unalterable; and no reason can be assigned why these qualities may not belong
to matter. As they are altogether unknown and inconceivable, they can never
be proved incompatible with it.

Add to this that in tracing an
eternal succession of objects it seems
absurd to inquire for a general cause or
first author. How can anything that exists from eternity have a cause, since
that relation implies a priority in time
and a beginning of existence?

In such a chain, too, or succession
of objects, each part is caused by that
which preceded it, and causes that which
succeeds it. Where then is the difficulty?
But the *whole*, you say, wants a cause. I
answer that the uniting of these parts
into a whole, like the uniting of several
distinct countries into one kingdom, or
several distinct members into one body,
is performed merely by an arbitrary act
of the mind, and has no influence on the
nature of things. Did I show you the particular causes of each individual in a collection of twenty particles of matter, I
should think it very unreasonable should
you afterwards ask me what was the
cause of the whole twenty. This is sufficiently explained in explaining the cause
of the parts.

Though the reasonings which you
have urged, Cleanthes, may well excuse
me, said Philo, from starting any further
difficulties, yet I cannot forbear insisting
still upon another topic. It is observed
by arithmeticians that the products of
9 compose always either 9 or some lesser
product of 9 if you add together all the
characters of which any of the former
products is composed. Thus, of 18, 27,
36, which are products of 9, you make
9 by adding 1 to 8, 2 to 7, 3 to 6.
Thus 369 is a product also of 9; and if
you add 3, 6, and 9, you make 18, a

lesser product of 9.[2] To a superficial
observer so wonderful a regularity may
be admired as the effect either of chance
or design; but a skilful algebraist immediately concludes it to be the work of
necessity, and demonstrates that it must
for ever result from the nature of these
numbers. Is it not probable, I ask, that
the whole economy of the universe is
conducted by a like necessity, though no
human algebra can furnish a key which
solves the difficulty? And instead of ad-
miring the order of natural beings, may
it not happen that, could we penetrate
into the intimate nature of bodies, we
should clearly see why it was absolutely
impossible they could ever admit of any
other disposition? So dangerous is it to
introduce this idea of necessity into the
present question! and so naturally does it
afford an inference directly opposite to
the religious hypothesis!

But dropping all these abstractions,
continued Philo, and confining ourselves
to more familiar topics, I shall venture
to add an observation that the argument
a priori has seldom been found very convincing, except to people of a metaphysical head who have accustomed themselves
to abstract reasoning, and who, finding
from mathematics that the understanding
frequently leads to truth through obscurity, and contrary to first appearances,
have transferred the same habit of thinking to subjects where it ought not to
have place. Other people, even of good
sense and the best inclined to religion,
feel always some deficiency in such arguments, though they are not perhaps able
to explain distinctly where it lies—a certain proof that men ever did and ever
will derive their religion from other
sources than from this species of reasoning.

[2] *Republique des Lettres*, Aut 1685.

A Reinterpretation of the Teleological Argument

F. R. TENNANT

In an exposition of the significance of the moral order for theistic philosophy, the first step is to point out that man belongs to Nature, and is an essential part of it, in such a sense that the world cannot be described or explained as a whole without taking him and his moral values into account. Prof. Pringle-Pattison, especially, has elaborated the doctrine that, as he expresses it, "man is organic to the world". What precisely this, or the similar phrase "man is the child of Nature", should mean, if either is to be more than a half-truth, needs to be made clear. Insofar as man's soul, i.e. man as *noümenon*, or (in the language of spiritualistic pluralism) the dominant monad in the empirical self, is concerned, we are not authorised by known facts to regard man as organic to Nature, or as the child of Nature, in the sense that he is an emergent product of cosmic evolution. We are rather forbidden by psychology to entertain any such notion. But, this proviso being observed—it must qualify all that is further said in the present connexion—we can affirm that man's body, with all its conditioning of his mentality, his sociality, knowledge and morality, is 'of a piece' with Nature; and that, in so far as he is a phenomenal being, man is organic to Nature, or a product of the world. And this fact is as significant for our estimation of Nature as for our anthropology. If man is Nature's child, Nature is the wonderful mother of such a child. Any account of her which ignores the fact of her maternity is scientifically partial and philosophically insignificant. Her capacity to produce man must be reckoned among her potencies, explain it how we may. And man is no monstrous birth out of due time,

no freak or sport. In respect of his body and the bodily conditioning of his mentality, man is like, and has genetic continuity with, Nature's humbler and earlier-born children. In the fulness of time Nature found self-utterance in a son possessed of the intelligent and moral status. Maybe she was pregnant with him from the beginning, and the world-ages are the period of her gestation. As to this anthropocentric view of the world-process, and its co-existensiveness with teleological interpretation, more will presently be said. But in the light of man's continuity with the rest of the world we can at once dismiss the view that Nature suddenly "stumbled" or "darkly blundered" on man, while "churning the universe with mindless motion". The world-process is a *praeparatio anthropologica,* whether designedly or not, and man is the culmination, up to the present stage of the knowable history of Nature, of a gradual ascent. We cannot explain man in terms of physical Nature; conceivably Nature may be found explicable—in another sense of the word—in terms of man, and can be called 'the threshold of spirit'. Judging the genealogical tree by its roots, naturalism once preached that Darwin had put an end to the assumption that man occupies an exceptional position on our planet; apparently implying that there is no difference of status between man and the primordial slime because stages between the two are traceable. But if we judge the tree by its fruits, Darwin may rather be said to have restored man to the position from which Copernicus seemed to have ousted him, in making it possible to read the humanising of Nature in the naturalising of man, and to regard man as not only the last term and the

FROM: *Philosophical Theology*, F. R. Tennant. (New York: Cambridge University Press, 1928), Vol. II, Chapter 4, p. 99–120. Reprinted by permission of Cambridge University Press.

crown of Nature's long upward effort, but also as its end or goal.[1]

The phrase 'organic to Nature', as applied to man, may serve to sum up other relations between humanity and the world besides that of parentage or blood-affinity. It implies also a denial of the assertion that man is an excrescence upon Nature in the sense of being an alien in a world that is indifferent to his moral aims, or hostile to his ideals. The most forcible presentation of this view, that the cosmic process and human morality are antithetical, is perhaps that contained in Huxley's *Romanes Lecture*. It is therefore here selected for examination. Huxley's first point was that the world, as involving struggle for existence and extermination of the less fit, is no "school of virtue". If that statement merely meant that it is not from Nature that we are to imbibe our ethical maxims, no one would wish to dispute it. But it would then overlook the fact that in other senses Nature may fairly be called a school of virtue. In the first place, Nature is largely a cosmos ruled by uniformity or law; and if Nature's uniformity and impartiality are a main source of the trouble to which man is born, they are also a precondition of all intelligent, and therefore of all moral, life. In this respect Nature is the power that makes it possible for noümenal man to be, as phenomenal man, a moral being. Further, it is partly through his being "the plaything of hazard and the prey of hardship" that man's moral virtues are acquired. The world is thus instrumental to the emergence, maintenance, and progressiveness, of morality. The second charge which Huxley preferred against the cosmos is that the physical world works upon man solely through his lower nature, his ingrained appetites, etc., and against his higher ethical interests. Nature is thus the cause of his 'original sin', and is diabolically provocative of his diverse immoralities. This also is true; but again it presents but one

aspect of the facts. For, apart from man's bodily appetites and impulses it is inconceivable that ethical principles should gain purchase on him. Hunger and sex are the bed-rock of human morality; and the self-determination which human morality presupposes is hardly possible without the conflict between moral reason and non-moral impulse. Morality cannot be made without raw material; and in providing this raw material Nature is once more instrumental to man's acquisition of the moral status. Morality thus has its roots in Nature, however indispensable be the innate and non-inherited potentialities of the pure ego or soul. The non-moral cosmos, personified into a morally evil world by pessimistic poets for the purpose of giving it, as Mr. Chesterton has said of one of them, a piece of their mind, has nevertheless subserved the moralisation of human souls, even when soliciting to carnality. And it is an exaggeration to say that Nature fosters only tendencies that issue in vice. We have seen before that there is such a thing as 'natural virtue', or 'original rectitude', as 'instinctive' as is self-seeking; and Nature plainly appraises health and vigor, thus inciting to temperance and self-control. Lastly, Huxley maintained that the world is indifferent to man's moral aspirations, in that they along with him are destined to be extinguished before the break-up of the solar system. Here he became unwarrantably dogmatical: for, apart from the fact that science's predictions are not unconditional, speculations as to the ruin of a fragment of the universe, based on partial knowledge of a larger fragment of what, for all we know, may be possessed of a power to make all things new, are too precarious to be considered exhaustive of the possibilities even as to our terrestrial home, let alone those as to a future life.

Nature, then, has produced moral beings, is instrumental to moral life and therefore amenable to 'instrumental' moral valuation, and is relatively modifiable by operative moral ideas—or, rather, by moral agents pursuing ideals.

[1] A. Seth Pringle-Pattison, *The Idea of God*, 1917, pp. 82 f.

Nature and moral man are not at strife, but are organically one. The whole process of Nature is capable of being regarded as instrumental to the development of intelligent and moral creatures. Acquisition of the moral status is in line with the other stages of the long 'ascent of man', and is its climax—unless we reserve that name for the morality which, tinged with sentiment transcending reverence for duty, passes into religion.

The more or less separable fields of fact which have now been surveyed may each be said to admit of teleological explanation even if explanation of the causal or the descriptive type be forthcoming in every case. None of them calls for resort to final causes merely because other kinds of causality, or linkage according to law, are not assignable. Theism no longer plants its God in the gaps between the explanatory achievements of natural science, which are apt to get scientifically closed up. Causal explanation and teleological explanation are not mutually exclusive alternatives; and neither can perform the function of the other. It is rather when these several fields of fact are no longer considered one by one, but as parts of the whole or terms of a continuous series, and when for their dovetailing and interconnectedness a sufficient ground is sought, such as mechanical and proximate causation no longer seems to supply, that divine design is forcibly suggested. Paley's watch is no analogue of the human eye; but it may none the less be an approximate analogue of Nature as a whole. Thus the wider teleological argument is not comparable with a chain whose strength is precisely that of its weakest link; it is comparable rather with a piece of chain-armour. And this can the better be seen if the relevant facts be presented again so as to display especially their connexions and their gradually increasing suggestiveness.

There is no intrinsic necessity that a world, or an assemblage of existents and happenings, indefinably and unaccountably 'standing out' as against nothingness, be a cosmos, even to the extent of any one existent being comparable with another or behaving in the same way twice. Reality, or the aggregate of those determinate beings, might conceivably be a 'chaos' of disparates and inconsistencies such that if any of its members possessed consciousness or awareness and the potentiality of intelligence, they would find the world presented to them utterly unintelligible. Our world is, however, a cosmos, at least in the humblest sense of the word, and the original determinateness of its terms or *posita* is such as to make it intelligible. This, of course, constitutes a teleological proof of theism no more than does the existence of the word afford a causal or cosmological proof. The mystery of mysteries is that something exists; and if the one underived or uncaused existent be God, the creator of all things else, God is "the last irrationality", and creation is the next to the last inexplicability. To replace absolute pluralism by theism is to reduce an indefinite number of separate inexplicabilities to these two alone; and so far economy, and therefore explicability of a kind, is secured. It is of no important kind, however: for there is no more wonder about a self-subsistent plurality than about a self-subsistent individual. But when the intelligibility of a cosmos, rather than the mere existence of a world of any sort, is the fact to be considered, teleological theism evinces more conspicuously its advantage, in other respects than that of economy, over absolute pluralism. For over and above the forthcomingness, conceived as self-subsistence, of the many existents, is their adaptiveness, inherent in their primary determinateness and relations, to the requirements of intelligibility. This further particularises their determinateness and so bespeaks more of coincidence in the 'fortuitous'. For cosmos-quality, or intelligibility, in our world, which conceivably might have been a determinate 'chaos', non-theistic philosophy can assign no reason. If the world 'made itself', so to say, or is the self-subsistent Absolute, its adaptiveness to understanding has simply happened, and is part and parcel of the pluralist's last irrationality. It gives him more to explain or to refuse to explain: for why should the many arrange themselves to form an intelligible and an organic whole? If, on the other hand, this be due to an intelligent Creator designing the world to be a theatre for rational life, mystery is minimised, and a possible and sufficient reason is assigned. More than this cannot be extracted out of the initial fact that the world is intelligible, in the sense that has as yet solely been in question; but if it be merely a hint that Nature's dice may be loaded, it is to be observed that the hint becomes broader as Nature is further examined, and as the knowledge-process is analysed. For instance, the particular species of intelligibility, in which the knowledge of common sense and science consists, is mediated by the 'real' categories; and they depend for their forthcomingness on the contingency that the dominant monad in man is embodied, or associated with monads such as also constitute Nature but which, in virtue of some mysterious affinity, are not merely bits of Nature to the soul but also its windows and telephonic exchange-office mediating to it all its knowledge whatsoever, even its self-knowledge. Thus, as step by step the machinery which produces intelligibility is scientifically explored and made manifest, the richer in specialised determinateness are some of the world's constituents found to be; and therefore the more suggestive is the intricate adaptiveness, involved in knowledge of the world by man, of pre-established harmony or immanent guidance, or both, and the less reasonable or credible becomes the alternative theory of cumulative groundless coincidence. The doctrine that man is organic to Nature can now be broadened out so as to embrace the fact that it is only in so far as he is part and parcel of Nature that he can ejectively make the knowledge-venture, and only in virtue of Nature's affinity with him that his postulatory categories receive pragmatic verification, and his assimilation-drafts are honoured. When the

impossible Cartesian rationalism is exchanged for the humanism or anthropism which, implicit in Kant, is explicitly demanded by more modern empirical knowledge of the human mind, the epistemological argument for theism begins to acquire a forcibleness that was lacking to the arbitrary, if not circular, reasoning of Descartes. It is, however, but a fragment of the epistemological argument to establish the anthropocentric theory of knowledge, which is ultimately based on the fact that between the soul and the world, in so far as knowledge of the one by the other is concerned, stands the body; and the epistemological line or mesh-work is but a fragment of the teleological argument as a whole.

Turning now from Nature's knowability to her structure and history, we may revert first to the fact of adaptiveness in the organic realm, which, so far, has only been found not to yield teleological proof of the narrower kind. Here adaptiveness, unhappily described as internal teleology, is not teleological at all in so far as it is internal to the organism. There is no end present to the agent. It is from the (*ps*) standpoint of the biologist, not from the (ψ) standpoint of the organism, that reference to the future is involved in organic adaptedness. Again, neither the occurrence nor the progressiveness of organic adaptations, taking *singillatim*, calls for other than natural, if non-mechanical, causation. It is true that the course of living Nature is not mere change, but change that admits of valuation, of one kind or another; of valuation not only in terms of fitness for survival but also in terms of differentiation or complexity of structure and function, and of subservience to further development culminating, in man, in rationality and morality. Despite cases of stagnancy and of degeneration, which equally with progress may ensure biological fitness, the plasticity, formative power, or *élan* in organic Nature secures not only self-conservation but also progress, morphological and ultimately mental, so that within the main line of development there has been a steady advance from amoeba to man. But each step and special adaptation, each case of emergence of something new and higher, in this long process, can be sufficiently accounted for in terms of natural, non-teleological causation. So far as the foregoing facts are concerned there is no need to resort to external teleology. It is not *necessary* to invoke design in order to find a guarantee for the stability, in face of the ever-present possibility of deletion of the 'higher' by the 'fitter', of the long and gradual ascent, remarkable as that is. It is rather when the essential part played by the environment, physical and organic, in the progressive development of the organic world, is appreciated, that non-teleological explanation ceases to be plausible in this sphere, and, conspiration being precluded, external design begins to be indicated or strongly suggested. It is the environment that is the selector, though 'selection' is a figurative expression when applied to non-intelligent Nature. Subjective selection, or the Lamarckean factor, may decide what shall arise; but the environment decides what shall stand. And before discussing the alternatives of theistic teleology and naturalistic Pyrrhonism (if the doctrine of fortuitousness or ungrounded coincidence may so be called), it may be submitted that the fact just mentioned restricts our choice to the one or the other of them, in that, when taken into account, it deprives the only other forthcoming alternative, viz. the theory of 'unconscious purpose', of such plausibility as, *prima facie*, it may seem to possess.

The phrases 'unconscious will' and 'unconscious purpose' are, of course, when taken literally, contradictions in terms. That, however, is unimportant. Overlooking the poetic licence evinced in such forms of speech, we may inquire what the writers who favour them mean by them, or what are their equivalents in scientific terminology. This is not always easy to ascertain with precision; but it would seem to amount to the assertion of an *élan vital* present in Nature as a whole, an intrinsic potency to strive blindly towards, and to attain by changes

that we valuing subjects call progressive from the lower to the higher, what, from the same intelligent point of view, are relative goals: not ends of a designer, nor merely temporally later stages in a process, but 'ends' in the sense of later stages that happen to be of higher value, of one kind or another, than the earlier stages, *as if* foreseen and striven for. This kind of *Zweckmässigkeit* without *Absichtlichkeit* has a parallel in human endeavours. Men have sometimes "built more wisely than they knew", and human societies may fashion institutions, beliefs, etc., without any of their members having a preconceived definite idea of the 'end' in which their activities are destined to issue. One thing that was willed leads on to other things that were not at first willed or even imagined, and *sometimes* these other things are found desirable, or are goods to be preserved. Sometimes, however, they are of the opposite kind, so that reforms or revolutions find place in human history. And here, if the theory before us be not misunderstood, this analogy breaks down. For the theory ascribes to Nature an intrinsic potency which, if it is to succeed in the absence of that self-correction by which erring human mentality can change its own course and avoid impending catastrophes, must inevitably go, like animal instinct, straight to its mark in all essentials and on all critical occasions. Nature's 'unconscious wisdom', in other words, must vastly exceed the sapience and foresight of humanity, liable as that is to errors which, save for reasoned amendment, might prove fatal. In fact the theory requires us to believe that Nature keeps her head, which *ex hypothesi* is brainless, through all the changes and chances of cosmic history.

Further, 'unconscious purpose', which has turned out to be as fatalistic as mechanism and yet as value-realising as man, does not seem, on examination, to be one and the same thing in the different kingdoms of Nature. In that part of the organic world that is (macroscopically) psychical it is said to be exemplified in animal impulse, or the non-volitional conation of individual organisms. But this subjective selectiveness of the individual, though essential to organic development, does not of itself suffice to secure it. The organism, in filling its skin, may get itself a better skin to fill, but on the other hand it might burst its skin; and blind or random movement, such as might secure escape from the painful or displeasing, may land 'out of the frying-pan into the fire'. Natural selection can only secure the progress of species in virtue of such individual catastrophes, misfits, etc., in organisms inspired with venturesomeness and *élan*. Individual variations are mostly indefinite or in many directions, not in the straight path of progress alone; and it is the environment, as censor, that plays the larger part in determining a steady and permanent advance, as contrasted with the sporadic and evanescent experiments which make progress a possibility. Thus the environment, the preponderating part of which is inorganic, as well as its organic denizens, needs to be accredited with 'unconscious purpose'; yet it lacks even the animal conatus and the vegetable 'formative power' which, though they are Actualities, are not unconsciously *purposive*, in that, of themselves, they are not fraught with an exclusively progressive trend. A formative power lodged in the physical, as science has hitherto understood it, making as if for a goal, is not an Actuality known to science. Consequently, it here becomes impossible to find any explanatoriness, and indeed any meaning, in 'unconscious purpose'. If it but asserts that in the inorganic world there is a potency of adaptiveness, that is but a new name for the fact that the environment is adapted; it but restates the fact to be explained, the problem to be solved, and proffers no explanation or solution. An explanation, however, is offered by teleology and theism. (It is a fact that Nature, as inorganic, is as much adapted to organic life as organic life is adaptive to physical environment; and it is not a matter of indifference whether we say "God has wisely willed it so" or "Nature

has wisely arranged this", simply because Nature has no wisdom wherewith to arrange anything. If Nature evinces wisdom, the wisdom is Another's.) The issue narrows to whether what we may generically call the order in Nature is to be accounted an outcome of wisdom or of undesigned coincidence. Indeed, in so far as the question is as to explicability, the issue narrows to the vanishing-point; for assertion of coincidence in the self-subsistent, wondrous in respect of its manifoldness and complex interlacingness, is, again, not explanation but statement of what calls for explanation.

The manifoldness of the coincidences on which the order in the world, including man, is conditional, has already been sufficiently illustrated, though it might be more minutely and extensively expounded. These coincidences, let it be repeated, are present in the determinate natures of the cosmic elements, the world's original existents and their primary collocations, in the adjustment of similarity to difference between them which is the ground of all the uniformity and variety, the stability and the progressiveness, of the irreversible process of becoming; in the alogical *posita*, their logico-mathematical relations, their determinate *rapport* which is such as to provide a law-making, and so a law-governed, world; a world instrumental to valuation and evocative of it, and intelligible in the peculiar anthropic sense which saturates the meaning of 'knowledge' whenever that word denotes the Actual processes in which the human mind comes to an understanding with Actuality. What is here being called coincidence is to be seen, again, in the stages of emergence of novelty which issue not, as conceivably they might and as mere mechanism suggests they perhaps should, in successive labile configurations of a cosmic dust-cloud blown by a changing cosmic wind, but in an evolutionary process in which much goes that comes, while nevertheless the unceasing flux is such that one whole world-state is, as it were, a built storey and a scaffolding for the erection of another. Emergents 'here' seem to 'take note of', or be relevant to, causally unconnected[2] emergents 'there', in both space and time, since an elaborate interlacing of contingencies is requisite to secure inorganic Nature's adaptedness to be a theatre of life. Any miscarriage in promiscuous 'naturation', such as might ruin the whole, as a puff of air may lay low the soaring house of cards, has been avoided in the making of *Natura naturata*; and though such possibilities do not suggest themselves to science contemplating Nature as a system of Lagrangean equations, the historical process conceivably might be seen to have teemed with critical moments and crucial situations by a visualising compeer of Laplace's calculator. Similarly in the organic world, erratic and venturesomely varying conative individuals may have constantly endangered, as much as they have provided for, the future of the world. Orderly progress, however, has been attained; and it has been ensured by the firm hand and the directivity of already stabilised environment. Organisms, and man in especial measure, have the world with them in their aspiringness. It is not so much the progressiveness displayed in the world-process as the intricate and harmonious interconnexion, rendering progress, intelligibility and intelligence, etc., possible, that in its marvellousness suggests intelligent art. On the other hand, it is the progressiveness which suggests that such art is directed toward an end—realisation of 'the good'.

So long as attention is paid exclusively to the universal, the logical and rational, as is necessary in the case of science but is arbitrary in the case of philosophy, the inner significance of this world, with all its particular 'thusness', will be missed. It is in the concrete or the historical, to which the universal is but incidental and of which the logical or rational is but one nexus among others, that meaning can be, and seems

[2] Causally unconnected in the sense in which experimental science must use the notion of causal connexion.

to be, conveyed: and as the history, made by the mindless or by practically infinitesimal minds, is on so grand a scale intelligible to universalising intellect, there would seem to be directive intelligence behind it. It is in the characteristics of *this* world, in the particular determinateness of the collocations prescriptive of its Actual course, and—not least—in the anthropism thrust by Nature on the non-anthropic pure egos out of which she has made men, and its affinity with the world in respect of both genetic continuity and epistemic capacity, that purposiveness lets itself be read. If we thus read things, a unique significance attaches to the realm of the moral, amongst other teleologically suggestive domains of fact, in that it enables us to advance from belief that the world is a work of art to belief that it is constructed for a purpose, and worthily specifies what the purpose is, or includes. If we decline to explain things thus, it would seem that the only alternative is to regard the self-subsistent entities, of which the world is constituted, as comparable with letters of type which have shuffled themselves not only into a book or a literature but also into a reader commanding the particular tongue in which the book utters its unintentional meaning. If the inference from cumulative adaptiveness to design be non-logical, as is admitted, it at least is not unreasonable.

Even critical and iconoclastic philosophers have treated with respect forms of teleological argument such as were current in their day. Hume denied that the argument is logically coercive, but he allows Philo, in the *Dialogues*, to admit that the fitness of final causes in the universe and its parts strikes us with such irresistible force that all objections to them appear cavils and sophisms. Kant, again, speaks of it as the clearest of the 'proofs', and as the one most in harmony with the common reason of mankind. Yet the more comprehensive and synoptic design-argument that is now producible is more imposing than any contemplated in their day. Hume almost ignored man and his moral status; while

Kant, who saw in man's moral faculty the central fact about the universe, so over-emphasised its purely rational functioning as to overlook its historical development, its alogical content, and the respects in which it is 'of a piece' with Nature. The greater strength claimed for the newer argument consists in its exhibition of the interconnexion and reciprocal adaptation between systems of fact which used to be treated as if isolated. It can now be submitted that if the uniformity of Nature rests on mechanical postulates, and the 'validity' of moral principles involves a moral postulate, the evolutionary progressiveness of the world points to a teleological postulate. And if this evolution is to be explained, or to be assigned a sufficient ground, instead of being merely accepted as a brute happening, the historical and alogical aspect of the world-process must not only be regarded as the primary reality *in ordine cognoscendi* but also as our clue to the *ordo*, and the *ratio, essendi.* Mechanism and the universalisings of pure rationality are tools as useless for this purpose as a typing-machine and a book of logarithms are for landscape-painting: for the problem is reducible to the question, *cui bono?* Teleological explanation is comparable with discernment of "the signs of the times" rather than of "the face of the sky"; and although to fail to discern cosmical signs of the former kind need not be to class oneself with the "hypocrites", to be indifferent as to whether there be such signs may be said to involve venturing less than the "all that doth become a man". Perhaps no thinking being is thus indifferent, or even uninquisitive. When the teleological or theistic explanation of the world is not adopted, it is because one's explanation-craving is satiated before the limit to which the theist presses is reached in the regress, or because a seemingly better explanation has been found, or because one has become convinced that none has been found that tallies with all the facts. Whether theism satisfies this last condition will be discussed in another chapter, and more remains to be said as to certain alternatives to theism; but it has perhaps already been shewn that no *explanation* is contained in the assertion that the world is an organic whole and consequently involves adaptiveness. That is only a restatement of the occult and wondrous fact that cries for explanation. The world's 'thusness' is explained, however, if it be attributable to the design and creativeness of a Being whose purpose is, or includes, the realisation of moral values. Further back than a creative Spirit it is neither needful nor possible to go. But further back than the world we can and must go, because the notion of a non-intelligent world that produces intelligent beings and makes itself intelligible, that can have no purpose and yet abundantly seems to bespeak one, and so forth, is not the clearest and most reason-satisfying conception that our minds can build wherein to rest. Moreover, as J. Ward has observed, the alternative that the world's evolution is ultimate, or its own sufficient reason, ignores the fact that we rational beings are part of the evolution, so that our demand for a sufficient reason is "a demand that the world itself has raised".

At more than one place in this chapter stress has been laid on the intelligibilty of the world to the specifically anthropic intelligence possessed by us, and on the connexion between the conditioning of that intelligibility, on the one hand, and the constitution and process of Nature, on the other hand. Thus a close relationship is indicated between teleological explanation and an anthropocentric world-view; and this relationship may now be more explicitly described.

Anthropocentrism, in some sense, is involved in cosmic teleology. It is useless for ethical theism to argue that the world evidences design unless the only rational and moral denizen of the world, in so far as it is known to us, be assumed to afford an indication as to what the designed end of the world-process is. And, as thus stated, anthropocentrism involves no human arrogance or self-exaltation. It does not assert that man, as a zoological species or genus whose geographical distribution is presumably confined to this planet, is the highest being under God, or the final stage of progressive cosmic evolution, or the end and the whole end of the divine design. It is compatible with belief in "thrones, dominions, principalities, powers", or angels and archangels, and in the possibility that in other worlds there are rational beings akin to us in being embodied and having their specific intelligence moulded thereby.[3] It is content to allow that the divine end, in its completeness, is unfathomable. Nor does it imply that lower creatures evolved in the world-process are necessarily of but instrumental value as stages or means to ends, and, when not figuring in man's genealogical tree, are mere by-products in the making of humanity. Anthropocentrism rather means that, whereas in the realm of Nature beneath man no final purpose can be discerned, such purpose may be discerned in beings possessed of rationality, appreciation, self-

[3] It is, of course, a matter of indifference to teleology and anthropocentric interpretation whether the material heavens contain a plurality of inhabited worlds. But it is interesting to find recent astronomy, as represented by Prof. Eddington, inclined to the views that the physical universe probably does not greatly extend beyond the range of human observation, and that the number of the heavenly bodies suitable for the maintenance of life (as it is conditioned on this earth) is extremely small. It is commonly deemed absurd to suppose that, out of the immense number of worlds known to astronomy, only one is peopled with living beings; yet it is not a question of numbers but of chemical and physiological conditions. Science pronounces the globes which satisfy these conditions to be, in all probability, very few; while organic life involving only inorganic chemistry, organisms adapted to the temperature of the burning fiery furnace, and so forth, are notions that hardly lie within the sphere of scientific imagination. If anyone likes to maintain that the Creator of the starry heaven is "mindful" *only* of man, neither will science accuse him of grotesque exaggeration nor will theism need to hope that he is absolutely accurate.

determination, and morality. Man may exhibit these powers and attributes in but a limited or humble degree. But, in its essence, intelligence may be common to a hierarchy of beings; and it is in virtue of his membership in that hierarchy, if such there be, rather than in his distinctive or specific and contingent characteristics, the anthropic or human, that man shares the privilege of being a bearer of the highest values, and of being in some relative, rather than in an absolute and exhaustive, sense bound up with the otherwise ineffable divine purpose. Teleology is interpretation of beginnings by *terminus ad quem*, lower stages by higher, process by product, and temporal becoming in terms of realisation of values; and the *terminus ad quem* of the world, so far as the world-process has as yet gone, and in so far as the world is known, is man. It is not that he is the last evolute in time; indeed his parasites should be later: but that he is the highest product in respect of value, and in the light of whose emergence all Nature, to which he is akin, seems to have its *raison d'être*. Hence the necessity of his figuring pre-eminently in theistic philosophy, if that is to be based on facts rather than on preconceived ideas, and is not to transcend fact save in the inevitable way of fact-controlled and reasonable extrapolation and idealisation. That the investigation, pursued in the preceding volume and in the present chapter, of man's rational and moral status and its conditioning by his physical and social environment, has involved more emphasising of what may be called man's anthropism than of his rationality, etc., in the abstract, is a necessity dictated by facts and by the empirical method. But now that the anthropocentric view of the world has been reached, and the facts which justify it have been set forth, our attention may move on from terrestrial contingencies, creaturely limitations, and specifically human characteristics, to the generic features which, from the point of view of theism, must be common to the mind of man and the Mind of God. The anthropocentric view of the world is a necessary step to the theistic interpretation of the world and man: it need not profess to be more.

The empirical approach to theism being essentially teleological, it is now necessary to raise the question, what an end or purpose, as attributable to the Deity, consists in. The idea of purpose is derived from the sphere of human activity; and such meaning as is imported into it from that context has necessary relevance only so long as that context is not transcended: such is the empirical doctrine as to the scope and validity of ideas or ideational propositions. But when applied to God, whose activities, by definition or *ex hypothesi*, include some that are unique, and whose intelligence is necessarily different in some respects from ours, the idea may become non-significant. Theism that would use the idea, it has sometimes been urged, must be unduly anthropomorphic. That need not be so, however, if such constituents of the complex idea of purpose as involve intrinsic limitations of human mentality and activity can be eliminated from it, while others, essential to the conception of purposiveness but separable from their human manifestation, can be isolated for legitimate transference to the sphere of divine activity. What elements require to be eliminated, modified, or newly related, in such recasting of the idea, has been differently decided by different exponents of theism; and perhaps it is premature to undertake the analysis and re-synthesis until an exposition has been given of one's conception of the nature and attributes of the Deity. In the absence of such preliminary discussion it may suffice to indicate possible divergences of view, as occasion calls.

In the conception of human purpose we may distinguish the following constituent elements: (1) the pre-conceived idea of a situation to be reached, (2) desire for that situation because of its value to the agent, (3) the use—in general—of means for the attainment of it, (4) the actualisation—generally by stages—of what was contemplated in thought and striven for. Into the first of these, and indeed into all of them, the idea of temporal succession enters: idea of the goal is previous to attainment of goal, desire to fruition, and so on. And whether the temporal form, characterising human experience, is to be carried over into the conception of God's activity and experience is a disputed question; that it has been variously answered is the chief source of divergence of view as to what exactly purpose, ascribed to the Deity, is. This question is not to be discussed for the present. It need only be remarked here that *if* it be possible to conceive of purposive activity as not necessarily involving the temporal stages which have been indicated, so that separation of ideated end and accomplished end be non-essential, and if concomitance of plan with actualised volition be as useful a notion as that of succession of the one upon the other, then the purposiveness of the world will consist in its being an organic system, or one in which the natures and interconnexions of the parts are determined by the whole, and in its being an expression of intelligence but not an actualisation of a *pre*-existent plan. According to this attenuated conception of purpose the relation of means to end, generally involved in human purposefulness, also vanishes.

The element of value, of desire and satisfaction, is not eliminable from the idea of purpose. Without it the category of end would lose its distinctiveness and become identical with some other, such as cause or ground, mechanism, or non-contradiction. The tendency to minimise or cancel valuation, in this connexion, and to speak of satisfactoriness as something of logical nature, conceivable in abstraction from satisfaction, is evinced by absolute monists rather than by theists. In whatever sense the world may be said to embody divine purpose, the least that can be meant is that the world contains what is of worth to the Supreme Being.

The third factor in human purposing, adaptation of means to end, is again one which some theists have been reluctant to admit into the conception of divine purpose: partly because of its temporal implication; partly because it is thought to bespeak limited power and need to overcome difficulties; and sometimes on the ground that the divine end is the world-process, not some perfected outcome of it, and that everything that we would regard as but a stage or a means toward something else is, for God, itself an end. This last issue may be considered immediately; but whether the relation of a determinate God to a determinate world, other than Himself, admits of being conceived without ascription to Him of some kinds of limitation such as do not render the distinction between means or stages and end obviously superfluous in the case of divine activity, is a question that will receive later the discussion for which it calls. The fourth of the factors into which the idea of purpose has been resolved presents no especial problem other than that already indicated when the first was touched upon.

It has been remarked before that Nature and man, empirically studied, may strongly suggest that the world is an outcome of intelligence and purpose, while *the* purpose or divine end which the universe and the world-process subserve may remain unknowable to us. But, as we have also seen, speculation on the latter subject must be allowed to influence views as to the nature of the purposiveness that is involved in the former assertion. The forthcoming alternative views, between which facts scarcely enable us to decide, may be briefly mentioned. The divine purposing may be conceived as pre-ordination, in which every detail is foreseen. An analogy is presented in Mozart's (alleged) method of composition, who is said to have imagined a movement—its themes, development, embroidery, counterpoint and orchestration—in all its detail and as a simultaneous whole, before he wrote it. If God's composition of the cosmos be regarded as similar to this, all its purposiveness will be expressed in the initial collocations, and evolution will be preformation. On the other hand, God's activity

might be conceived as fluent, or even as "increasing", rather than as wholly static, purpose. It might then be compared, in relevant respects, with the work of a dramatist or a novelist such, perhaps, as Thackeray, who seems to have moulded his characters and plot, to some extent, as he wrote. And it would appear that the divine purposiveness must be partly thus conceived if conative creaturely activity may either co-operate or clash with the Creator's, so that providential control and adaptation to the emergent must enter into the realisation of the divine plan.

Again, though the divine end is usually construed eschatologically, there is an alternative interpretation. It may be that there is no "far off divine event" toward which creation was predestined to move: the process itself may constitute the end. Certainly progress has a unique value, incapable of the absorption or transmutation which some values undergo; and the conception of the divine end as a perfected society of ethical individuals, and a philosophy of history such as is based on that presupposition, are not free from difficulties. At any rate the securing of the consummation will need to be so conceived as not to involve sacrifice of the ethical dignity of the individual person as an end for himself, and no mere instrument to the future perfecting of others. The social good may but be good in that it ministers to the goodness of individuals, each of whom—as the Christian conception of the Fatherhood of God implies—is singly an end for God. Position in the time-series, or the progress-series of social development towards perfection, may be of no moment as compared with the individual's use of his opportunities, such as they may be: timelessness, in the sense of indifference to axiological rank as temporally circumstanced, may characterise the valuation he receives from God, who seeth not as man seeth, and may read the heart rather than 'Objectively' estimate the actual output of the will. If so, asymptotic attainment of ethical perfection, and the ideal consummation, may be contingent or conditional aspects of the divine end, while progressive becoming, throughout all reaches and domains of the universe, may be its ultimate essence. These alternative conceivabilities are here merely mentioned; their relative tenability is not to be investigated. But it may further be observed that if evolution is itself an end and not a means to an end, the hard dualism of means and end must vanish. Childhood, for instance, will not be merely a stage in the making of a man; nor will groping past generations have worked merely to provide their posterity with better opportunities for making further advance. As a rose-bud has a beauty or perfection different from but quite equal to that of the full-blown rose, so may each stage in the life of the individual or the race have, along with its appropriate work, an intrinsic value, or be an end in itself as well as a means to something beyond. The only conclusion now to be elicited from the foregoing remarks is that teleology and theism may admit of statement in terms of other than the static concepts, and the abstractions such as perfection that is of no *kind*, which dominated thought until a century or so ago, and which, within the spheres of philosophy and theology, still impose themselves on some evolutionists.

The teleological approach to theism, with which this chapter has been concerned, has been made from the fact that conformity to law is intrinsic to the world, and from the conclusion that such order belongs to the world as ontal. It has already been found not to be blocked by science or by mechanistic philosophy of Nature and its law-abidingness. Besides being a cosmos explicable, in one general sense, in terms of its structure and scientific intelligibility, the world is a bearer and a producer of values in that in our *rapport* with it we are affected by it. The world is not com-

pletely described if this aspect of it is left out: less than all the data would but then be taken account of. The Actual or historical world-process, from which mechanism is an abstraction, is characterised by irreversibility, epigenesis, progressiveness of development, and by manifold adaptations which adaptedly interlace. It evokes explanation, consequently, of a different type from that pursued by physical science; and it accords pragmatic verification to use of the category of design for this new kind of explanation, as well as to use of the causal category for scientific explanation. If reason stand to formal rationality in a relation similar to that in which philosophy stands to mechanical science, philosophical reasonableness cannot be a mere extension of scientific, or of logico-mathematical, rationality; and if existential 'knowledge' is allowed its postulates, it seems but partial to disallow to 'knowledge' concerning the value-aspect of Actuality the postulate that is similarly needful to it. *Homo* who provides the *mensura* for all and every kind of intelligibility needs not to blind himself to the fact that he is more than a logical thinker, or to the fact that he stands in other relations with the universe than that of knowing about its structure. He cannot but have other problems besides that of the relation of being to thought. Philosophy in other words, is an affair of living as well as a mode of thinking. All causal knowledge is, in the last resort, but reasonable and postulatory: teleology is therefore a development from science along its own lines, or a continuation, by extrapolation, of the plotted curve which comprehensively describes its knowledge. And this is the *apologia* of theism such as professes to be reasonable belief for the guidance of life, when arranged by science and logic—or by more pretentious theology.

A Critique of the Cosmological and Teleological Arguments

C. J. DUCASSE

THE COSMOLOGICAL ARGUMENT FOR EXISTENCE OF THE GOD OF MONOTHEISM

From time to time, articles or books are written concerning the question whether sea serpents really exist, or whether on the contrary the serious reports of a specimen's having been sighted are explicable as due to malobservation. If, when this question arises, one were to reply that of course sea serpents exist, namely the well-known *Hydrophidae*, which live in the warmer parts of the Indian and Pacific oceans, are viviparous, feed on fishes, have a flattened tail, and so on, one would immediately be told that although these reptiles are serpents and live in the sea, they are not what one means when one asks whether sea serpents exist.

This example brings out the basic fact that no question as to the existence or nonexistence of something is even theoretically capable of answer unless one understands to begin with *what kind of thing* it is, about which that question is being asked. If one were to accost a person and simply ask him: "Are there any?" he would naturally ask us at once: "Any what?" Lacking specification of this, one's question is completely insoluble because completely ambiguous.

The bearing of these considerations on the question as to whether a God exists is evident. It is capable of an answer—in principle at least, even if perhaps not at a given time—only if one understands what sort of a being is meant by the word God, which is used in the question. In the classical arguments for the existence of a God, the god meant has been that of monotheism, and conceived mainly in the cosmological role commented upon above. It has been a God conceived as a person, in the sense of possessed of will, feelings, knowledge, and power; but as superperson in the sense of being infinite instead of, like human persons, finite; and "perfect," i.e., omnipotent, omniscient, and wholly good. The characteristic of infinity is made a part of the definition not here simply, as Leupa suggests in a different connection, out of man's insatiable megalomania, but in order to entail uniqueness of the God defined, i.e., to entail monotheism; the reasoning being that if one God's power is unlimited, then there can be no other god since the power of another would automatically limit that of the former.

The first of the three classical arguments for the existence of a God as so conceived is called the Cosmological Argument and takes as its major premise that nothing can exist or occur without a sufficient cause. It is then pointed out that no man or other thing in the world caused itself, but that each was caused by something antecedent. The same thing is true, however, of that antecedent itself, and of the antecedent of it, and so on; so that, it is argued, one must come at last to a first cause, which is God, and without which nothing at all would have come to be. This argument has been put in a variety of forms, and is the most popular. It is implicit in the common reference to God as "the Creator."

Considered by daylight, however, this "proof" is at once seen to be a logical monstrosity, since it attempts to prove its conclusion, viz., that something (to wit, God) exists without a cause, by taking as premise the very contradictory of this, viz., that nothing exists without a cause. This is exactly like arguing that, since all crows are black, therefore one crow is not black. As Schopenhauer puts the point, the law of universal causation

FROM: *A Philosophical Scrutiny of Religion*, C. J. Ducasse. (New York: The Ronald Press Company, 1953), pp. 333–339 and pp. 342–346. Reprinted by permission of the Ronald Press Company.

"is not so accommodating as to let itself be used like a hired cab, which we dismiss when we have reached our destination";[1] rather, if we start riding it, we have to keep on riding, without end.

But, it is sometimes objected, the universe *must* have had a beginning. The alleged necessity of this, however, is not evident. Many of the persons who assert it seem to have no difficulty in believing that the universe, in one form or another, or at the very least, human souls, will continue existing through infinite time. And, if infinitely prolonged existence in the forward direction is conceivable without contradiction, it is equally conceivable in the backward direction. That there must have been a beginning is no more self-evident than that there will have to be an end.

As an example of the kind of logic sometimes used in attempts to save Cosmological Argument, may be mentioned the following purported demonstration that an infinite regress of causes is impossible. It is based on the assertion that nowhere in the backward series of causes can there be found an "adequately sufficient reason" for the existence of any one member, say *A*, of the series. This is supposedly proved by observing that "if the *adequately sufficient reason* for *A*'s existence could be found in any one such cause or group of causes, then all causes in the series prior to this group could be considered as nonexisting as far as their requirement for *A*'s existence is concerned. But if any cause in the series is considered as nonexisting, then all subsequent causes in the series must be considered as nonexisting and hence *A* as nonexisting. Hence the hypothesis, that any cause in the series can give an adequately sufficient reason for *A*'s existence, results in the absurd conclusion that *A* cannot be existing."[2]

Obviously, however, if this proves anything at all, it is only that any *one* cause, or *finite number* of causes, cannot be an "adequately sufficient reason" for the existence of *A*; whereas what needed to be proved was that *the whole* of an *infinite* series of prior causes is not an "adequately sufficient reason" for the existence of *A*. But nothing in the article cited contributes in the least to show this.

A few words may be added concerning the contradiction alleged by the French philosopher Renouvier to be involved in the supposition that an infinite series of events have already taken place. As summarized by Ferm,[3] it is that if the sum total of past events "is already infinite, nothing more can be added since the infinite cannot be made greater than itself. Thus no further events would be possible since the infinite is already reached and cannot be added to or increased—a *reductio ad absurdum.*"

The reply, of course, is that infinite series, of which there are several kinds, have peculiar properties. For instance, in an infinite series, certain parts of it have as many items as the whole of it; for example, there are just as many even numbers—namely, an infinity—as there are numbers altogether; for the number series, and the even-number series which is only a part of it, can be put in one-to-one correspondence, as follows:

$$1, \; 2, \; 3, \; 4, \; 5, \; 6, \; 7, \ldots$$
$$2, \; 4, \; 6, \; 8, \; 10, \; 12, \; 14, \ldots$$

In doing this, one would *never* run out of even numbers in the lower line, with which to match the numbers in the upper.

Again, it can be shown that an infinite series, each member of which consists of an infinite series of whole numbers, contains no more numbers altogether than does the series of the whole numbers. But it can also be shown that there are more numerous ways of ordering the items of the series of the whole numbers than there are whole

[1] Arthur Schopenhauer, *The Fourfold Root of the Principle of Sufficient Reason,* trans. Mme Karl Hillebrand (London: Bell and Sons, 1891), pp. 42–43.

[2] "Science and True Religion," by the Rev. John S. O'Conor, *The Scientific Monthly* (February, 1941), 177.

[3] Ferm, *First Chapters in Religious Philosophy,* p. 124 n.

numbers altogether, so that certain infinite collections have more items than certain other infinite collections! Also, and more directly relevant to Renouvier's contention, some infinite series do—paradoxical as it sounds—have both a first and last term; for example, the series of fractions between and including ¼ and ½. To this infinite series, it is perfectly possible to add any finite number of other fractions we please, for instance, $11\frac{1}{16}$, ⅝ and ¾; or an infinite number of other fractions, for instance, all those between ½ and ¾. But although such addition is possible, the numerousness of the sum is exactly the same as that of the fractions between and including ¼ and ½.[4] Infinite series are queer things indeed, but if one is going to bring them into an argument for the existence of a God, one has to take them with the properties they do have, queer as these may be.

An attempt is sometimes made to evade the contradiction in terms, which as Schopenhauer points out is contained in the expression "the first cause," by introducing the notion of immanent cause, or *causa sui*, and applying it to the postulated first cause, saying that it too is indeed caused, but is *self*-caused.

Causes and effects, however, are essentially events and essentially successive, so that—unless "cause" in *causa sui* is used in some sense radically other than its common one—the expression *causa sui* too is a contradiction in terms, implying as it does that the cause concerned exists before it yet exists. The right emblem for *causa sui*, Schopenhauer pointedly remarks, "is Baron Münchhausen, sinking on horseback into the water, clinging by the legs to his horse and pulling both himself and the animal out by his own pigtail."[5]

The relation, however, which the expressions *causa sui* and "immanent cause" are intended to refer to, is not causality at all in its ordinary sense, but is the kind of relation which would obtain in the case of something whose existence would follow with *logical* necessity from its *essence*, i.e., from its nature or description. But this kind of relation, which as we shall see is the one invoked in the famous but fallacious "Ontological Proof" of the existence of God, is another monstrosity, born of confusion between, or of the dire need for one's purposes to confuse, the two distinct notions of *cause* (of the existence of something) and of *evidence* (of the truth of a proposition).[6]

In the attempt to save the Cosmological Argument's validity, it is sometimes urged that the law of universal causality applies only to things or events whose existence is "contingent," i.e., dependent on something external to themselves, and not to something, namely, God, which being *causa sui*, is "absolutely necessary." But if it were possible at all for anything to be "self-caused," then no reason appears why the world as a whole, i.e., the *entire* series of contingent things and events, might not itself be so. The expression "absolute necessity," however, is itself internally contradictory no less than is *causa sui*, for necessity is the *relation* between something necessitated and something necessitating it, and yet "absolute necessity" would mean necessity that is *not relational*.

On the other hand; if, in the expression "absolute necessity," the qualification "absolute" is not intended to negate the relational nature of necessity, then the only meaning left for "absolute" is "categorical" (as opposed to "hypothetical"). But, that existence of something B is categorically necessary means (1) that B is so related to something else A that *if* A exists, *then* necessarily B exists; *and* (2) that A *does* exist. Hence, to

---

[4] An illuminating discussion of the concept of infinity, readable without special mathematical training, is E. V. Huntington, *The Continuum as a Type of Order* (Cambridge: Harvard University Press).

[5] Schopenhauer, *op. cit.*, p. 17.

[6] That this confusion pervades Spinoza's *Ethics* is clearly shown by Schopenhauer, *op. cit.*, pp. 13–20, who calls attention to the fact that Spinoza finds himself forced to write again and again, *"ratio seu causa."*

prove that existence of B is necessary "absolutely," i.e., categorically, one must first have proved not only that if A exists then B necessarily exists, but also have somehow proved *that* A *does exist*. And, of course, the Cosmological Argument does not do this at all.

Again, it is sometimes contended that although the existence of any particular thing or event in the causal series is accounted for by reference to its immediate cause in the series, and so on backwards *ad infinitum*, nevertheless the series as a whole, i.e., the world, could conceivably have been more or less different from what it actually has been, and therefore that a cause external to the whole series (namely, God) is required to account for its being what it actually has been, rather than different. But if this argument has any force at all, it requires us then to ask in turn for the cause of that external cause, and for the cause of its cause, etc., thus leading us only to another causal series, at right angles as it were to the series constituting the universe, but like it infinitely regressive, i.e., without a first term.

Finally, if instead of taking as major premise that nothing can exist without a cause, one were to take instead that nothing except God can exist without a cause, then no use could be made of *this* premise to show that a God exists; for it would constitute only a covert declaration that, by the word "God," one *means* a being who can exist without a cause; and the question would then remain whether any such being does or does not exist.

THE ARGUMENT FROM DESIGN

Kant, Schopenhauer, and some other critics of the classical arguments for the existence of the monotheistic God have regarded the logic of the Argument from Design as somewhat more respectable than that of the other two. It has, however, been severely criticized by Hume and, as we shall see, has ultimately the same defects as that of the Cosmological Argument.

As impressive a way as any to state the argument from design would probably be the following. Suppose that man eventually manages to reach the moon, and that when the crew of the first rocket arrives it finds not only the uninhabited and uninhabitable lifeless body astronomers had predicted they would, but also, on some rock there, a complete camera quite similar to those manufactured on earth. How could its existence there be explained?

Someone might answer that, after all, the surface of the moon has been subjected for ages to violent bombardment by meteorites, and has probably been also churned by volcanic phenomena, so that, in the billions of years of its existence, almost any imaginable arrangement of its various materials is very likely to have occurred automatically; and that the camera happens to be merely one of these chance combinations.

This explanation would of course at once be rejected as impossible on the ground that the kinds of things which the forces invoked are known to be capable of producing are radically different from the kind of thing a camera is. For example, those forces in fact do not polish but scratch and crack such pieces of glass as they may happen to work on; nor are those forces capable of cutting fine screw threads, such as exist in the lens mounting and on the lens retainer, to say nothing of them screwing the latter into the former, with the lens between. And so on.

The supposition that the camera found on the moon came into existence in this manner would therefore rightly be judged preposterous. The camera, it would be said, is an object in which every part—lens, shutter, diaphragm, focusing mechanism, shutter speed regulator, dark chamber, light-sensitive film— and the relations in space of these parts to one another, are precisely what they would have to be if a photograph is to result when the shutter release is depressed; and the only hypothesis at all plausible, to account for the existence of such a complex and special arrangement of materials, is that some intelligent being conceived the idea of photographs, desired to be able to take them, designed an apparatus which would make this possible, and constructed it.

But now it is asked, if this is the only adequate explanation of the existence of a camera, is it not then necessarily also the only adequate explanation of the existence of man's eye, which in every essential part is itself literally a camera? Man, however, neither designs nor constructs his own eye. Therefore some other intelligently purposive being —namely, God—must have done so. Hence, the argument concludes, a God must exist. The same conclusion is drawn, of course, from the existence of the numerous other specialized organs of the bodies of men and of other living beings, and is extended to the specialized conditions of temperature, moisture, composition of the atmosphere, etc., indispensable to life.[7]

Obviously, however, if such capacities as the eye possesses are explicable only as products of the intelligent activity of a purposive being, the capacities of that being himself are quite as remarkable as those of the eye he designed, and are themselves then explicable only by postulation of a purposive designer of the designer of the eye—just as a designer of men is postulated to account for the fact that men have such capacities as that of designing and constructing cameras.

But explanation thus in terms of intelligently purposive causation, instead of in terms of blind causation, still has for its major premise that nothing exists without a sufficient cause (whether blind or purposive) for its being; and from this premise, as we have seen, what follows is not that a first cause, itself uncaused, must exist, but on the contrary that none such can exist. An infinite regress—here of intelligent designer-constructors—is what the mode of explanation postulated by the Design Argument logically entails; and, as we have also seen, no logical contradiction is contained

in this entailed consequence, whatever may be its merits in other respects.

A second point is that, if indeed a designer or a series of designers needs to be postulated to account for the facts in view, then such a designer need not be an omnipotent, omniscient, and wholly good being, but one only potent, intelligent, and good enough to design and create the kind of world which actually exists—a world which indeed contains many clever adjustments and felicitous adaptions, but which also contains a vast amount of evil, waste, disease, maladjustment and frustration. For if man is assumed competent to perceive correctly that the universe contains many good things and exhibits much teleology, there is then no ground to deny him equal competence to perceive also correctly that the universe contains numerous evils and much dysteleology. The pious admonitions to distrust his competence to judge that one thing or another is really an evil, which are addressed to him by writers of theodicies, are called for equally with regard to man's judgment that this or that thing is really good, if they are called for at all.

It is well to bear in mind further that a designer is not necessarily superior in every respect to what he designs and constructs: man, for instance, designs and constructs many instruments —microscopes, electronic computers, steam shovels, etc.—whose capacities to do certain things vastly exceed his own. Indeed, even the simplest of the innumerable tools man makes is constructed by him because he himself lacks capacities the tool possesses: even a crude knife or axe has a better cutting edge than have man's teeth or nails.

At this point, however, we may return to the comparison of the eye to the camera, and ask whether it is indeed true, as the Argument from Design asserts, that only intelligent plan and construction can account for the existence of such highly adapted structures. The answer, as Hume points out, is that this is only one of the ways in which, according to experience, such structures actually come

[7] Wm. Paley, *Natural Theology* (New York: Harper's Family Library, 1840) is a classical instance of such a train of thought.

into being. Natural growth, vegetable and animal, is another actual way; and if, instead of starting with the camera, we should elect to start with the eye, then, if we had not observed how cameras are constructed, what the similarity of the camera to the eye would suggest to us would be that the camera too must be somehow a product of *natural growth*. To suppose it, of course, would be to speculate—to postulate that the process of coming to be, in a case, viz., the camera's, where we did not observe it, is of the same kind, viz., growth, as in the case of the eye, where we do observe it taking place—ontogenetically through cell division, and phylogenetically through mutation and automatic elimination of mutations disadvantageous to preservation of life. But the converse supposition, viz., that the eye comes into existence as does the camera, is speculation too and speculation quite as wild; for in the production of the eye we do not observe any hands, lens-polishing instruments, or other tools such as produce a camera. Nor do we observe any designer at work. Moreover, if we speculatively postulate one, we have to postulate in addition that he is capable of doing in some wholly mysterious manner without hands or tools what camera makers can do only by means of these. And further, if we proceed on the supposition that the eye comes into existence, like the camera, by design and intelligent construction, then what the supposition suggests is not one infinitely wise and potent designer-constructor, but much rather a plurality of finite designers and artisans, collaborating to turn out a generally neat but by no means perfect piece of work—indeed, sometimes one so defective that a camera maker that did no better would soon go bankrupt.

Rather than all this, however, we can suppose more economically but quite as explanatorily that the eye is, as Schopenhauer would have said, an automatic objectification of an obscure craving or felt need to see; the hand, of a craving to grasp, etc. Such craving, however, not being *purpose* since purpose implies not only a craving but in addition an idea of what would satisfy the craving; and still less being *intelligent* purpose since this implies not only a craving and an idea of what would satisfy it, but in addition knowledge, or at least beliefs, as to what actions would or might bring into existence that which would satisfy the craving. It may be objected that we do not understand *how* an obscure craving to see can generate an eye or at least the bodily variations which gradually culminate in an eye. But we do not understand in the least better *how* the craving of a designer external to man, that man shall have an eye, can generate without hands or tools that eye in man. Hence, if we suppose a craving to be somehow capable of doing the trick, it is more economical to locate it in the animal himself, who at least is known to exist, than in an external designer, whose existence is purely suppositious and not in the least more explanatory.

The considerations appealed to by the Argument from Design thus do not, when their implications are developed logically, contribute anything that would support the hypothesis of an omniscient, and perfectly good designer. Rather, they militate against it. The only sort of God compatible with, though not evidenced by, the observable facts would be, as John Stuart Mill perceived, a God possibly great but nevertheless limited in power, or knowledge, or goodness, or in any two or all three of these respects.

The
Moral
Argument

Immanuel Kant offers an argument which, in effect, attempts to base religion on morality. The conclusion can perhaps best be stated in these terms: It is reasonable to believe that there is a morally perfect Being possessed of sufficient power to guarantee justice. Often, at least, Kant uses "knowledge" in such a way that only what is empirically testable can count as knowledge; so we cannot, for Kant, *know* that God exists. The ontological, cosmological, and teleological proofs are all, in Kant's opinion, unsuccessful. But by means of his version of the moral argument, we can, he suggests, rationally justify the belief that God exists in the sense that this claim is presupposed by morality. But we must be careful in putting Kant's view even in this way, for normally "P presupposes Q" means " that Q is false entails that P is false," while Kant holds that all our moral obligations but one would remain intact even were "God exists" known to be false.

With a minimum of oversimplification, Kant's argument can be stated in these terms: (1) The highest good includes two elements—worthiness of being happy and actually possessing happiness; (2) it is possible that one possess one of the elements but not the other, for good men can be unhappy and happy men can be evil. (These claims are to be found in Kant's Introduction; hereafter we will be dealing with Section Five.) (3) Everyone is obligated to seek the highest good, in the sense that he is obligated to seek a state of affairs in which each man receives happiness proportionate to his worthiness of it. (4) Whatever everyone is obligated to seek can be attained; thus the highest good can be attained. (5) No man can guarantee that he himself or anyone else gains whatever happiness he is worthy of; so (6) unless there is a being both powerful enough to bring about this proportionment and good enough always to do so, the highest good will not be attained. Hence (7) there must be a being of this sort.

Kant does not claim that this argument shows that we have a duty to believe in God, nor (as we have mentioned) would any duty except that specified in (3) be canceled were (7) known to be false. Further, it should be mentioned that Kant develops his argument in the context of a moral and teleological system; he refers to some of the elements of this system in the selection that follows. Even if the specific argument under review should fail, it is possible that the system as a whole could be revised and defended. But that is too large an issue for consideration here. The last two sections of our selection from Kant offer further explication of the sense in which Kant believes that he has established (7) as a postulate.

However, we do not, on Kant's own terms, have the obligation specified in (3). We are, perhaps, under the obligation to do what we can to further the highest good, but—for the very reason specified in (6)—we are not obligated to seek the highest good. The difference between these obligations is not hard to understand. Consider the difference between (A) Jones is obligated to eliminate all the suffering in the world, and (B) Jones is obligated to eliminate whatever suffering he can eliminate. There is no problem in seeing how (B) could express an obligation that Jones has, while (A), being well beyond Jones's capacities, expresses no obligation that Jones has. Analogously, one could have an obligation to do what he can to further progress toward the highest good, but not have an obligation to seek or attain the highest good. One could make the same point by noting that (3) is ambiguous as between these obligations and is acceptable only on the weaker interpretation. So (3) is incorrect, and (5) is thus unsupported. Hence we have no proof of (7).

The Existence of God Is a Justified Postulate
IMMANUEL KANT

OF THE DIALECTIC
OF PURE REASON
IN DEFINING THE CONCEPTION
OF THE "SUMMUM BONUM"

*T*he conception of the *summum* itself contains an ambiguity which might occasion needless disputes if we did not attend to it. The *summum* may mean either the supreme (*supremum*) or the perfect (*consummatum*). The former is that condition which is itself unconditioned, *i.e.* is not subordinate to any other (*originarium*); the second is that whole which is not a part of a greater whole of the same kind (*perfectissimum*). It has been shown in the Analytic that *virtue* (as worthiness to be happy) is the *supreme condition* of all that can appear to us desirable, and consequently of all our pursuit of happiness, and is therefore the *supreme* good. But it does not follow that it is the whole and perfect good as the object of the desires of rational finite beings; for this requires happiness also, and that not merely in the partial eyes of the person who makes himself an end, but even in the judgment of an impartial reason, which regards persons in general as ends in themselves. For to need happiness, to deserve it (247) and yet at the same time not to participate in it, cannot be consistent with the perfect volition of a rational being possessed at the same time of all power, if, for the sake of experiment, we conceive such a being. Now inasmuch as virtue and happiness together constitute the possession of the *summum bonum* in a person, and the distribution of happiness in exact proportion to morality (which is the worth of the person, and his worthiness to be happy) constitutes the *summum bonum* of a possible world; hence this *summum bonum* expresses the whole, the perfect good, in which, however, virtue as the condition is always the supreme good, since it has no condition above it; whereas happiness, while it is pleasant to the possessor of it, is not of itself absolutely and in all respects good, but always presupposes morally right behaviour as its condition. (216)

When two elements are *necessarily* united in one concept, they must be connected as reason and consequence, and this either so that their unity is considered as *analytical* (logical connexion), or as *synthetical* (real connexion)—the former following the law of identity, the latter that of causality. The connexion of virtue and happiness may therefore be understood in two ways: either the endeavour to be virtuous and the rational pursuit of happiness are not two distinct actions, but absolutely identical, in which case no maxim need be made the principle of the former, other than what serves for the latter; or the connexion consists in this, that virtue produces happiness as something distinct from the consciousness of virtue, as a cause produces an effect.

The ancient Greek schools were, properly speaking, only two, and in determining the conception of the *summum bonum* these followed in fact one and the same method, inasmuch as they did not allow virtue and happiness to be regarded as two distinct elements of the *summum bonum*, and consequently sought (248) the unity of the principle by the rule of identity; but they differed as to which of the two was to be taken

FROM: *Kant's Critique of Practical Reason and Other Works on the Theory of Ethics*, T. K. Abbott. (Essex, England: Longmans Green and Co., Ltd.,) pp. 206–209, 220–231, 240–246. Reprinted by permission of Longmans Green and Co., Ltd. (originally published in 1788). The numbers in brackets in the text refer to the corresponding pages of the 1838 Rosencranz and Schubert edition, Vol. VIII.

as the fundamental notion. The *Epicurean* said: To be conscious that one's maxims lead to happiness is virtue; the *Stoic* said: To be conscious of one's virtue is happiness. With the former, *Prudence* was equivalent to morality; with the latter, who chose a higher designation for virtue, morality alone was true wisdom.

While we must admire the men who in such early times tried all imaginable ways of extending the domain of philosophy, we must at the same time lament that their acuteness was unfortunately misapplied in trying to trace out identity between two extremely heterogeneous notions, those of happiness and virtue. But it agrees with the dialectical spirit of their times (and subtle minds are even now sometimes misled in the same way) to get rid of irreconcilable differences in principle by seeking to change them into a mere contest about words, and thus apparently working out the identity of the notion under different names, and this usually occurs in cases where the combination of heterogeneous principles lies so deep or so high, or would require so complete a transformation of the doctrines assumed in the rest of the philosophical system, that men are afraid to penetrate deeply into the real difference, and prefer treating it as a difference in matters of form.

While both schools sought to trace out the identity of the practical principles of virtue and happiness, they were not agreed as to the way in which they tried to force this identity, but were separated infinitely from one another, the one placing its principle on the side of sense, the other on that of reason; the one in the consciousness of sensible wants, the other in the independence of practical reason (249) on all sensible grounds of determination. According to the Epicurean the notion of virtue was already involved in the maxim: To promote one's own happiness; according to the Stoics, on the other hand, the feeling of happiness was already contained in the consciousness of virtue. Now

whatever is contained in another notion is identical with part of the containing notion, but not with the whole, and moreover two wholes may be specifically distinct, although they consist of the same parts, namely, if the parts are united into a whole in totally different ways. The Stoic maintained that virtue was the *whole summum bonum*, and happiness only the consciousness of possessing it, as making part of the state of the subject. The Epicurean maintained that happiness was the *whole summum bonum*, and virtue only the form of the maxim for its pursuit, viz. the rational use of the means for attaining it.

Now it is clear from the Analytic that the maxims of virtue and those of private happiness are quite heterogeneous as to their supreme practical principle; and although they belong to one *summum bonum* which together they make possible, yet they are so far from coinciding that they restrict and check one another very much in the same subject. Thus the question, *How is the summum bonum* practically possible? still remains an unsolved problem, notwithstanding all the *attempts at coalition* that have hitherto been made. The Analytic has, however, shown what it is that makes the problem difficult to solve; namely, that happiness and morality are two specifically *distinct elements of the summum bonum*, and therefore their combination *cannot* be *analytically* cognized (as if the man that seeks his own happiness should find by mere analysis of his conception that in so acting he is virtuous, or as if the man that follows virtue should in the consciousness of such conduct find that he is already happy *ipso facto*) (250), but must be a *synthesis* of concepts. Now since this combination is recognized as *à priori*, and therefore as practically necessary, and consequently not as derived from experience, so that the possibility of the *summum bonum* does not rest on any empirical principle, it follows that the *deduction* [legitimation] of this concept must be *transcendental*. It is *à priori* (morally) necessary to *produce the summum bonum by freedom of will*: therefore the condition of its possibility must rest solely on *à priori* principles of cognition. . .

THE EXISTENCE OF GOD AS A POSTULATE OF PURE PRACTICAL REASON

In the foregoing analysis the moral law led to a practical problem which is prescribed by pure reason alone, without the aid of any sensible motives, namely, that of the necessary completeness of the first and principal element of the *summum bonum*, viz. Morality; and as this can be perfectly solved only in eternity, to the postulate of *immorality*. The same law must also lead us to affirm the possibility of the second element of the *summum bonum*, viz. Happiness proportioned to that morality, and this on grounds as disinterested as before, and solely from impartial reason; that is, it must lead to the supposition of the existence of a cause adequate to this effect; in other words, it must postulate the *existence of God*, as the necessary condition of the possibility of the *summum bonum* (an object of the will which is necessarily connected with the moral legislation of pure reason). We proceed to exhibit this connexion in a convincing manner.

Happiness is the condition of a rational being in the world with whom *everything goes according to his wish and will*; it rests, therefore, on the harmony of physical nature with his whole end, and likewise with the essential determining principle of his will. Now the moral law as a law of freedom commands by determining principles (266), which ought to be quite independent on nature and on its harmony with our faculty of desire (as springs). But the acting rational being in the world is not the cause of the world and of nature itself. There is not the least ground, therefore, in the moral law for a necessary connexion between morality and proportionate happiness in a being that belongs to the world as part of it, and therefore dependent on it, and which for that rea-

son cannot by his will be a cause of this nature, nor by his own power make it thoroughly harmonize, as far as his happiness is concerned, with his practical principles. Nevertheless, in the practical problem of pure reason, *i.e.* the necessary pursuit of the *summum bonum*, such a connexion is postulated as necessary: we ought to endeavour to promote the *summum bonum*, which, therefore, must be possible. Accordingly, the existence of a cause of all nature, distinct from nature itself, and containing the principle of this connexion, namely, of the exact harmony of happiness with morality, is also *postulated*. Now, this supreme cause must contain the principle of the harmony of nature, not merely with a law of the will of rational beings, but with the conception of this *law*, in so far as they make it the *supreme determining principle of the will*, and consequently not merely with the form of morals, but with their morality as their motive, that is, with their moral character. Therefore, the *summum bonum* is possible in the world only on the supposition of a Supreme Being[1] having a causality corresponding to moral character. Now a being that is capable of acting on the conception of laws is an *intelligence* (a rational being), and the causality of such a being according to this conception of laws is his *will*; therefore the supreme cause of nature, which must be presupposed as a condition of the *summum bonum* (267) is a being which is the cause of nature by *intelligence* and *will*, consequently its author, that is God. It follows that the postulate of the possibility of the *highest derived good* (the best world) is likewise the postulate of the reality of a *highest original good*, that is to say, of the existence of God. Now it was seen to be a duty for us to promote the *summum bonum*; consequently it is not merely allowable,

[1] [The original has "a Supreme Nature." "*Natur*," however, almost invariably means "physical nature"; therefore Hartenstein supplies the words "cause of" before "nature." More probably "Nature" is a slip for "Ursache," "cause."]

but it is a necessity connected with duty as a requisite, that we should presuppose the possibility of this *summum bonum*; and as this is possible only on condition of the existence of God, it inseparably connects the supposition of this with duty; that is, it is morally necessary to assume the existence of God.

It must be remembered here that this moral necessity is *subjective*, that is, it is a want, and not *objective*, that is, itself a duty, for there cannot be a duty to suppose the existence of anything (since this concerns only the theoretical employment of reason). Moreover, it is not meant by this that it is necessary to suppose the existence of God *as a basis of all obligation in general* (for this rests, as has been sufficiently proved, simply on the autonomy of reason itself). What belongs to duty here is only the endeavour to realize and promote the *summum bonum* in the world, the possibility of which can therefore be postulated; and as our reason finds it not conceivable except on the supposition of a supreme intelligence, the admission of this existence is therefore connected with the consciousness of our duty, although the admission itself belongs to the domain of speculative reason. Considered in respect of this alone, as a principle of explanation, it may be called a *hypothesis*, but in reference to the intelligibility of an object given us by the moral law (the *summum bonum*), and consequently of a requirement for practical purposes, it may be called *faith*, that is to say a pure *rational faith*, since pure reason (268) (both in its theoretical and its practical use) is the sole source from which it springs.

From this *deduction* it is now intelligible why the *Greek* schools could never attain the solution of their problem of the practical possibility of the *summum bonum*, because they made the rule of the use which the will of man makes of his freedom the sole and sufficient ground of this possibility, thinking that they had no need for that purpose of the existence of God. No doubt they were so far right

that they established the principle of morals of itself independently on this postulate, from the relation of reason only to the will, and consequently made it the *supreme* practical condition of the *summum bonum*; but it was not therefore the *whole* condition of its possibility. The *Epicureans* had indeed assumed as the supreme principle of morality a wholly false one, namely, that of happiness, and had substituted for a law a maxim of arbitrary choice according to every man's inclination; they proceeded, however, *consistently* enough in this, that they degraded their *summum bonum* likewise just in proportion to the meanness of their fundamental principle, and looked for no greater happiness than can be attained by human prudence (including temperance and moderation of the inclinations), and this, as we know, would be scanty enough and would be very different according to circumstances; not to mention the exceptions that their maxims must perpetually admit and which make them incapable of being laws. The *Stoics*, on the contrary, had chosen their supreme practical principle quite rightly, making virtue the condition of the *summum bonum*; but when they represented the degree of virtue required by its pure law as fully attainable in this life, they not only strained the moral powers of the *man* whom they called *the wise* beyond all the limits of his nature, and assumed (269) a thing that contradicts all our knowledge of men, but also and principally they would not allow the second *element* of the *summum bonum*, namely, happiness, to be properly a special object of human desire, but made their *wise man*, like a divinity in his consciousness of the excellence of his person, wholly independent on nature (as regards his own contentment); they exposed him indeed to the evils of life, but made him not subject to them (at the same time representing him also as free from moral evil). They thus, in fact, left out the second element of the *summum bonum*, namely, personal happiness, placing it solely in action and satisfaction with one's own personal worth, thus including it in the consciousness of being morally minded, in which they might have been sufficiently refuted by the voice of their own nature.

The doctrine of Christianity,[2] even

[2] It is commonly held that the Christian precept of morality has no advantage in respect of purity over the moral conceptions of the Stoics; the distinction between them is, however, very obvious. The Stoic system made the consciousness of strength of mind the pivot on which all moral dispositions should turn; and although its disciples spoke of duties and even defined them very well, yet they placed the spring and proper determining principle of the will in an elevation of the mind above the lower springs of the senses, which owe their power only to weakness of mind. With them, therefore, virtue was a sort of heroism in the *wise man* who, raising himself above the animal nature of man, is sufficient for himself, and while he prescribes duties to others is himself raised above them, and is not subject to any temptation to transgress the moral law. All this, however, they could not have done if they had conceived this law in all its purity and strictness, as the precept of the Gospel does. When I give the name *idea* to a perfection to which nothing adequate can be given in experience, it does not follow that the moral ideas are something transcendent, that is something of which we could not even determine the concept adequately, or of which it is uncertain whether there is any object corresponding to it at all (270), as is the case with the ideas of speculative reason; on the contrary, being types of practical perfection, they serve as the indispensable rule of conduct and likewise as the *standard of comparison.* Now if I consider *Christian morals* on their philosophical side, then compared with the ideas of the Greek schools they would appear as follows: the ideas of the *Cynics,* the *Epicureans,* the *Stoics,* and the *Christians* are: *simplicity of nature, prudence, wisdom,* and *holiness.* In respect of the way of attaining them, the Greek schools were distinguished from one another thus, that the Cynics only required *common sense,* the others the path of *science,* but both found the mere *use of natural powers* sufficient for the purpose. Christian morality, because its precept is framed (as a moral precept must be) so pure and unyielding, takes from man all

if we do not consider it as a religious doctrine, gives, touching this point (269), a conception of the *summum bonum* (the kingdom of God), which alone satisfies the strictest demand of practical reason. The moral law is holy (unyielding) and demands holiness of morals, although all the moral perfection to which man can attain is still only virtue, that is, a rightful disposition arising from *respect* for the law, implying consciousness of a constant propensity to transgression, or at least a want of purity, that is, a mixture of many spurious (not moral) motives of obedience to the law, consequently a self-esteem combined with humility. In respect, then, of the holiness which the Christian law requires, this leaves the creature nothing but a progress in *infinitum,* but for that very reason it justifies him in hoping for an endless duration of his existence. The *worth* of a character *perfectly* accordant with the moral law is infinite, since (270) the only restriction on all possible happiness in the judgment of a wise and all-powerful distributor of it is the absence of conformity of rational beings to their duty. But the moral law of itself does not *promise* any happiness, for according to our conceptions of an order of nature in general, this is not necessarily connected with obedience to the law. Now Christian morality supplies this defect (of the second indispensable element of the *summum bonum*) by representing the world, in which rational beings devote themselves with all their soul to the moral law, as a *kingdom of God,* in which nature and morality are brought into a harmony foreign to each of itself, by a holy Author who makes the derived *summum bonum* possible. *Holiness* of life is prescribed to them as

confidence that he can be fully adequate to it, at least in this life, but again sets it up by enabling us to hope that if we act as well as it is in our *power* to do, then what is not in our power will come in to our aid from another source, whether we know how this may be or not. *Aristotle* and *Plato* differed only as to the *origin* of our moral conceptions.

a rule even in this life, while the welfare proportioned to it, namely, *bliss*, is represented as attainable only in an eternity; because the *former* must always be the pattern of their conduct in every state, and progress towards it is already possible and necessary in this life; while the *latter*, under the name of happiness, cannot be attained at all in this world (so far as our own power is concerned), and therefore is made simply an object of hope. Nevertheless, the Christian principle of *morality* itself is not theological (so as to be heteronomy), but is autonomy of pure practical reason, since it does not make the knowledge of God and His will the foundation of these laws, but only of the attainment of the *summum bonum*, on condition of following these laws, and it does not even place the proper *spring* of this obedience in the desired results, but solely in the conception of duty, as that of which the faithful observance alone constitutes the worthiness to obtain those happy consequences.

In this manner the moral laws lead through the conception of the *summum bonum* as the object and final end of pure practical reason to *religion* (271), that is, to the *recognition of all duties as divine commands, not as sanctions,*[3] *that is to say, arbitrary ordinances of a foreign will and contingent in themselves,* but as essential *laws* of every free will in itself, which, nevertheless, must be regarded as commands of the Supreme Being, because it is only from a morally perfect (holy and good) and at the same time all-powerful will, and consequently only through harmony with this will, that we can hope to attain the *summum bonum* which the moral law makes it our duty to take as the object of our endeavours. Here again, then, all remains disinterested and founded merely on duty; neither fear nor hope being made the fundamental springs, which if taken as principles would destroy the whole moral

---

[3] [The word 'sanction' is here used in the technical German sense, which is familiar to students of history in connexion with the 'Pragmatic Sanction.']

worth of actions. The moral law commands me to make the highest possible good in a world the ultimate object of all my conduct. But I cannot hope to effect this otherwise than by the harmony of my will with that of a holy and good Author of the world; and although the conception of the *summum bonum* as a whole, in which the greatest happiness is conceived as combined in the most exact proportion with the highest degree of moral perfection (possible in creatures), includes *my own happiness*, yet it is not this that is the determining principle of the will which is enjoined to promote the *summum bonum*, but the moral law, which, on the contrary, limits by strict conditions my unbounded desire of happiness.

Hence also morality is not properly the doctrine how we should *make* ourselves happy, but how we should become *worthy* of happiness. It is only when religion is added that there also comes in the hope of participating some day in happiness in proportion as we have endeavoured to be not unworthy of it.

(272) A man is *worthy* to possess a thing or a state when his possession of it is in harmony with the *summum bonum*. We can now easily see that all worthiness depends on moral conduct, since in the conception of the *summum bonum* this constitutes the condition of the rest (which belongs to one's state), namely, the participation of happiness. Now it follows from this that *morality* should never be treated as a *doctrine of happiness*, that is, an instruction how to become happy; for it has to do simply with the rational condition (*conditio sine qua non*) of happiness, not with the means of attaining it. But when morality has been completely expounded (which merely imposes duties instead of providing rules for selfish desires), then first, after the moral desire to promote the *summum bonum* (to bring the kingdom of God to us) has been awakened, a desire founded on a law, and which could not previously arise in any selfish mind, and when for the behoof of this desire the step to religion has been taken, then

this ethical doctrine may be also called a doctrine of happiness because the *hope* of happiness first begins with religion only.

We can also see from this that, when we ask what is *God's ultimate end* in creating the world, we must not name the *happiness* of the rational beings in it, but the *summum bonum*, which adds a further condition to that wish of such beings, namely, the condition of being worthy of happiness, that is, the *morality* of these same rational beings, a condition which alone contains the rule by which only they can hope to share in the former at the hand of a *wise* Author. For as *wisdom* theoretically considered signifies *the knowledge of the summum bonum*, and practically *the accordance of the will with the summum bonum*, we cannot attribute to a supreme independent wisdom an end based merely on *goodness* (273). For we cannot conceive the action of this goodness (in respect of the happiness of rational beings) as suitable to the highest original good, except under the restrictive conditions of harmony with the holiness of His will. Therefore those who placed the end of creation in the glory of God (provided that this is not conceived anthropomorphically as a desire to be praised) have perhaps hit upon the best expression. For nothing glorifies God more than that which is the most estimable thing in the world, respect for His command, the observance of the holy duty that His law imposes on us, when there is added thereto His glorious plan of crowning such a beautiful order of things with corresponding happiness. If the latter (to speak humanly) makes Him worthy of love, by the *former* He is an object of adoration. Even men can never acquire respect by benevolence alone, though they may gain love, so that the greatest beneficence only procures them honour when it is regulated by worthiness.[5]

[5] In order to make these characteristics of these conceptions clear, I add the remark that whilst we ascribe to God various attributes, the quality of which we also find applicable to creatures, only that in Him

That in the order of ends, man (and with him every rational being) is *an end in himself*, that is, that he can never be used merely as a means by any (274) (not even by God) without being at the same time an end also himself, that therefore *humanity* in our person must be *holy* to ourselves, this follows now of itself because he is the *subject*[6] *of the moral law*, in other words, of that which is holy in itself, and on account of which and in agreement with which alone can anything be termed holy. For this moral law is founded on the autonomy of his will, as a free will which by its universal laws must necessarily be able to agree with that to which it is to submit itself.

OF THE POSTULATES OF PURE PRACTICAL REASON IN GENERAL

They all proceed from the principle of morality, which is not a postulate but a law, by which reason determines the will directly, which will, because it is so determined as a pure will, requires these necessary conditions of obedience to its precept. These postulates are not theoretical dogmas but, suppositions practically necessary; while then they do [not][7] extend our speculative knowledge, they give

they are raised to the highest degree, *e.g.* power, knowledge, presence, goodness, &c., under the designations of omnipotence, omniscience, omnipresence, &c., there are three that are ascribed to God exclusively, and yet without the addition of greatness, and which are all moral. He is the *only holy*, the *only blessed*, the *only wise*, because these conceptions already imply the absence of limitation. In the order of these attributes He is also the *holy lawgiver* (and creator), the *good governor* (and preserver), and the *just judge*, three attributes which include everything by which God is the object of religion, and conformity with which the metaphysical perfections are added of themselves in the reason.

[6] [That the ambiguity of the word *subject* may not mislead the reader, it may be remarked that it is here used in the psychological sense *subjectum legis*, not *subjectus legi*.]

[7] [Absent from the original text.]

objective reality to the ideas of speculative reason in general (by means of their reference to what is practical), and give it a right to concepts, the possibility even of which it could not otherwise venture to affirm.

These postulates are those *of immortality, freedom* positively considered (as the causality of a being so far as he belongs to the intelligible world), and the *existence of God*. The *first* results from the practically necessary condition of a duration (275) adequate to the complete fulfilment of the moral law; the *second* from the necessary supposition of independence on the sensible world, and of the faculty of determining one's will according to the law of an intelligible world, that is, of freedom; the *third* from the necessary condition of the existence of the *summum bonum* in such an intelligible world, by the supposition of the supreme independent good, that is, the existence of God.

Thus the fact that respect for the moral law necessarily makes the *summum bonum* an object of our endeavours, and the supposition thence resulting of its objective reality, lead through the postulates of practical reason to conceptions which speculative reason might indeed present as problems, but could never solve. Thus it leads—1. To that one in the solution of which the latter could do nothing but commit *paralogisms* (namely, that of immortality), because it could not lay hold of the character of permanence, by which to complete the psychological conception of an ultimate subject necessarily ascribed to the soul in self-consciousness, so as to make it the real conception of a substance, a character which practical reason furnishes by the postulate of a duration required for accordance with the moral law in the *summum bonum*, which is the whole end of practical reason. 2. It leads to that of which speculative reason contained nothing but *antinomy*, the solution of which it could only found on a notion problematically conceivable indeed, but whose objective reality it could not prove or determine, namely, the *cosmological* idea of an intel-

ligible world and the consciousness of our existence in it, by means of the postulate of freedom (the reality of which it lays down by virtue of the moral law), and with it likewise the law of an intelligible world, to which speculative reason could only point, but could not define its conception. 3. What speculative reason was able to think, but was obliged to leave undetermined as a mere transcendental *ideal* (276), viz. the *theological* conception of the First Being, to this it gives significance (in a practical view, that is, as a condition of the possibility of the object of a will determined by that law), namely, as the supreme principle of the *summum bonum* in an intelligible world, by means of moral legislation in it invested with sovereign power.

Is our knowledge, however, actually extended in this way by pure practical reason, and is that *immanent* in practical reason which for the speculative was only *transcendent*? Certainly, but *only in a practical point of view*. For we do not thereby take knowledge of the nature of our souls, nor of the intelligible world, nor of the Supreme Being, with respect to what they are in themselves, but we have merely combined the conceptions of them in the *practical* concept of the *summum bonum* as the object of our will, and this altogether *à priori*, but only by means of the moral law, and merely in reference to it, in respect of the object which it commands. But how freedom is possible, and how we are to conceive this kind of causality theoretically and positively, is not thereby discovered; but only that there is such a causality is postulated by the moral law and in its behoof. It is the same with the remaining ideas, the possibility of which no human intelligence will ever fathom, but the truth of which, on the other hand, no sophistry will ever wrest from the conviction even of the commonest man.

OF BELIEF FROM A REQUIREMENT OF PURE REASON

A want or requirement of pure reason in its speculative use leads only to a *hypothesis*; that of pure practical reason to a *postulate*; for in the former case I ascend from the result as high as I please in the series of causes, not in order to give objective reality to the result (*e.g.* the causal connexion of things and changes in the world), but in order thoroughly to satisfy my inquiring reason in respect of it. Thus I see before me order and design in nature, and need not resort to speculation to assure myself of their *reality*, but to *explain* them I have *to pre-suppose a Deity* as their cause; and then since the inference from an effect to a definite cause is always uncertain and doubtful, especially to a cause so precise and so perfectly defined as we have to conceive in God, hence the highest degree of certainty to which this pre-supposition can be brought is, that it is the most rational opinion for us men[8] (288). On the other hand, a requirement of pure *practical* reason is based on a *duty*, that of making something (the *summum bonum*) the object of my will so as to promote it with all my powers; in which case I must suppose its possibility, and consequently also the conditions necessary thereto, namely, God, freedom, and immortality; since I cannot prove these by my speculative reason, although neither can I refute them. This duty is founded on something that is indeed quite independent on these

[8] But even here we should not be able to allege a requirement *of reason*, if we had not before our eyes a problematical, but yet inevitable, conception of reason, namely, that of an absolutely necessary being. This conception now seeks to be defined, and this, in addition to the tendency to extend itself, is the objective ground of a requirement of speculative reason, namely, to have a more precise definition of the conception of a necessary being which is to serve as the first cause of other beings, so as to make these* latter knowable by some means. Without such antecedent necessary problems there are no *requirements*—at least not of *pure reason*—the rest are requirements of *inclination*.

* I read 'diese' with the ed. of 1791. Rosenkranz and Hartenstein both read 'dieses,' 'this being.'

suppositions, and is of itself apodictically certain, namely, the moral law; and so far it needs no further support by theoretical views as to the inner constitution of things, the secret final aim of the order of the world, or a presiding ruler thereof, in order to bind me in the most perfect manner to act in unconditional conformity to the law. But the subjective effect of this law, namely, the mental *disposition* conformed to it and made necessary by it, to promote the practically possible *summum bonum*, this pre-supposes at least that the latter is *possible*, for it would be practically impossible to strive after the object of a conception which at bottom was empty and had no object. Now the above-mentioned postulates concern only the physical or metaphysical conditions of the *possibility* of the *summum bonum* (289); in a word, those which lie in the nature of things; not however, for the sake of an arbitrary speculative purpose, but of a practically necessary end of a pure rational will, which in this case does not *choose*, but *obeys* an inexorable command of reason, the foundation of which is *objective*, in the constitution of things as they must be universally judged by pure reason, and is not based on *inclination*; for we are in nowise justified in assuming, on account of what we *wish* on merely *subjective* grounds, that the means thereto are possible or that its object is real. This, then, is an absolutely necessary requirement, and what it pre-supposes is not merely justified as an allowable hypothesis, but as a postulate in a practical point of view; and admitting that the pure moral law inexorably binds every man as a command (not as a rule of prudence), the righteous man may say: I *will* that there be a God, that my existence in this world be also an existence outside the chain of physical causes, and in a pure world of the understanding, and lastly, that my duration be endless; I firmly abide by this, and will not let this faith be taken from me; for in this instance alone my interest, because I *must* not relax anything of it, inevitably determines my judgment, without regarding sophistries, however unable I may be to answer them or to oppose them with others more plausible.[9]

. . . .

(290) In order to prevent misconception in the use of a notion as yet so unusual as that of a faith of pure practical reason, let me be permitted to add one more remark. It might almost seem as if this rational faith were here announced as itself a *command*, namely, that we should assume the *summum bonum* as possible. But a faith that is commanded is nonsense. Let the preceding analysis, however, be remembered of what is required to be supposed in the conception of the *summum bonum*, and it will be seen that it cannot be commanded to assume this possibility, and no practical disposition of mind is required

[9] In the *Deutsches Museum,* February, 1787, there is a dissertation by a very subtle and clear-headed man, the late *Wizenmann,* whose early death is to be lamented, in which he disputes the right to argue from a want to the objective reality of its object, and illustrates the point by the example of *a man in love,* who, having fooled himself into an idea of beauty, which is merely a chimera of his own brain, would fain conclude that such an object really exists somewhere (290). I quite agree with him in this, in all cases where the want is founded on *inclination,* which cannot necessarily postulate the existence of its object even for the man that is affected by it, much less can it contain a demand valid for everyone, and therefore it is merely a *subjective* ground of the wish. But in the present case we have a want of reason springing from an objective determining principle of the will, namely, the moral law, which necessarily binds every rational being, and therefore justifies him in assuming *à priori* in nature the conditions proper for it, and makes the latter inseparable from the complete practical use of reason. It is a duty to realize the *summum bonum* to the utmost of our power, therefore it must be possible, consequently it is unavoidable for every rational being in the world to assume what is necessary for its objective possibility. The assumption is as necessary as the moral law, in connexion with which alone it is valid.

to *admit* it; but that speculative reason must concede it without being asked, for no one can affirm that it is *impossible* in itself that rational beings in the world should at the same time be worthy of happiness in conformity with the moral law, and also possess this happiness proportionately. Now in respect of the first element of the *summum bonum,* namely, that which concerns morality, the moral law gives merely a command, and to doubt the possibility of that element would be the same as to call in question the moral law itself (291). But as regards the second element of that object, namely, happiness perfectly proportioned to that worthiness, it is true that there is no need of a command to admit its possibility in general, for theoretical reason has nothing to say against it; but *the manner* in which we have to conceive this harmony of the laws of nature with those of freedom has in it something in respect of which we have a *choice,* because theoretical reason decides nothing with apodictic certainty about it, and in respect of this there may be a moral interest which turns the scale.

I had said above that in a mere course of nature in the world an accurate correspondence between happiness and moral worth is not to be expected, and must be regarded as impossible, and that therefore the possibility of the *summum bonum* cannot be admitted from this side except on the supposition of a moral Author of the world. I purposely reserved the restriction of this judgment to the *subjective* conditions of our reason, in order not to make use of it until the manner of this belief should be defined more precisely. The fact is that the impossibility referred to is *merely subjective,* that is, our reason finds it *impossible for it* to render conceivable in the way of a mere course of nature a connexion so exactly proportioned and so thoroughly adapted to an end, between two sets of events happening according to such distinct laws; although, as with everything else in nature that is adapted to an end, it cannot prove, that is, show by sufficient objective reasons, that it is not possible by universal laws of nature.

Now, however, a deciding principle of a different kind comes into play to turn the scale in this uncertainty of speculative reason. The command to promote the *summum bonum* is established on an objective basis (in practical reason); the possibility of the same in general is likewise established on an objective basis (292) (in theoretical reason, which has nothing to say against it). But reason cannot decide objectively in what way we are to conceive this possibility; whether by universal laws of nature without a wise Author presiding over nature, or only on supposition of such an Author. Now here there comes in a *subjective* condition of reason; the only way theoretically possible for it, of conceiving the exact harmony of the kingdom of nature with the kingdom of morals, which is the condition of the possibility of the *summum bonum*; and at the same time the only one conducive to morality (which depends on an objective law of reason). Now since the promotion of this *summum bonum*, and therefore the supposition of its possibility, are *objectively* necessary (though only as a result of practical reason), while at the same time the manner in which we would conceive it rests with our own choice, and in this choice a free interest of pure practical reason decides for the assumption of a wise Author of the world; it is clear that the principle that herein determines our judgment, though as a want it is *subjective*, yet at the same time being the means of promoting what is *objectively* (practically) necessary, is the foundation of a *maxim* of belief in a moral point of view, that is, a *faith of pure practical reason*. This, then, is not commanded, but being a voluntary determination of our judgment, conducive to the moral (commanded) purpose, and moreover harmonizing with the theoretical requirement of reason, to assume that existence and to make it the foundation of our further employment of reason, it has itself sprung from the moral disposition of mind; it may there-

fore at times waver even in the well-disposed, but can never be reduced to unbelief.

OF THE WISE ADAPTATION OF MAN'S COGNITIVE FACULTIES TO HIS PRACTICAL DESTINATION

(293) If human nature is destined to endeavour after the *summum bonum*, we must suppose also that the measure of its cognitive faculties, and particularly their relation to one another, is suitable to this end. Now the Critique of Pure *Speculative* Reason proves that this is incapable of solving satisfactorily the most weighty problems that are proposed to it, although it does not ignore the natural and important hints received from the same reason, nor the great steps that it can make to approach to this great goal that is set before it, which, however, it can never reach of itself, even with the help of the greatest knowledge of nature. Nature then seems here to have provided us only in a *step-motherly* fashion with the faculty required for our end.

Suppose now that in this matter nature had conformed to our wish, and had given us that capacity of discernment or that enlightenment which we would gladly possess, or which some *imagine* they actually possess, what would in all probability be the consequence? Unless our whole nature were at the same time changed, our inclinations, which always have the first word, would first of all demand their own satisfaction, and joined with rational reflection, the greatest possible and most lasting satisfaction, under the name of happiness; the moral law (294) would afterwards speak, in order to keep them within their proper bounds, and even to subject them all to a higher end, which has no regard to inclination. But instead of the conflict that the moral disposition has now to carry on with the inclinations, in which, though after some defeats, moral strength of mind may be gradually acquired, *God* and *eternity* with their *awful majesty* would stand unceasingly *before our eyes* (for what we can prove perfectly is to us as certain as that of which we are assured by the sight of our eyes). Transgression of the law, would, no doubt, be avoided; what is commanded would be done; but the mental *disposition*, from which actions ought to proceed, cannot be infused by any command, and in this case the spur of action is ever active and *external*, so that reason has no need to exert itself in order to gather strength to resist the inclinations by a lively representation of the dignity of the law: hence most of the actions that conformed to the law would be done from fear, a few only from hope, and none at all from duty, and the moral worth of actions, on which alone in the eyes of supreme wisdom the worth of the person and even that of the world depends, would cease to exist. As long as the nature of man remains what it is, his conduct would thus be changed into mere mechanism, in which, as in a puppet-show, everything would *gesticulate* well, but there would be *no life* in the figures. Now, when it is quite otherwise with us, when with all the effort of our reason we have only a very obscure and doubtful view into the future, when the Governor of the world allows us only to conjecture His existence and His majesty, not to behold them or prove them clearly; and, on the other hand, the moral law within us, without promising or threatening anything with certainty, demands of us disinterested respect; and only when this respect has become active (295) and dominant does it allow us by means of it a prospect into the world of the supersensible, and then only with weak glances; all this being so, there is room for true moral disposition, immediately devoted to the law, and a rational creature can become worthy of sharing in the *summum bonum* that corresponds to the worth of his person and not merely to his actions. Thus what the study of nature and of man teaches us sufficiently elsewhere may well be true here also; that the unsearchable wisdom by which we exist is not less worthy of admiration in what it has denied than in what it has granted.

Does Evil
Prove
That God
Does Not Exist?

*T*he problem of evil can be stated fairly simply. According to traditional theism, God, is all-knowing, all-powerful, and all-good. He created the world from nothing and providentially governs the course of history. Nonetheless, there is evil in the world—pain and suffering that apparently serve no good purpose, natural disasters that kill and maim and destroy, murder and malice that hurt all parties concerned. Why, if God exists and has the nature ascribed to Him (and, for traditional theism, if no being having that nature exists, then God does not exist), is there any evil, let alone so much of it?

There are at least three distinct questions here. The purpose of this introduction is to sort them out and to indicate some of the answers given in the selections that follow. The three questions are:

(I) Are the statements (1) "God (an all-knowing, all-powerful, all-good being) exists" and (2) "There is evil" logically incompatible, so that if (2) is true, then (1) is false?

(II) If (1) and (2) are logically compatible, does (2) nonetheless provide strong *evidence* against (1)? Two statements can be logically compatible (both *can* be true without contradiction) while the truth of one of them constitutes strong evidence against the truth of the other. For example: (3) Jones was the only man in the near vicinity of Smith when Smith was murdered, and Jones was the only man who would profit from Smith's death, and (4) Jones did not murder Smith, are compatible but (3) provides reasons relevant to showing (4) to be false. Our question is: Does (2) provide a reason relevant to showing (1) to be false?

(III) *Why* is evil permitted by God, granting that God does exist? To attempt to answer this question is to offer a *theodicy*, an explanation of the role of evil in the plans of providence.

(I) Philosophers differ greatly as to the answer to our question. J. L. Mackie takes it to be *obvious* that (1) and (2) are incompatible, so much so that any attempt to show that they are compatible *must* somehow be mistaken. In contrast, Nelson Pike categorically denies that they are incompatible and doubts that any argument to show that they are incompatible could be effective.

Mackie admits that (1) and (2) *alone* are not incompatible; he says that "we need some additional premises, or perhaps some quasi-logical rules connecting the terms 'good,' 'evil,' and 'omnipotent.' " The admission is important: even for Mackie, (1) and (2) *by themselves* are not incompatible. Pike, however, is dubious that any additional premises are available which are true and will, with (1) and (2), yield a contradiction. If (5) every evil there is serves some morally sufficient purpose (Pike offers some remarks to clarify the phrase "morally sufficient purpose") is true, then it is dubious that there are any further premises that will serve Mackie's purposes. And, Pike remarks, until (5) is proven false, Hume's argument (and Mackie's as well) "against the existence of God is not finished. And it is not at all obvious that it is *capable* of effective completion." So far as these selections go, then, the critic needs a proof of (5) to make good his case, and no proof of (5) is offered. Pike is dubious that there is any, and he may be right.

(II) But if one grants that (1) and (2) are compatible, (2) may still be evidence against (1). Many of Mackie's comments could be reinterpreted along these lines, and much of Hume's Part XI is also capable of being interpreted in this manner. Two comments will, I believe, clarify this aspect of the discussion. One is that, as Pike notes, Philo (or Hume through Philo) uses (2) in a specific way. He does not use (2), primarily at least, as evidence against (1). Rather, he argues that if (1) is inferred from data we get by observing natural phenomena and human conduct, we must use *all* the data obtained from such observation. Among these data is the existence of evil. Not only (as we noted in the section on the cosmological and teleological arguments) are we at most entitled to infer a *somewhat* knowledgeable and powerful Designer from these data, but we are *at most* entitled to infer a *somewhat* good being. Philo remarks: "I am sceptic enough to allow that the bad appearances [i.e., evil] . . . may be compatible with such attributes as you suppose, but surely they can never prove these attributes." The fact of evil prevents us from inferring from the existence and character of the natural and human environment to an all-good Deity, even if in fact God is all-good. So used, as Pike notes, (2) is not an objection to a theology that takes the existence of God as a datum of faith though it may be an objection to a theology that infers from the phenomena of nature and history to an all-good Deity.

But (2) *has* been used as evidence against (1). One important way (see Mackie's article) in which this has been done is by suggesting that God could have created a better world than our own—for example by not permitting such things as pain, fear, temptation, and the like, and by having created men so that they were morally perfect. The response has traditionally been made that these evils are justified in that they make certain virtues possible. Ninian Smart offers a fresh and powerful statement of this line of argument. His thesis is that the *meaning* of the claims that God could create morally perfect men and that it would be better for there to be no pain, fear, or temptation is unclear. As Smart puts it, "the point [is] that moral discourse is embedded in the cosmic status quo." Since our appraisal of a man as good is closely tied to how he reacts in contexts that involve fear, pain, temptation, and the like, the more we alter these contexts the less clear it is when a man should be called "good" or what would be *meant* by calling him "good." Evaluation of Smart's argument is a complex matter. Perhaps *some* alteration for the better of some kinds or degrees are consistent with our using our moral terms as we now do, but not other kinds or degrees of alteration of present conditions. However this issue is to be resolved, Smart raises a significant question as to how clear it is that claims of the form "It would obviously be better had God created the world so that . . ." are true, or even intelligible. Of course there are other ways in which (2) has been used as putative evidence against (1).

(III) There is disagreement as to how important it is for a theist to attempt some answer to our third question—that is, offer some kind of theodicy. Mackie, taking the problem of evil to be intractable, would of course deny that any theodicy could possibly succeed. Pike, however, says that for a theology that does not attempt to infer (1) from empirical and evaluative data—as opposed to accepting (1) on the basis of an a priori proof such as Anselm's or taking (1) as a datum of faith—"The problem of evil can only be the problem of discovering a *specific* theodicy which is adequate." But given (1), there must be a morally sufficient reason for whatever evils there are, and "once it is granted that there is some specific reason for evil, there is a sense in which it is no longer vital to find it."

Hume, however, raises several questions, which anyone who wishes to offer a theodicy will attempt to answer. Whether it is *necessary* for a theist to offer a theodicy is, as noted, open to question. It would seem, however, that he only strengthens his claim that (2) does not constitute evidence against (1) as he succeeds in the difficult (perhaps even presumptuous) task of writing a theodicy.

Not every issue raised in the following selections fits neatly in the above classification. Two such issues are particularly important and deserve mention. One is this: In "God is good," to what degree is "good" identical in meaning and function to the word "good" in "Jones (a particular man) is good." There is the danger that in attempting to be reverent, a theist may claim that the sense in which God is good is incomprehensible to us, that we just do not know what "God is good" means. But if this view is held, it is altogether problematic as to why God should be revered, or even respected.

The other issue is that each of the writers assumes that (2) is true—that there *is* evil in the universe in some nonarbitrary sense of "evil." This claim is not itself indubitable, as it requires that moral claims—(2) at least—be known or reasonably believed to be true. This in turn raises the question whether moral sentences *have* truth value and *can* be rationally appraised. (See *Theory of Knowledge*: "Is Moral Knowledge Possible?" and *Ethics*: "How Can Ethical Viewpoints Be Evaluated?")

The Existence of Evil Does Prove That God Does Not Exist
DAVID HUME

X

*I*t *is my opinion*, I own, replied Demea, that each man feels, in a manner, the truth of religion within his own breast, and, from a consciousness of his imbecility and misery rather than from any reasoning, is led to seek protection from that Being on whom he and all nature is dependent. So anxious or so tedious are even the best scenes of life that futurity is still the object of all our hopes and fears. We incessantly look forward and endeavour, by prayers, adoration, and sacrifice, to appease those unknown powers whom we find, by experience, so able to afflict and oppress us. Wretched creatures that we are! What resource for us amidst the innumerable ills of life did not religion suggest some methods of atonement, and appease those terrors with which we are incessantly agitated and tormented?

I am indeed persuaded, said Philo, that the best and indeed the only method of bringing everyone to a due sense of religion is by just representations of the misery and wickedness of men. And for that purpose a talent of eloquence and strong imagery is more requisite than that of reasoning and argument. For is it necessary to prove what everyone feels within himself? It is only necessary to make us feel it, if possible, more intimately and sensibly.

The people, indeed, replied Demea, are sufficiently convinced of this great and melancholy truth. The miseries of life, the unhappiness of man, the general corruptions of our nature, the unsatisfactory enjoyment of pleasures, riches, honours—these phrases have become almost proverbial in all languages. And who can doubt of what all men declare from their own immediate feeling and experience?

In this point, said Philo, the learned are perfectly agreed with the vulgar; and in all letters, *sacred* and *profane*, the topic of human misery has been insisted on with the most pathetic eloquence that sorrow and melancholy could inspire. The poets, who speak from sentiment, without a system, and whose testimony has therefore the more authority, abound in images of this nature. From Homer down to Dr. Young, the whole inspired tribe have ever been sensible that no other representation of things would suit the feeling and observation of each individual.

As to authorities, replied Demea, you need not seek them. Look round this library of Cleanthes. I shall venture to

FROM: *Dialogues Concerning Natural Religion*, David Hume. Parts 10 and 11 (originally published in 1779).

affirm that, except authors of particular sciences, such as chemistry or botany, who have no occasion to treat of human life, (there is scarce) one of those innumerable writers) from whom (the sense of human misery has not, in some passage or other, (extorted a complaint and confession of it.) At least, the chance is entirely on that side; and no one author has ever, so far as I can recollect, been so extravagant as to deny it.

There you must excuse me, said Philo: Leibniz has denied it, and is perhaps the first[1] who ventured upon so bold and paradoxical an opinion; at least, the first who made it essential to his philosophical system.

And by being the first, replied Demea, might he not have been sensible of his error? For is this a subject in which philosophers can propose to make discoveries especially in so late an age? And can any man hope by a simple denial (for the subject scarcely admits of reasoning) to bear down the united testimony of mankind, founded on sense and consciousness?

And why should man, added he, pretend to an exemption from the lot of all other animals? The whole earth, believe me, Philo, is cursed and polluted. A perpetual war is kindled amongst all living creatures. Necessity, hunger, want stimulate the strong and courageous; fear, anxiety, terror agitate the weak and infirm. The first entrance into life gives anguish to the new-born infant and to its wretched parent; weakness, impotence, distress attend each stage of that life, and it is, at last, finished in agony and horror.

Observe, too, says Philo, the curious artifices of nature in order to embitter the life of every living being. The stronger prey upon the weaker and keep them in perpetual terror and anxiety. The weaker, too, in their turn, often prey upon the stronger, and vex and molest them without relaxation. Consider that innumerable race of insects, which either are bred on the body of each animal or, flying about, infix their stings in him. These insects have others still less than themselves which torment them. And thus on each hand, before and behind, above and below, every animal is surrounded with enemies which incessantly seek his misery and destruction.

Man alone, said Demea, seems to be, in part, an exception to this rule. For by combination in society he can easily master lions, tigers, and bears, whose greater strength and agility naturally enable them to prey upon him.

On the contrary, it is here chiefly, cried Philo, that the uniform and equal maxims of nature are most apparent. Man, it is true, can, by combination, surmount all his *real* enemies and become master of the whole animal creation; but does he not immediately raise up to himself *imaginary* enemies, the demons of his fancy, who haunt him with superstitious terrors and blast every enjoyment of life? His pleasure, as he imagines, becomes in their eyes a crime; his food and repose give them umbrage and offence; his very sleep and dreams furnish new materials to anxious fear; and even death, his refuge from every other ill, presents only the dread of endless and innumerable woes. Nor does the wolf molest more the timid flock than superstition does the anxious breast of wretched mortals.

Besides, consider, Demea: This very society by which we surmount those wild beasts, our natural enemies, what new enemies does it not raise to us? What woe and misery does it not occasion? Man is the greatest enemy of man. Oppression, injustice, contempt, contumely, violence, sedition, war, calumny, treachery, fraud—by these they mutually torment each other, and they would soon dissolve that society which they had formed were it not for the dread of still greater ills which must attend their separation.

But though these external insults, said Demea, from animals, from men,

[1] That sentiment had been maintained by Dr. King and some few others before Leibniz, though by none of so great fame as that German philosopher.

from all the elements, which assault us form a frightful catalogue of woes, they are nothing in comparison of those which arise within ourselves, from the distempered condition of our mind and body. How many lie under the lingering torment of diseases? Hear the pathetic enumeration of the great poet.

Intestine stone and ulcer, colic-pangs,
Demoniac frenzy, moping melancholy,
And moon-struck madness, pining
    atrophy,
Marasmus, and wide-wasting pestilence.
Dire was the tossing, deep the groans:
    Despair
Tended the sick, busiest from couch to
    couch.
And over them triumphant Death *his dart*
Shook: but delay'd to strike, though oft
    invok'd
With vows, as their chief good and final
    hope.[2]

The disorders of the mind, continued Demea, though more secret, are not perhaps less dismal and vexatious. Remorse, shame, anguish, rage, disappointment, anxiety, fear, dejection, despair— who has ever passed through life without cruel inroads from these tormentors? How many have scarcely ever felt any better sensations? Labour and poverty, so abhorred by everyone, are the certain lot of the far greater number; and those few privileged persons who enjoy ease and opulence never reach contentment or true felicity. All the goods of life united would not make a very happy man, but all the ills united would make a wretch indeed; and any one of them almost (and who can be free from every one?), nay, often the absence of one good (and who can possess all?) is sufficient to render life ineligible.

Were a stranger to drop on a sudden into this world, I would show him, as a specimen of its ills, an hospital full of diseases, a prison crowded with malefactors and debtors, a field of battle strewed with carcases, a fleet foundering in the ocean, a nation languishing under tyranny, famine, or pestilence. To turn the gay side of life to him and give him a notion of its pleasures—whither should I conduct him? To a ball, to an opera, to court? He might justly think that I was only showing him a diversity of distress and sorrow.

There is no evading such striking instances, said Philo, but by apologies which still further aggravate the charge. Why have all men, I ask, in all ages, complained incessantly of the miseries of life? . . . They have no just reason, says one: these complaints proceed only from their discontented, repining, anxious disposition. . . . And can there possibly, I reply, be a more certain foundation of misery than such a wretched temper?

But if they were really as unhappy as they pretend, says my antagonist, why do they remain in life? . . .

Not satisfied with life, afraid of death—this is the secret chain, say I, that holds us. We are terrified, not bribed to the continuance of our existence.

It is only a false delicacy, he may insist, which a few refined spirits indulge, and which has spread these complaints among the whole race of mankind. . . . And what is this delicacy, I ask, which you blame? Is it anything but a greater sensibility to all the pleasures and pains of life? And if the man of a delicate, refined temper, by being so much more alive than the rest of the world, is only so much more unhappy, what judgment must we form in general of human life?

Let men remain at rest, says our adversary, and they will be easy. They are willing artificers of their own misery. . . . No! reply I: an anxious languor follows their repose; disappointment, vexation, trouble, their activity and ambition.

I can observe something like what you mention in some others, replied Cleanthes, but I confess I feel little or nothing of it in myself, and hope that it is not so common as you represent it.

If you feel not human misery yourself, cried Demea, I congratulate you on so happy a singularity. Others, seemingly

---

[2] [Milton: *Paradise Lost*, Bk. XI.]

the most prosperous, have not been ashamed to vent their complaints in the most melancholy strains. Let us attend to the great, the fortunate emperor, Charles V, when, tired with human grandeur, he resigned all his extensive dominions into the hands of his son. In the last harangue which he made on that memorable occasion, he publicly avowed *that the greatest prosperities which he had ever enjoyed had been mixed with so many adversities that he might truly say he had never enjoyed any satisfaction or contentment.* But did the retired life in which he sought for shelter afford him any greater happiness? If we may credit his son's account, his repentance commenced the very day of his resignation.

Cicero's fortune, from small beginnings, rose to the greatest lustre and renown; yet what pathetic complaints of the ills of life do his familiar letters, as well as philosophical discourses, contain? And suitably to his own experience, he introduces Cato, the great, the fortunate Cato protesting in his old age that had he a new life in his offer he would reject the present.

Ask yourself, ask any of your acquaintance, whether they would live over again the last ten or twenty years of their life. No! but the next twenty, they say, will be better:

And from the dregs of life, hope to receive
What the first sprightly running could not give[3]

Thus, at last, they find (such is the greatness of human misery, it reconciles even contradictions) that they complain at once of the shortness of life and of its vanity and sorrow.

And is it possible, Cleanthes, said Philo, that after all these reflections, and infinitely more which might be suggested, you can still persevere in your anthropomorphism, and assert the moral at-

[3] [John Dryden, *Aureng-Zebe*, Act IV, sc. 1.]

tributes of the Deity, his justice, benevolence, mercy, and rectitude, to be of the same nature with these virtues in human creatures? His power, we allow, is infinite; whatever he wills is executed; but neither man nor any other animal is happy; therefore, he does not will their happiness. His wisdom is infinite; he is never mistaken in choosing the means to any end; but the course of nature tends not to human or animal felicity; therefore, it is not established for that purpose. Through the whole compass of human knowledge there are no inferences more certain and infallible than these. In what respect, then, do his benevolence and mercy resemble the benevolence and mercy of men?

Epicurus' old questions are yet unanswered.

Is he willing to prevent evil, but not able? then is he impotent. Is he able, but not willing? then he is malevolent. Is he both able and willing? whence then is evil?

You ascribe, Cleanthes, (and I believe justly) a purpose and intention to nature. But what, I beseech you, is the object of that curious artifice and machinery which she has displayed in all animals—the preservation alone of individuals, and propagation of the species? It seems enough for her purpose if such a rank be barely upheld in the universe, without any care or concern for the happiness of the members that compose it. No resource for this purpose: no machinery in order merely to give pleasure or ease; no fund of pure joy and contentment; no indulgence without some want or necessity accompanying it. At least, the few phenomena of this nature are overbalanced by opposite phenomena of still greater importance.

Our sense of music, harmony, and indeed beauty of all kinds, gives satisfaction, without being absolutely necessary to the preservation and propagation of the species. But what racking pains, on the other hand, arise from gouts, gravels, megrims, toothaches, rheumatisms, where the injury to the animal machinery is either small or incurable?

Mirth, laughter, play, frolic seem gratuitous satisfactions which have no further tendency; spleen, melancholy, discontent, superstition are pains of the same nature. How then does the Divine benevolence display itself, in the sense of your anthropomorphites? None but we mystics, as you were pleased to call us, can account for this strange mixture of phenomena, by deriving it from attributes infinitely perfect but incomprehensible.

And have you, at last, said Cleanthes smiling, betrayed your intentions, Philo? Your long agreement with Demea did indeed a little surprise me, but I find you were all the while erecting a concealed battery against me. And I must confess that you have now fallen upon a subject worthy of your noble spirit of opposition and controversy. If you can make out the present point, and prove mankind to be unhappy or corrupted, there is an end at once of all religion. For to what purpose establish the natural attributes of the Deity, while the moral are still doubtful and uncertain?

You take umbrage very easily, replied Demea, at opinions the most innocent and the most generally received, even amongst the religious and devout themselves; and nothing can be more surprising than to find a topic like this—concerning the wickedness and misery of man—charged with no less than atheism and profaneness. Have not all pious divines and preachers who have indulged their rhetoric on so fertile a subject, have they not easily, I say, given a solution of any difficulties which may attend it? This world is but a point in comparison of the universe; this life but a moment in comparison of eternity. The present evil phenomena, therefore, are rectified in other regions, and in some future period of existence. And the eyes of men, being then opened to larger views of things, see the whole connection of general laws, and trace, with adoration, the benevolence and rectitude of the Deity through all the mazes and intricacies of his providence.

No! replied Cleanthes, no! These arbitrary suppositions can never be admitted, contrary to matter of fact, visible and uncontroverted. Whence can any cause be known but from its known effects? Whence can any hypothesis be proved but from the apparent phenomena? To establish one hypothesis upon another is building entirely in the air; and the utmost we ever attain by these conjectures and fictions is to ascertain the bare possibility of our opinion, but never can we, upon such terms, establish its reality.

The only method of supporting Divine benevolence—and it is what I willingly embrace—is to deny absolutely the misery and wickedness of man. Your representations are exaggerated; your melancholy views mostly fictitious; your inferences contrary to fact and experience. Health is more common than sickness; pleasure than pain; happiness than misery. And for one vexation which we meet with, we attain, upon computation, a hundred enjoyments.

Admitting your position, replied Philo, which yet is extremely doubtful, you must at the same time allow that, if pain be less frequent than pleasure, it is infinitely more violent and durable. One hour of it is often able to outweigh a day, a week, a month of our common insipid enjoyments; and how many days, weeks, and months are passed by several in the most acute torments? Pleasure, scarcely in one instance, is ever able to reach ecstasy and rapture; and in no one instance can it continue for any time at its highest pitch and altitude. The spirits evaporate, the nerves relax, the fabric is disordered, and the enjoyment quickly degenerates into fatigue and uneasiness. But pain often, good God, how often! rises to torture and agony; and the longer it continues, it becomes still more genuine agony and torture. Patience is exhausted, courage languishes, melancholy seizes us, and nothing terminates our misery but the removal of its cause or another event which is the sole cure of all evil, but which, from our natural folly, we regard with still greater horror and consternation.

But not to insist upon these topics, continued Philo, though most obvious, certain, and important, I must use the freedom to admonish you, Cleanthes, that you have put the controversy upon a most dangerous issue, and are unawares introducing a total scepticism into the most essential articles of natural and revealed theology. What! no method of fixing a just foundation for religion unless we allow the happiness of human life, and maintain a continued existence even in this world, with all our present pains, infirmities, vexations, and follies, to be eligible and desirable! But this is contrary to everyone's feeling and experience; it is contrary to an authority so established as nothing can subvert. No decisive proofs can ever be produced against this authority; nor is it possible for you to compute, estimate, and compare all the pains and all the pleasures in the lives of all men and of all animals; and thus, by your resting the whole system of religion on a point which, from its very nature, must for ever be uncertain, you tacitly confess that that system is equally uncertain.

But allowing you what never will be believed, at least, what you never possibly can prove, that animal or, at least, human happiness in this life exceeds its misery, you have yet done nothing; for this is not, by any means, what we expect from infinite power, infinite wisdom, and infinite goodness. Why is there any misery at all in the world? Not by chance, surely. From some cause then. Is it from the intention of the Deity? But he is perfectly benevolent. Is it contrary to his intention? But he is almighty. Nothing can shake the solidity of this reasoning, so short, so clear, so decisive, except we assert that these subjects exceed all human capacity, and that our common measures of truth and falsehood are not applicable to them—a topic which I have all along insisted on, but which you have, from the beginning, rejected with scorn and indignation.

But I will be contented to retire still from this intrenchment, for I deny that you can ever force me in it. I will allow that pain or misery in man is *compatible* with infinite power and goodness in the Deity, even in your sense of these attributes: what are you advanced by all these concessions? A mere possible compatibility is not sufficient. You must *prove* these pure, unmixed, and uncontrollable attributes from the present mixed and confused phenomena, and from these alone. A hopeful undertaking! Were the phenomena ever so pure and unmixed, yet, being finite, they would be insufficient for that purpose. How much more, where they are also so jarring and discordant!

Here, Cleanthes, I find myself at ease in my argument. Here I triumph. Formerly, when we argued concerning the natural attributes of intelligence and design, I needed all my sceptical and metaphysical subtlety to elude your grasp. In many views of the universe and of its parts, particularly the latter, the beauty and fitness of final causes strike us with such irresistible force that all objections appear (what I believe they really are) mere cavils and sophisms; nor can we then imagine how it was ever possible for us to repose any weight on them. But there is no view of human life or of the condition of mankind from which, without the greatest violence, we can infer the moral attributes or learn that infinite benevolence, conjoined with infinite power and infinite wisdom, which we must discover by the eyes of faith alone. It is your turn now to tug the labouring oar, and to support your philosophical subtleties against the dictates of plain reason and experience.

XI

I scruple not to allow, said Cleanthes, that I have been apt to suspect the frequent repetition of the word *infinite*, which we meet with in all theological writers, to savour more of panegyric than of philosophy, and that any purposes of reasoning, and even of religion, would be better served were we to rest contented with more accurate and more modern expressions. The terms *admirable, excellent, superlatively great, wise,* and *holy*—

these sufficiently fill the imaginations of men, and anything beyond, besides that it leads into absurdities, has no influence on the affections or sentiments. Thus in the present subject, if we abandon all human analogy, as seems your intention, Demea, I am afraid we abandon all religion and retain no conception of the great object of our adoration. If we preserve human analogy, we must forever find it impossible to reconcile any mixture of evil in the universe with infinite attributes; much less can we ever prove the latter from the former. But supposing the Author of nature to be finitely perfect though far exceeding mankind, a satisfactory account may then be given of natural and moral evil, and every untoward phenomenon be explained and adjusted. A lesser evil may then be chosen in order to avoid a greater; inconveniences be submitted to in order to reach a desirable end; and, in a word, benevolence, regulated by wisdom and limited by necessity, may produce just such a world as the present. You, Philo, who are so prompt at starting views and reflections and analogies, I would gladly hear, at length, without interruption, your opinion of this new theory; and if it deserve our attention, we may afterwards, at more leisure, reduce it into form.

My sentiments, replied Philo, are not worth being made a mystery of; and, therefore, without any ceremony, I shall deliver what occurs to me with regard to the present subject. It must, I think, be allowed that, if a very limited intelligence whom we shall suppose utterly unacquainted with the universe were assured that it were the production of a very good, wise, and powerful Being, however finite, he would, from his conjectures, form *beforehand* a different notion of it from what we find it to be by experience; nor would he ever imagine, merely from these attributes of the cause of which he is informed, that the effect could be so full of vice and misery and disorder, as it appears in this life. Supposing now that this person were brought into the world, still assured that

it was the workmanship of such a sublime and benevolent Being, he might, perhaps, be surprised at the disappointment, but would never retract his former belief if founded on any very solid argument, since such a limited intelligence must be sensible of his own blindness and ignorance, and must allow that there may be many solutions of those phenomena which will for ever escape his comprehension. But supposing, which is the real case with regard to man, that this creature is not antecedently convinced of a supreme intelligence, benevolent, and powerful, but is left to gather such a belief from the appearances of things— this entirely alters the case, nor will he ever find any reason for such a conclusion. He may be fully convinced of the narrow limits of his understanding, but this will not help him in forming an inference concerning the goodness of superior powers, since he must form that inference from what he knows, not from what he is ignorant of. The more you exaggerate his weakness and ignorance, the more diffident you render him, and give him the greater suspicion that such subjects are beyond the reach of his faculties. You are obliged, therefore, to reason with him merely from the known phenomena, and to drop arbitrary supposition or conjecture.

Did I show you a house or palace where there was not one apartment convenient or agreeable, where the windows, doors, fires, passages, stairs, and the whole economy of the building were the source of noise, confusion, fatigue, darkness, and the extremes of heat and cold, you would certainly blame the contrivance, without any further examination. The architect would in vain display his subtilty, and prove to you that, if this door or that window were altered, greater ills would ensue. What he says may be strictly true: the alteration of one particular, while the other parts of the building remain, may only augment the inconveniences. But still you would assert in general that, if the architect had had skill and good intentions, he might have formed such a plan of the whole, and might have adjusted the parts in such a manner as would have remedied all or most of these inconveniences. His ignorance, or even your own ignorance of such a plan, will never convince you of the impossibility of it. If you find any inconveniences and deformities in the building, you will always, without entering into any detail, condemn the architect.

In short, I repeat the question: Is the world, considered in general and as it appears to us in this life, different from what a man or such a limited being would, *beforehand*, expect from a very powerful, wise, and benevolent Deity? It must be strange prejudice to assert the contrary. And from thence I conclude that, however consistent the world may be, allowing certain suppositions and conjectures with the idea of such a Deity, it can never afford us an inference concerning his existence. The consistency is not absolutely denied, only the inference. Conjectures, especially where infinity is excluded from the Divine attributes, may perhaps be sufficient to prove a consistency, but can never be foundations for any inference.

There seem to be *four* circumstances on which depend all or the greatest part of the ills that molest sensible creatures; and it is not impossible but all these circumstances may be necessary and unavoidable. We know so little beyond common life, or even of common life, that, with regard to the economy of a universe, there is no conjecture, however wild, which may not be just, nor any one, however plausible, which may not be erroneous. All that belongs to human understanding, in this deep ignorance and obscurity, is to be skeptical or at least cautious, and not to admit of any hypothesis whatever, much less of any which is supported by no appearance of probability. Now this I assert to be the case with regard to all the causes of evil and the circumstances on which it depends. None of them appear to human reason in the least degree necessary or unavoidable, nor can we suppose them

such, without the utmost license of imagination.

The *first* circumstance which introduces evil is that contrivance or economy of the animal creation by which pains, as well as pleasures, are employed to excite all creatures to action, and make them vigilant in the great work of self-preservation. Now pleasure alone, in its various degrees, seems to human understanding sufficient for this purpose. All animals might be constantly in a state of enjoyment; but when urged by any of the necessities of nature, such as thirst, hunger, weariness, instead of pain, they might feel a diminution of pleasure by which they might be prompted to seek that object which is necessary to their subsistence. Men pursue pleasure as eagerly as they avoid pain; at least, they might have been so constituted. It seems, therefore, plainly possible to carry on the business of life without any pain. Why then is any animal ever rendered susceptible of such a sensation? If animals can be free from it an hour, they might enjoy a perpetual exemption from it, and it required as particular a contrivance of their organs to produce that feeling as to endow them with sight, hearing, or any of the senses. Shall we conjecture that such a contrivance was necessary, without any appearance of reason, and shall we build on that conjecture as on the most certain truth?

But a capacity of pain would not alone produce pain were it not for the *second* circumstance, viz., the conducting of the world by general laws; and this seems nowise necessary to a very perfect Being. It is true, if everything were conducted by particular volitions, the course of nature would be perpetually broken, and no man could employ his reason in the conduct of life. But might not other particular volitions remedy this inconvenience? In short, might not the Deity exterminate all ill, wherever it were to be found, and produce all good, without any preparation or long progress of causes and effects?

Besides, we must consider that, according to the present economy of the world, the course of nature, though supposed exactly regular, yet to us appears not so, and many events are uncertain, and many disappoint our expectations. Health and sickness, calm and tempest, with an infinite number of other accidents whose causes are unknown and variable, have a great influence both on the fortunes of particular persons and on the prosperity of public societies; and indeed all human life, in a manner, depends on such accidents. A being, therefore, who knows the secret springs of the universe might easily, by particular volitions, turn all these accidents to the good of mankind and render the whole world happy, without discovering himself in any operation. A fleet whose purposes were salutary to society might always meet a fair wind. Good princes enjoy sound health and long life. Persons born to power and authority be framed with good tempers and virtuous dispositions. A few such events as these, regularly and wisely conducted, would change the face of the world, and yet would no more seem to disturb the course of nature or confound human conduct than the present economy of things where the causes are secret and variable and compounded. Some small touches given to Caligula's brain in his infancy might have converted him into a Trajan. One wave, a little higher than the rest, by burying Caesar and his fortune in the bottom of the ocean, might have restored liberty to a considerable part of mankind. There may, for aught we know, be good reasons why Providence interposes not in this manner, but they are unknown to us; and, though the mere supposition that such reasons exist may be sufficient to *save* the conclusion concerning the Divine attributes, yet surely it can never be sufficient to *establish* that conclusion.

If everything in the universe be conducted by general laws, and if animals be rendered susceptible of pain, it scarcely seems possible but some ill must arise in the various shocks of matter and the various concurrence and opposition of general laws; but this ill would be very rare were it not for the *third* circumstance which I proposed to mention, viz., the great frugality with which all powers and faculties are distributed to every particular being. So well adjusted are the organs and capacities of all animals, and so well fitted to their preservation, that, as far as history or tradition reaches, there appears not to be any single species which has yet been extinguished in the universe. Every animal has the requisite endowments, but these endowments are bestowed with so scrupulous an economy that any considerable diminution must entirely destroy the creature. Wherever one power is increased, there is a proportional abatement in the others. Animals which excel in swiftness are commonly defective in force. Those which possess both are either imperfect in some of their senses or are oppressed with the most craving wants. The human species, whose chief excellence is reason and sagacity, is of all others the most necessitous, and the most deficient in bodily advantages, without clothes, without arms, without food, without lodging, without any convenience of life, except what they owe to their own skill and industry. In short, nature seems to have formed an exact calculation of the necessities of her creatures, and, like a *rigid master*, has afforded them little more powers or endowments than what are strictly sufficient to supply those necessities. An *indulgent parent* would have bestowed a large stock in order to guard against accidents, and secure the happiness and welfare of the creature in the most unfortunate concurrence of circumstances. Every course of life would not have been so surrounded with precipices that the least departure from the true path, by mistake or necessity, must involve us in misery and ruin. Some reserve, some fund, would have been provided to ensure happiness, nor would the powers and the necessities have been adjusted with so rigid an economy. The Author of nature is inconceivably powerful; his force is supposed great, if not altogether inexhaustible, nor is there any reason, as far as we can judge, to make him observe this strict frugality in his dealings with his creatures. It would have been better, were his power extremely limited, to have created fewer animals, and to have endowed these with more faculties for their happiness and preservation. A builder is never esteemed prudent who undertakes a plan beyond what his stock will enable him to finish.

In order to cure most of the ills of human life, I require not that man should have the wings of the eagle, the swiftness of the stag, the force of the ox, the arms of the lion, the scales of the crocodile or rhinoceros; much less do I demand the sagacity of an angel or cherubim. I am contented to take an increase in one single power or faculty of his soul. Let him be endowed with a greater propensity to industry and labour, a more vigorous spring and activity of mind, a more constant bent to business and application. Let the whole species possess naturally an equal diligence with that which many individuals are able to attain by habit and reflection, and the most beneficial consequences, without any allay of ills, is the immediate and necessary result of this endowment. Almost all the moral as well as natural evils of human life arise from idleness; and were our species, by the original constitution of their frame, exempt from this vice or infirmity, the perfect cultivation of land, the improvement of arts and manufactures, the exact execution of every office and duty, immediately follows; and men at once may fully reach that state of society which is so imperfectly attained by the best regulated government. But as industry is a power, and the most valuable of any, nature seems determined, suitably to her usual maxims, to bestow it on men with a very sparing hand, and rather to punish him severely for his deficiency in it than to reward him for his attainments. She has so contrived his frame that nothing but the most violent necessity can oblige him to labour; and she employs all his other wants to overcome, at least in part, the want of diligence, and to endow him with some share of a faculty of which she has thought fit naturally to bereave him. Here our demands may be allowed very humble, and therefore the more reasonable. If we required the endowments of superior penetration and judgment, of a more delicate taste of beauty, of a nicer sensibility to benevolence and friendship, we might be told that we impiously pretend to break the order of nature, that we want to exalt ourselves into a higher rank of being, that the presents which we require, not being suitable to our state and condition, would only be pernicious to us. But it is hard, I dare to repeat it, it is hard that, being placed in a world so full of wants and necessities, where almost every being and element is either our foe or refuses its assistance . . . we should also have our own temper to struggle with, and should be deprived of that faculty which can alone fence against these multiplied evils.

The *fourth* circumstance whence arises the misery and ill of the universe is the inaccurate workmanship of all the springs and principles of the great machine of nature. It must be acknowledged that there are few parts of the universe which seem not to serve some purpose, and whose removal would not produce a visible defect and disorder in the whole. The parts hang all together, nor can one be touched without effecting the rest, in a greater or less degree. But at the same time, it must be observed that none of these parts or principles, however useful, are so accurately adjusted as to keep precisely within those bounds in which their utility consists; but they are, all of them, apt, on every occasion, to run into the one extreme or the other. One would imagine that this grand production had not received the last hand of the maker—so little finished is every part, and so coarse are the strokes with which it is executed. Thus the winds are requisite to convey the vapours along the surface of the globe, and to assist men in navigation; but how often, rising up to tempests and hurricanes, do they become pernicious? Rains are necessary to nourish all the plants and animals of the earth; but how often are they defective? how often excessive? Heat is requisite to all life and vegetation, but is not always found in the due proportion. On the mixture and secretion of the humours and juices of the body depend the health and prosperity of the animal; but the parts perform not regularly their proper function. What more useful than all the passions of the mind, ambition, vanity, love, anger? But how often do they break their bounds and cause the greatest convulsions in society? There is nothing so advantageous in the universe but what frequently becomes pernicious, by its excess or defect; nor has nature guarded, with the requisite accuracy, against all disorder or confusion. The irregularity is never perhaps so great as to destroy any species, but is often sufficient to involve the individuals in ruin and misery.

On the concurrence, then, of these *four* circumstances does all or the greatest part of natural evil depend. Were all living creatures incapable of pain, or were the world administered by particular volitions, evil never could have found access into the universe; and were animals endowed with a large stock of powers and faculties, beyond what strict necessity requires, or were the several springs and principles of the universe so accurately framed as to preserve always the just temperament and medium, there must have been very little ill in comparison of what we feel at present. What then shall we pronounce on this occasion? Shall we say that these circumstances are not necessary, and that they might easily have been altered in the contrivance of the universe? This decision seems too presumptuous for creatures so blind and ignorant. Let us be more modest in our conclusions. Let us allow that, if the goodness of the Deity (I mean a goodness like the human) could be established on any tolerable reasons *a priori*, these phenomena, however untoward, would not be sufficient to subvert that principle, but might easily, in some unknown manner, be reconcilable to it. But let us still assert that, as this goodness is not antecedently established but must be inferred from the phenomena, there can be no grounds for such an inference while there are so many ills in the universe, and while these ills might so easily have been remedied, as far as human understanding can be allowed to judge on such a subject. I am sceptic enough to allow that the bad appearances, notwithstanding all my reasonings, may be compatible with such attributes as you suppose, but surely they can never prove these attributes. Such a conclusion cannot result from scepticism, but must arise from the phenomena, and from our confidence in the reasonings which we deduce from these phenomena.

Look round this universe. What an immense profusion of beings animated and organized, sensible and active! You admire this prodigious variety and fecundity. But inspect a little more narrowly these living existences, the only beings worth regarding. How hostile and destructive to each other! How insufficient all of them for their own happiness! How contemptible or odious to the spectator! The whole presents nothing but the idea of a blind nature, impregnated by a great vivifying principle, and pouring forth from her lap, without discernment or parental care, her maimed and abortive children!

Here the Manichaean system occurs as a proper hypothesis to solve the difficulty; and, no doubt, in some respects it is very specious and has more probability than the common hypothesis, by giving a plausible account of the strange mixture of good and ill which appears in life. But if we consider, on the other hand, the perfect uniformity and agreement of the parts of the universe, we shall not discover in it any marks of the combat of a malevolent with a benevolent being. There is indeed an opposition of pains and pleasures in the feelings of sensible creatures; but are not all the operations of nature carried on by an opposition of principles, of hot and cold, moist and dry, light and heavy? The true conclusion is that the original Source of all things is entirely indifferent to all these principles, and has no more regard to good above ill than to heat above cold, or to drought above moisture, or to light above heavy.

There may *four* hypotheses be framed concerning the first causes of the universe: that they are endowed with perfect goodness; that they have perfect malice; that they are opposite and have both goodness and malice; that they have neither goodness nor malice. Mixed phenomena can never prove the two former unmixed principles; and the uniformity and steadiness of general laws seem to oppose the third. The fourth, therefore, seems by far the most probable.

What I have said concerning natural evil will apply to moral with little or no variation; and we have no more reason to infer that the rectitude of the Supreme Being resembles human rectitude than that his benevolence resembles the human. Nay, it will be thought that we have still greater cause to exclude from him moral sentiments, such as we feel them, since moral evil, in the opinion of many, is much more predominant above moral good than natural evil above natural good.

But even though this should not be allowed, and though the virtue which is in mankind should be acknowledged much superior to the vice, yet, so long as there is any vice at all in the universe, it will very much puzzle you anthropomorphites how to account for it. You must assign a cause for it, without having recourse to the first cause. But as every effect must have a cause, and that cause another, you must either carry on the progression in *infinitum* or rest on that original principle, who is the ultimate cause of all things. . . .

Hold! hold! cried Demea: Whither does your imagination hurry you? I joined in alliance with you in order to prove the incomprehensible nature of the Divine Being, and refute the principles of Cleanthes, who would measure everything by human rule and standard. But I now find you running into all the topics of the greatest libertines and infidels, and betraying that holy cause which you seemingly espoused. Are you secretly, then, a more dangerous enemy than Cleanthes himself?

And are you so late in perceiving it? replied Cleanthes. Believe me, Demea, your friend Philo, from the beginning, has been amusing himself at both our expense; and it must be confessed that the injudicious reasoning of our vulgar theology has given him but too just a handle of ridicule. The total infirmity of human reason, the absolute incomprehensibility of the Divine Nature, the great and universal misery, and still greater wickedness of men—these are strange topics, surely, to be so fondly cherished by orthodox divines and doctors. In ages of stupidity and ignorance, indeed, these principles may safely be espoused; and perhaps no views of things are more proper to promote superstition than such as encourage the blind amazement, the diffidence, and melancholy of mankind. But at present . . .

Blame not so much, interposed Philo, the ignorance of these reverend gentlemen. They know how to change their style with the times. Formerly, it was a most popular theological topic to maintain that human life was vanity and misery, and to exaggerate all the ills and pains which are incident to men. But of late years, divines, we find, begin to retract this position and maintain, though still with some hesitation, that there are more goods than evils, more pleasures than pains, even in this life. When religion stood entirely upon temper and education, it was thought proper to encourage melancholy, as indeed, mankind never have recourse to superior powers so readily as in that disposition. But as men have now learned to form principles and to draw consequences, it is necessary to change the batteries, and to make use of such arguments as will endure at least some scrutiny and examination. This variation is the same (and from the same causes) with that which I formerly remarked with regard to scepticism.

Thus Philo continued to the last

his spirit of opposition, and his censure of established opinions. But I could observe that Demea did not at all relish the latter part of the discourse; and he took occasion soon after, on some pretence or other, to leave the company.

A Critique of Hume
NELSON PIKE

*I*n parts *X and XI* of the *Dialogues Concerning Natural Religion*, Hume sets forth his views on the traditional theological problem of evil. Hume's remarks on this topic seem to me to contain a rich mixture of insight and oversight. It will be my purpose in this paper to disentangle these contrasting elements of his discussion.[1]

PHILO'S FIRST POSITION
(A) God, according to the traditional Christian view put forward by Cleanthes in the *Dialogues*, is all-powerful, all-knowing, and perfectly good. And it is clear that for Cleanthes, the terms "powerful," "knowing," and "good" apply to God in exactly the same sense in which these terms apply to men. Philo argues as follows. If God is to be all-powerful, all-knowing, and perfectly good (using all key terms in their ordinary sense), then to claim that God exists is to preclude the possibility of admitting that there occur instances of evil; that is, is to preclude the possibility of admitting that there occur instances of suffering, pain, superstition, wickedness, and so forth.[2] The statements "God exists" and

"There occur instances of suffering" are logically incompatible. Of course, no one could deny that there occur instances of suffering. Such a denial would plainly conflict with common experience.[3] Thus it follows from obvious fact that God (having the attributes assigned to Him by Cleanthes) does not exist.

This argument against the existence of God has enjoyed considerable popularity since Hume wrote the *Dialogues*. Concerning the traditional theological problem of evil, F. H. Bradley comments as follows:

The trouble has come from the idea that the Absolute is a moral person. If you start from that basis, then the relation of evil to the Absolute presents at once an irreducible dilemma. The problem then becomes insoluble, but not because it is obscure or in any way mysterious. To

least on the particularities of the logic of this term. At one point in Part X, for example, Philo formulates his challenge to Cleanthes without using "evil." Here he speaks only of *misery*. In what is to follow, I shall (following Hume) make little use of "evil." Also, I shall use "suffering" as short for "suffering pain, superstition, wickedness, and so on."

[1] See preceding essay.

[2] It is clear that, for Philo, the term "evil" is used simply as a tag for the class containing all instances of suffering, pain and so on. Philo offers no analysis of "evil" nor does his challenge to Cleanthes rest in the

[3] Had Philo been dealing with "evil" (defined in some special way) instead of "suffering," this move in the argument might not have been open to him.

FROM: *The Philosophical Review*, Vol. LXXII, No. 2 (1963). Reprinted by permission of the editors of *The Philosophical Review* and the author.

anyone who has the sense and courage to see things as they are, and is resolved not to mystify others or himself, there is really no question to discuss. The dilemma is plainly insoluble because it is based on a clear self-contradiction.[4]

John Stuart Mill,[5] J. E. McTaggart,[6] Antony Flew,[7] H. D. Aiken,[8] J. L. Mackie,[9] C. J. Ducasse,[10] and H. J. McCloskey[11] are but a few of the many others who have echoed Philo's finalistic dismissal of traditional theism after making reference to the logical incompatibility of "God exists" and "There occur instances of suffering." W. T. Stace refers to Hume's discussion of the matter as follows:

(Assuming that "good" and "powerful" are used in theology as they are used in ordinary discourse), we have to say that Hume was right. The charge has never been answered and never will be. The simultaneous attribution of all-power and all-goodness to the Creator of the whole world is logically incompatible with the existence of evil and pain in the world, for which reason the conception of a

[4] *Appearance and Reality* (London: Oxford University Press, 1930), p. 174. Italics mine.

[5] *Theism* (New York: The Liberal Arts Press, 1957), p. 40. See also *The Utility of Religion* (New York: The Liberal Arts Press, 1957), pp. 73ff.

[6] *Some Dogmas of Religion* (London: Edward Arnold, Ltd., 1906), pp. 212f.

[7] "Theology and Falsification," in *New Essays in Philosophical Theology*, A. Flew and A. MacIntyre, eds. (New York: The Macmillan Company, 1955), p. 108.

[8] "God and Evil: Some Relations Between Faith and Morals," *Ethics*, Vol. LXVIII (1958), p. 77ff.

[9] "Evil and Omnipotence," *Mind*, Vol. LXIV (1955).

[10] *A Philosophical Scrutiny of Religion* (New York: The Ronald Press Company, 1953), Chap. 16.

[11] "God and Evil," *The Philosophical Quarterly*, Vol. X (1960).

finite God, who is not all-powerful . . . has become popular in some quarters.[12]

In the first and second sections of this paper, I shall argue that the argument against the existence of God presented in Part X of the *Dialogues* is quite unconvincing. It is not clear at all that "God exists" and "There occur instances of suffering" are logically incompatible statements.

(B) Moving now to the details of the matter, we may, I think, formulate Philo's first challenge to Cleanthes as follows:

(1) The world contains instances of suffering.

(2) God exists—and is omnipotent and omniscient.

(3) God exists—and is perfectly good.

According to the view advanced by Philo, these three statements constitute an "inconsistent triad". Any two of them might be held together. But if any two of them are endorsed, the third must be denied. Philo argues that to say of God that he is omnipotent and omniscient is to say that he *could* prevent suffering if he wanted to. Unless God could prevent suffering, he would not qualify as both omnipotent and omniscient. But, Philo continues, to say of God that he is perfectly good is to say that God *would* prevent suffering if he could. A being who would not prevent suffering when it was within his power to do so would not qualify as perfectly good. Thus, to affirm propositions (2) and (3) is to affirm the existence of a being who both could prevent suffering if he wanted to and who would prevent suffering if he could. This, of course, is to deny the truth of proposition (1). By similar reasoning, Philo would insist, to affirm (1) and (2) is to deny the truth of (3). And to affirm (1) and (3) is to deny the truth of (2). But, as conceived by

[12] *Time and Eternity* (Princeton: Princeton University Press, 1952), p. 56.

Cleanthes, God is both omnipotent-omniscient and perfectly good. Thus, as understood by Cleanthes, "God exists" and "There occur instances of suffering" are logically incompatible statements. Since the latter of these statements is obviously true, the former must be false. Philo reflects: "Nothing can shake the solidarity of this reasoning, so short, so clear (and) so decisive".

It seems to me that this argument is deficient. I do not think it follows from the claim that a being is perfectly good that he would prevent suffering if he could.

Consider this case. A parent forces a child to take a spoonful of bitter medicine. The parent thus brings about an instance of discomfort—suffering. The parent could have refrained from administering the medicine; and he knew that the child would suffer discomfort if he did administer it. Yet, when we are assured that the parent acted in the interest of the child's health and happiness, the fact that he knowingly caused discomfort is not sufficient to remove the parent from the class of perfectly good beings. If the parent fails to fit into this class, it is not because he caused *this* instance of suffering.

Given only that the parent knowingly caused an instance of discomfort, we are tempted to *blame* him for his action—that is, to exclude him from the class of perfectly good beings. But when the full circumstances are known, blame becomes inappropriate. In this case, there is what I shall call a "morally sufficient reason" for the parent's action. To say that there is a morally sufficient reason for his action is simply to say that there is a circumstance or condition which, when known, renders *blame* (though, of course, not *responsibility*) for the action inappropriate. As a general statement, a being who permits (or brings about) an instance of suffering might be perfectly good providing only that there is a morally sufficient reason for his action. Thus, it does not follow from the claim that God is perfectly good that he would prevent suffering if he could. God might

fail to prevent suffering or himself bring about suffering, while remaining perfectly good. It is required only that there be a morally sufficient reason for his action.

(C) In the light of these reflections, let us now attempt to put Philo's challenge to Cleanthes in sharper form.

(4) The world contains instances of suffering.

(5) God exists—and is omnipotent, omniscient, and perfectly good.

(6) An omnipotent and omniscient being would have no morally sufficient reason for allowing instances of suffering.

This sequence is logically tight. Suppose (6) and (4) true. If an omnipotent and omniscient being would have no morally sufficient reason for allowing instances of suffering, then, in a world containing such instances, either there would be no omnipotent and omniscient being or that being would be blameworthy. On either of these last alternatives, proposition (5) would be false. Thus, if (6) and (4) are true, (5) must be false. In similar fashion, suppose (6) and (5) true. If an omnipotent and omniscient being would have no morally sufficient reason for allowing suffering, then, if there existed an omnipotent and omniscient being who was also perfectly good, there would occur no suffering. Thus, if (6) and (5) are true, (4) must be false. Lastly, suppose (5) and (4) true. If there existed an omnipotent and omniscient being who was also perfectly good, then if there occurred suffering, the omnipotent and omniscient being (being also perfectly good) would have to have a morally sufficient reason for permitting it. Thus, if (5) and (4) are true, (6) must be false.

Now, according to Philo (and all others concerned), proposition (4) is surely true. And proposition (6)—well, what about proposition (6)? At this point, two observations are needed.

First, it would not serve Philo's purpose were he to argue the truth of proposition (6) by enumerating a number of reasons for permitting suffering (which might be assigned to an omnipotent and omniscient being) and then by showing that in each case the reason offered is not a morally sufficient reason (when assigned to an omnipotent and omniscient being). Philo could never claim to have explained all of the possibilities. And at any given point in the argument, Cleanthes could always claim that God's reason for permitting suffering is one which Philo has not yet considered. A retreat to unexamined reasons would remain open to Cleanthes regardless of how complete the list of examined reasons seemed to be.

Second, the position held by Philo in Part X of the *Dialogues* demands that he affirm proposition (6) as a *necessary truth*. If this is not already clear, consider the following inconsistent triad.

(7) All swans are white.
(8) Some swans are not large.
(9) All white things are large.

Suppose (9) true, but not necessarily true. Either (7) or (8) must be false. But the conjunction of (7) and (8) is not contradictory. If the conjunction of (7) and (8) were contradictory, then (9) would be necessary truth. Thus, unless (9) is a necessary truth, the conjunction of (7) and (8) is not contradictory. Note what happens to this antilogism when "colored" is substituted for "large." Now (9) becomes a necessary truth and, correspondingly, (7) and (8) become logically incompatible. The same holds for the inconsistent triad we are now considering. As already discovered, Philo holds that "There are instances of suffering" (proposition 4) and "God exists" (proposition 5) are logically incompatible. But (4) and (5) will be logically incompatible only if (6) is a necessary truth. Thus, if Philo is to argue that (4) and (5) are logically incompatible, he must be prepared to affirm (6) as a necessary truth.

We may now reconstitute Philo's challenge to the position held by Cleanthes.

Proposition (4) is obviously true. No one could deny that there occur in-

stances of suffering. But proposition (6) is a necessary truth. An omnipotent and omniscient being would have no morally sufficient reason for allowing instances of suffering—just as a bachelor would have no wife. Thus, there exists no being who is, at once, omnipotent, omniscient, and perfectly good. Proposition (5) must be false.

(D) This is a formidable challenge to Cleanthes' position. Its strength can best be exposed by reflecting on some of the circumstances or conditions which, in ordinary life, and with respect to ordinary agents, are usually counted as morally sufficient reasons for failing to prevent (or relieve) some given instance of suffering. Let me list five such reasons.

First, consider an agent who lacked physical ability to prevent some instance of suffering. Such an agent could claim to have had a morally sufficient reason for not preventing the instance in question.

Second, consider an agent who lacked knowledge of (or the means of knowing about) a given instance of suffering. Such an agent could claim to have had a morally sufficient reason for not preventing the suffering, even if (on all other counts) he had the ability to prevent it.

Third, consider an agent who knew of an instance of suffering and had the physical ability to prevent it, but did not *realize* that he had this ability. Such an agent could usually claim to have had a morally sufficient reason for not preventing the suffering. Example: if I push the button on the wall, the torment of the man in the next room will cease. I have the physical ability to push the button. I know that the man in the next room is in pain. But I do not know that pushing the button will relieve the torment. I do not push the button and thus do not relieve the suffering.

Fourth, consider an agent who had the ability to prevent an instance of suffering, knew of the suffering, knew that he had the ability to prevent it, but did not prevent it because he believed (rightly or wrongly) that to do so would be to fail to effect some future good which would outweigh the negative value of the suffering. Such an agent might well claim to have had a morally sufficient reason for not preventing the suffering. Example: go back to the case of the parent causing discomfort by administering bitter medicine to the child.

Fifth, consider an agent who had the ability to prevent an instance of suffering, knew of the suffering, knew that he had the ability to prevent it, but failed to prevent it because to do so would have involved his preventing a prior good which outweighed the negative value of the suffering. Such an agent might claim to have had a morally sufficient reason for not preventing the suffering. Example: a parent permits a child to eat some birthday cake knowing that his eating the cake will result in the child's feeling slightly ill later in the day. The parent estimates that the child's pleasure of the moment outweighs the discomfort which will result.

Up to this point, Philo would insist, we have not hit on a circumstance or condition which could be used by Cleanthes when constructing a "theodicy," that is, when attempting to identify the morally sufficient reason God has for permitting instances of suffering.

The first three entries on the list are obviously not available. Each makes explicit mention of some lack of knowledge or power on the part of the agent. Nothing more need be said about them.

A theologian might, however, be tempted to use a reason for the fourth type when constructing a theodicy. He might propose that suffering *results in goods* which outweigh the negative value of the suffering. Famine (hunger) leads man to industry and progress. Disease (pain) leads man to knowledge and understanding. Philo suggests that no theodicy of this kind can be successful. An omnipotent and omniscient being could find other means of bringing about the same results. The mere fact that evils give rise to goods cannot serve as a morally sufficient reason for an omnipotent and omniscient being to permit suffering.

A theologian might also be tempted to use reasons of the fifth type when constructing a theodicy. He might propose that instances of suffering *result from goods* which outweigh the negative value of the suffering. That the world is run in accordance with natural law is good. But any such regular operation will result in suffering. That men have the ability to make free choices is good. But free choice will sometimes result in wrong choice and suffering. Philo argues that it is not at all clear that a world run in accordance with natural law is better than one not so regulated. And one might issue a similar challenge with respect to free will. But a more general argument has been offered in the contemporary literature on evil which is exactly analogous to the one suggested by Philo above. According to H. J. McCloskey, an omnipotent and omniscient being could devise a law-governed world which would not include suffering.[13] And according to J. L. Mackie, an omnipotent and omniscient being could create a world containing free agents which would include no suffering or wrong-doing.[14] The import of both of these suggestions is that an omnipotent and omniscient being could create a world containing whatever is good (regularity, free will, and so on) without allowing the suffering which (only factually) results from these goods. The mere fact that suffering results from good cannot serve as a morally sufficient reason for an omnipotent and omniscient being to allow suffering.

Though the above reflections may be far from conclusive, let us grant that, of the morally sufficient reasons so far considered, none could be assigned to an omnipotent and omniscient being. This, of course, is not to say that proposition (6) is true—let alone necessarily true. As mentioned earlier, proposition (6) will not be shown true by an enumerative procedure of the above kind. But consider the matter less rigorously.

[13] "God and Evil."

[14] "Evil and Omnipotence."

If none of the reasons so far considered could be assigned to an omnipotent and omniscient being, ought this not to raise a suspicion? Might there not be a principle operating in each of these reasons which guarantees that *no* morally sufficient reason for permitting suffering *could* be assigned to an omnipotent and omniscient being? Such a principle immediately suggests itself. Men are sometimes excused for allowing suffering. But in these cases, men are excused only because they lack the knowledge or power to prevent suffering, or because they lack the knowledge or power to bring about goods (which are causally related to suffering) without also bringing about suffering. In other words, men are excusable only because they are limited. Having a morally sufficient reason for permitting suffering *entails* having some lack of knowledge or power. If this principle is sound (and, indeed, it is initially plausible) then proposition (6) must surely be listed as a necessary truth.

DEMEA'S THEODICY

But the issue is not yet decided. Demea has offered a theodicy which does not fit any of the forms outlined above. And Philo must be willing to consider all proposals if he is to claim "decisiveness" for his argument against Cleanthes.

Demea reasons as follows:

This world is but a point in comparison of the universe; this life but a moment in comparison of eternity. The present evil phenomena, therefore, are rectified in other regions, and in some future period of existence. And the eyes of men, being then opened to larger views of things, see the whole connection of general laws, and trace with adoration, the benevolence and rectitude of the Deity through all mazes and intricacies of his providence.

It might be useful if we had a second statement of this theodicy, one taken from a traditional theological source. In Chapter LXXI of the *Summa Contra Gentiles*, St. Thomas argues as follows:

The good of the whole is of more account than the good of the part. Therefore, it belongs to a prudent governor to overlook a lack of goodness in a part, that there may be an increase of goodness in the whole. Thus, the builder hides the foundation of a house underground, that the whole house may stand firm. Now, if evil were taken away from certain parts of the universe, the perfection of the universe would be much diminished, since its beauty results from the ordered unity of good and evil things, seeing that evil arises from the failure of good, and yet certain goods are occasioned from those very evils through the providence of the governor, even as the silent pause gives sweetness to the chant. Therefore, evil should not be excluded from things by the divine providence.

Neither of these statements seems entirely satisfactory. Demea might be suggesting that the world is good on the whole—that the suffering we discover in our world is, as it were, made up for in other regions of creation. God here appears as the husband who beats his wife on occasion but makes up for it with favors at other times. In St. Thomas' statement, there are unmistakable hints of causal reasoning. Certain goods are "occasioned" by evils, as the foundation of the house permits the house to stand firm. But in both of these statements another theme is at least suggested. Let me state and explain it in my own way without pretense of historical accuracy.

I have a set of ten wooden blocks. There is a T-shaped block, an L-shaped block, an F-shaped block, and so on. No two blocks have the same shape. Let us assign each block a value—say an aesthetic value—making the T-shaped block most valuable and the L-shaped block least valuable. Now the blocks may be fitted together into formations. And let us suppose that the blocks are so shaped that there is one and only one subset of the blocks which will fit together into a square. The L-shaped block is a member of that subset. Further, let us stipulate that any formation of blocks (consisting of two or more blocks fitted together) will have more aesthetic value than any of the blocks taken individually or any subset of the blocks taken as a mere collection. And, as a last assumption, let us say that the square formation has greater aesthetic value than any other logically possible block formation. The L-shaped block is a necessary component of the square formation; that is, the L-shaped block is logically indispensable to the square formation. Thus the L-shaped block is a necessary component of the best of all possible block formations. Hence, the block with the least aesthetic value is logically indispensable to the best of all possible block formations. Without this very block, it would be logically impossible to create the best of all possible block formations.

Working from this model, let us understand Demea's theodicy as follows. Put aside the claim that instances of suffering are *de facto* causes or consequences of greater goods. God, being a perfectly good, omniscient, and omnipotent being, would create the best of all possible worlds. But the best of all possible worlds must contain instances of suffering: they are logically indispensable components. This is why there are instances of suffering in the world which God created.

What shall we say about this theodicy? Philo expresses no opinion on the subject.

Consider this reply to Demea's reasonings. A world containing instances of suffering as necessary components might be the best of all possible worlds. And if a world containing instances of suffering as necessary components were the best of all possible worlds, an omnipotent and omniscient being would have a morally sufficient reason for permitting instances of suffering. But how are we to know that, in fact, instances of suffering are logically indispensable components of the best of all possible worlds? There would appear to be no way of establishing this claim short of assuming that God does in fact exist and then concluding (as did Leibniz) that the world (containing suffering) which he did in fact create is the best of all possible

worlds. But, this procedure assumes that God exists. And this latter is precisely the question now at issue.

It seems to me that this reply to Demea's theodicy has considerable merit. First, my hypothetical objector is probably right in suggesting that the only way one could show that the best of all possible worlds must contain instances of suffering would be via the above argument in which the existence of God is assumed. Second, I think my objector is right in allowing that if instances of suffering were logically indispensable components of the best of all possible worlds, this would provide a morally sufficient reason for an omnipotent and omniscient being to permit instances of suffering. And, third, I think that my objector exhibits considerable discretion in not challenging the claim that the best of all possible worlds *might* contain instances of suffering as necessary components. I know of no argument which will show this claim to be true. But on the other hand, I know of no argument which will show this claim to be false. (I shall elaborate this last point directly.)

Thus, as I have said, the above evaluation of the theodicy advanced by Demea seems to have considerable merit. But this evaluation, *if correct*, seems to be sufficient to refute Philo's claim that "God exists" and "There occur instances of suffering" are logically incompatible statements. If instances of suffering were necessary components of the best of all possible worlds, then an omnipotent and omniscient being would have a morally sufficient reason for permitting instances of suffering. Thus, if it is *possible* that instances of suffering are necessary components of the best of all possible worlds, then there *might be* a morally sufficient reason for an omnipotent and omniscient being to permit instances of suffering. Thus if the statement "Instances of suffering are necessary components of the best of all possible worlds" is not contradictory, then proposition (6) is not a necessary truth. And, as we have seen, if proposition (6) is not a necessary truth, then "God exists" and "There occur instances of suffering" are not logically incompatible statements.

What shall we say? Is the statement "Instances of suffering are logically indispensable components of the best of all possible worlds" contradictory? That it is is simply assumed in Philo's first position. But, surely, this is not a trivial assumption. If it is correct, it must be shown to be so; it is not *obviously* correct. And how shall we argue that it is correct? Shall we, for example, assume that any case of suffering contained in any complex of events detracts from the value of the complex? If this principle were analytic, then a world containing an instance of suffering could not be the best of all possible worlds. But G. E. Moore has taught us to be suspicious of any such principle.[15] And John Wisdom has provided a series of counter-examples which tend to show that this very principle is, in fact, not analytic. Example: if I believe (rightly or wrongly) that you are in pain and become unhappy as a result of that belief, the resulting complex would appear to be better by virtue of my unhappiness (suffering) than it would have been had I believed you to be in pain but had not become unhappy (or had become happy) as a result.[16] Philo's argument against the existence of God is not finished. And it is not at all obvious that it is *capable* of effective completion. It is, I submit, far from clear that God and evil could not exist together in the same universe.

PHILO'S SECOND POSITION

At the end of Part X, Philo agrees to "retire" from his first position. He now concedes that "God exists" and "There occur instances of suffering" are not logically incompatible statements. (It is clear from the context that this adjustment in Philo's thinking is made only for purposes of argument and

[15] I refer here to Moore's discussion of "organic unities" in *Principia Ethica* (London: Macmillan & Co., Ltd., 1903), pp. 28ff.

[16] "God and Evil," *Mind*, Vol. XLIV (1935), 13f. I have modified Wisdom's example slightly.

not because Hume senses any inadequacy in Philo's first position.) Most contemporary philosophers think that Hume's major contribution to the literature on evil was made in Part X of the *Dialogues*. But it seems to me that what is of really lasting value in Hume's reflections on this subject is to be found not in Part X, but in the discussion in Part XI which follows Philo's "retirement" from his first position.

(A) Consider, first of all, a theology in which the existence of God is accepted on the basis of what is taken to be a conclusive (a priori) demonstration. (A theology in which the existence of God is taken as an item of faith can be considered here as well.) On this view, that God exists is a settled matter, not subject to review or challenge. It is, as it were, axiomatic to further theological debate. According to Philo, evil in the world presents no special problem for a theology of this sort:

Let us allow that, if the goodness of the Deity (I mean a goodness like the human) could be established on any tolerable reasons a priori, these (evil) phenomena, however untoward, would not be sufficient to subvert that principle, but might easily, in some unknown manner, be reconcilable to it.

This point, I think, is essentially correct, but it must be put more firmly.

Recalling the remarks advanced when discussing the inconsistent nature of propositions (4) through (6) above, a theologian who accepts the existence of God (either as an item of faith or on the basis of an a priori argument) must conclude either that there is some morally sufficient reason for God's allowing suffering in the world, or that there are no instances of suffering in the world. He will, of course, choose the first alternative. Thus, in a theology of the sort now under consideration, the theologian begins by affirming the existence of God and by acknowledging the occurrence of suffering. It follows *logically* that God has some morally sufficient reason for allowing instances of suffering. The conclusion is not, as Philo suggests, that there *might be* a morally sufficient reason for evil. The conclusion is, rather, that there *must be* such a reason. It *could not be otherwise.*

What then of the traditional theological problem of evil? Within a theology of the above type, the problem of evil can only be the problem of discovering a *specific* theodicy which is adequate —that is, of discovering which, if any, of the specific proposals which might be advanced really describes God's morally sufficient reason for allowing instances of suffering. This problem, of course, is not a major one for the theologian. If the problem of evil is simply the problem of uncovering the specific reason for evil— given assurance that there is (and must be) some such reason—it can hardly be counted as a critical problem. Once it is granted that there is some specific reason for evil, there is a sense in which it is no longer vital to find it. A theologian of the type we are now considering might never arrive at a satisfactory theodicy. (Philo's "unknown" reason might remain forever unknown.) He might condemn as erroneous all existing theodices and might despair of ever discovering the morally sufficient reason in question. A charge of incompleteness would be the worst that could be leveled at his world view.

(B) Cleanthes is not, of course, a theologian of the sort just described. He does not accept the existence of God as an item of faith, nor on the basis of an a priori argument. In the *Dialogues,* Cleanthes supports his theological position with an a posteriori argument from design. He argues that "order" in the universe provides sufficient evidence that the world was created by an omnipotent, omniscient, and perfectly good being.[17]

[17] It is interesting to notice that, in many cases, theologians who have used an argument from design have not attempted to argue that "order" in the world proves the existence of a perfectly moral being. For example, in St. Thomas' "fifth way" and in William Paley's *Natural Theology,* "order" is used to show only that the creator of the world was *intelligent.* There are, however,

He proposes the existence of God as a quasi-scientific explanatory hypothesis, arguing its truth via the claim that it provides an adequate explanation for observed facts.

Philo has two comments to make regarding the relevance of suffering in the world for a theology of this kind.

The first is a comment with which Philo is obviously well pleased. It is offered at the end of Part X and is repeated no less than three times in Part XI. It is this: even if the existence of God and the occurrence of suffering in the world are logically compatible, one cannot argue from a world containing suffering to the existence of an omnipotent, omniscient, and perfectly good creator. This observation, I think all would agree, is correct. Given only a painting containing vast areas of green, one could not effectively argue that its creator disliked using green. There would be no *logical* conflict in holding that a painter who disliked using green painted a picture containing vast areas of green. But given *only* the picture (and no further information), the hypothesis that its creator disliked using green would be poorly supported indeed.

It is clear that in this first comment Philo has offered a criticism of Cleanthes' *argument* for the existence of God. He explicitly says that this complaint is against Cleanthes' *inference* from a world containing instances of suffering to the existence of an omnipotent, omniscient, and perfectly good creator. Philo's second comment, however, is more forceful than this. It is a challenge of the *truth* of Cleanthes' *hypothesis.*

Philo argues as follows:

Look round this universe. What an immense profusion of beings, animated and organized, sensible and active! You admire this prodigious variety and fecun-

historical instances of the argument from design being used to prove the goodness as well as the intelligence of a creator. For example, Bishop Berkeley argues this way in the second of the *Dialogues Between Hylas and Philonous.*

dity. But inspect a little more narrowly these living existences, the only beings worth regarding. How hostile and destructive to each other! How insufficient all of them for their own happiness! . . . There is indeed an opposition of pains and pleasures in the feelings of sensible creatures; but are not all the operations of nature carried on by an opposition of principles, of hot and cold, moist and dry, light and heavy! The true conclusion is that the original Source of all things is entirely indifferent to all these principles, and has no more regard to good above ill than to heat above cold, or to drought above moisture, or to light above heavy.

Philo claims that *there is* an "original Source of all things" and that this source is indifferent with respect to matters of good and evil. He pretends to be inferring this conclusion from observed data. This represents a departure from Philo's much professed skepticism in the *Dialogues*. And, no doubt, many of the criticisms of Cleanthes' position which Philo advanced earlier in the *Dialogues* would apply with equal force to the inference Philo has just offered. But I shall not dwell on this last point. I think the center of Philo's remarks in this passage must be located in their skeptical rather than their metaphysical import. Philo has proposed a hypothesis which is counter to the one offered by Cleanthes. And he claims that his hypothesis is the "true conclusion" to be drawn from the observed data. But the point is not, I think, that Philo's new hypothesis is true, or even probable. The conclusion is, rather, that the hypothesis advanced by Cleanthes is false, or very improbable. When claiming that evil in the world *supports* a hypothesis which is counter to the one offered by Cleanthes, I think Philo simply means to be calling attention to the fact that evil in the world provides *evidence against* Cleanthes' theological position.

Consider the following analogy which, I think, will help expose this point. I am given certain astronomical data. In order to explain the data, I introduce the hypothesis that there exists a planet which has not yet been observed but will be observable at such and such a place in the sky at such and such a time. No other hypothesis seems as good. The anticipated hour arrives and the telescopes are trained on the designated area. No planet appears. Now, either one of two conclusions may be drawn. First, I might conclude that there is no planet there to be seen. This requires either that I reject the original astronomical data or that I admit that what seemed the best explanation of the data is not, in fact, the true explanation. Second, I might conclude that there is a planet there to be seen, but that something in the observational set-up went amiss. Perhaps the equipment was faulty, perhaps there were clouds, and so on. Which conclusion is correct? The answer is not straightforward. I must check both possibilities.

Suppose I find nothing in the observational set-up which is in the least out of order. My equipment is in good working condition, I find no clouds, and so on. To decide to retain the planet hypothesis in the face of the recalcitrant datum (my failure to observe the planet) is, in part, to decide that there is some circumstance (as yet unknown) which explains the datum *other* than the non-existence of the planet in question. But a decision to retain the planet hypothesis (in the face of my failure to observe the planet and in the absence of an explicit explanation which "squares" this failure with the planet hypothesis) is made correctly *only* when the *evidence for* the planet hypothesis is such as to render its negation less plausible than would be the assumption of a (as yet unknown) circumstance which explains the observation failure. This, I think, is part of the very notion of dealing reasonably with an explanatory hypothesis.

Now Cleanthes has introduced the claim that there exists an omnipotent, omniscient, and perfectly good being as a way of explaining "order" in the world. And Philo, throughout the *Dialogues* (up to and including most of Part XI), has

been concerned to show that this procedure provides very little (if any) solid
evidence for the existence of God. The
inference from the data to the hypothesis is extremely tenuous. Philo is now
set for his final thrust at Cleanthes' position. Granting that God and evil are not
logically incompatible, the existence of
human suffering in the world must still
be taken as a recalcitrant datum with
respect to Cleanthes' hypothesis. Suffering, as Philo says, is not what we should
antecedently expect in a world created
by an omnipotent, omniscient, and
perfectly good being. Since Cleanthes
has offered nothing in the way of
an explicit theodicy (that is, an explanation of the recalcitrant datum which
would "square" it with his hypothesis)
and since the *evidence for* his hypothesis
is extremely weak and generally ineffective, there is pretty good reason for
thinking that Cleanthes' hypothesis is
false.

This, I think, is the skeptical import
of Philo's closing remarks in Part XI.
On this reading nothing is said about
an "original Source of all things" which
is indifferent with respect to matters of
good and evil. Philo is simply making
clear the negative force of the fact of evil
in the world for a hypothesis such as
the one offered by Cleanthes.

It ought not to go unnoticed that
Philo's closing attack on Cleanthes' position has extremely limited application.
Evil in the world has central negative
importance for theology only when
theology is approached as a quasi-
scientific subject, as by Cleanthes. That
it is seldom approached in this way will
be evident to anyone who has studied the
history of theology. Within most theological positions, the existence of God is
taken as an item of faith or embraced
on the basis of an a priori argument.
Under these circumstances, where there
is nothing to qualify as a "hypothesis"
capable of having either negative or positive "evidence," the fact of evil in the
world presents no special problem for
theology. As Philo himself has suggested,
when the existence of God is accepted
prior to any rational consideration of the
status of evil in the world, the traditional
problem of evil reduces to a noncrucial
perplexity of relatively minor importance.

On the Failure of All Philosophical Essays in Theodicy
IMMANUEL KANT

*B*y a *theodicée* is understood the defense of the supreme wisdom of the
Author of the world against the accusa-
tion of that wisdom by reason, from what
is contrary-to-end in the world.—This
is named, defending the cause of God;
though at bottom it may be nothing more
than the cause of our assuming reason,
mistaking its limits, which cause is not
indeed the very best one, but must be
so far approved, as (setting aside that
self-conceit) man, as a rational being,
has a right to prove all assertions, all
the doctrines which reverence imposes
on him, before he submits himself to
them, in order that this reverence may
be sincere and not hypocritical.

To this justification, now, is required that the opiniative advocate of
God shall prove, either that that, which
we judge in the world as contrary-to-end,
is not so; or that, were it so, it must by no
means be judged as a fact, but as an
invariable consequence of the nature of
things; or lastly, that it must at least be
considered not as a fact of the Supreme

FROM: *Essays and Treatises*, W. Richardson, trans. in 1799 (originally published in 1791). Translation slightly emended.

Author of all things, but merely of mundane beings, to whom something can be imputed, that is, men (perhaps higher, good or bad, spiritual beings also).

The author of a Theodicée consents, then, that this action shall be brought before the court of reason; engages himself as counsel for the defendant, by formally refuting all the charges preferred by the plaintiff; and during the course of law must not put him off by an authoritative decision on the incompetency of the tribunal of reason (*exceptionem fori*), that is, must not dispatch the charges by imposing on the plaintiff a concession of the supreme wisdom of the Author of the world, which directly declares groundless, even without inquiry, all doubts that may be started; but must attend to the objections and as they by no means derogate from the conception of the supreme wisdom* by

* The proper conception of *wisdom* represents but the property of a will, to harmonize with the chief good, as the final end or *scope* of all things, *art* on the other hand, but the faculty in the use of the fittest means to *ends laid down at pleasure*; art, when it proves itself as such (which is adequate to ideas, whose possibility transcends all interpretation of human reason, for instance, when mean and end as in organized bodies, produce one another reciprocally) as a *divine art*, may not be improperly distinguished by the name of wisdom, yet in order not to permute the conceptions, by the name of a wisdom of art of the Author of the world, for the purpose of distinguishing it from his *moral wisdom*. Teleology (and by it physicothelogy) gives abundant proofs of the former in experience. But from it no inference to the moral wisdom of the Author of the world is valid, because law of nature and moral law require quite heterogeneous principles and the proof of the latter wisdom must be given *a priori* totally, therefore absolutely not grounded upon experience of what happens in the world. As now the conception of God, that shall be fit for religion (for we use it not for the behoof of the explanation of nature, of course in a speculative view) must be a conception of him as a moral Being; as this conception, as little can it be grounded upon experience, just as little

clearing them up and removing them, render everything comprehensible.—One thing, however, he has no occasion to enter on, namely to prove the supreme wisdom of God from what experience teaches of this world, for in this he would not succeed, as omniscience is thereto requisite, in order in a given world (as it gives to cognize itself in experience) to cognize that perfection, of which may be said with certainty that there is nowhere any greater in the creation and its government possible.

The contrary-to-end (*Das Zweckwidridge*) in the world, which may be opposed to the wisdom of its Author, is of a three-fold nature: I. The absolute contrary-to-end, which can be approved and desired by wisdom, neither as an end, nor as a mean. II. The conditional contrary-to-end, which consents with the wisdom of a will, indeed never as an end, but yet as a mean. The *first* is the moral contrary-to-end, as the proper evil (sin); the *second* the physical contrary-to-end, evil (pain).—But there is a conformity-to-end (*Zweckmässigkeit*) in the relation of the evils to the moral evil, as the latter once exists and neither can nor ought to be diminished; namely, in the conjunction of evils and pains, as punishments, with the evil, as a crime; and relatively to this conformity-to-end in the world the question is, whether in this justice be done to every one in the world. Consequently still a III. species of the contrary-to-end in the world must be conceived, namely, the disproportion of crimes and punishments in the world. [I.e., Kant suggests that moral evil (sin), physical evil (pain) and injustice are three kinds of evil, that every evil is of one of these kinds, and that one offering a theodicy must deal with each kind of evil. Ed.]

The attributes of the supreme wis-

can it be exhibited from merely transcendental conceptions of an absolutely necessary being, who is to us totally transcendent; so it is sufficiently evident that the proof of the existence of such a Being can be no more than a moral one.

dom of the Author of the world, against which those contraries-to-end appear as objections, are likewise three:

First, his HOLINESS, as LEGISLATOR (Creator), in contradistinction to the moral bad in the world.

Secondly, his GOODNESS, as GOVERNOR (Preserver), contrasted with the innumerable evils and pains of the rational mundane beings.

Thirdly, his JUSTICE, as JUDGE, in comparison with the evil state, in which the disproportion between the impunity of the vicious and their crimes seems to show itself in the world.*

* These three attributes, of which the one can by no means be reduced to the others, for instance justice to goodness, and so the whole to a smaller number, constitute the moral conception of God. Nor can their order be altered (as for example to make the goodness the chief condition of the creation of the world, to which the holiness of legislation is subordinated), without derogating from religion, which bottoms upon this very moral conception. Our own pure (practical) reason determines this order of rank, as, when the legislation confirms itself to the goodness, there is no more dignity of it and no firm conception of duties. Man wishes first of all, it is true, to be happy; but perspects, and grants (though unwillingly) that the worthiness of being happy, that is, the consension of the use of his liberty with the holy law, must in the decree of the Author be the condition of its validity and therefore necessarily precede. For the wish, which the subjective end (of self-love) has at bottom, cannot determine the objective end (of wisdom), which the law, that gives the will unconditionally the rule, prescribes—Punishment in the exercise of justice is by no means grounded as a mean, but as an end in the legislative wisdom; the transgression is combined with evils, not in order that another good may arise, but because the combination is, in itself, *id est*, morally and necessarily, good. Justice, it is true, presupposes goodness of the legislator (for if his will did not tend to the weal of his subjects, it could not oblige them to obey him), it is not, however goodness, but as justice essentially different from it, though comprehended in the universal conception of wisdom. Hence the complaint of the wont of

The answer to those three impeachments must be represented in the abovementioned threefold different manner, and proved according to their validity.

I. The first vindication of the holiness of the Divine will on account of the moral evil, which is complained of as disfiguring the world, his work, consists in this:

a. That there is by no means such an absolute contrary-to-end, as we take the transgression of the pure laws of our reason to be, but that it is only a fault in the eye of human wisdom; that the Divine judges them according to quite other rules incomprehensible to us, so that what we indeed find rejectable with reason relatively to our practical reason and its determination, may perhaps, in relation to Divine ends and supreme wisdom, be the fittest mean, as well for our particular weal, as for the good of the world in general; that the ways of the Supreme are not our ways (*sunt Superis sua jura*), and we err, when we judge that, which is a law but relatively for men in this life to be absolute, and thus hold that, which seems contrary-to-end to our contemplation of things from a station so low, to be so likewise, when contemplated from the highest station.—This apology, in which the defence is worse than the charge, requires no refutation, and may certainly be freely left to the detestation of every person, who has the smallest sentiment of morality. [I.e., Kant is asserting that to deny that actions condemned by the moral law are really wrong—or to say that they are wrong merely from our point of view but not from God's—does

justice, which shows itself in the lot that falls to men here in the world, is not that the good do not fare *well* here, but that the bad do not fare *ill* (though, when the former is superadded to the latter, the contrast still augments this difficulty). For in a divine government even the best man cannot ground his wish for well-being upon the divine justice, but must always [ground it] on his goodness; because he who does his duty merely, can lay no claim to the favor of God.

justice neither to morality nor to divine goodness. Eds.]

b. The second pretended vindication grants, it is true, the actuality of the moral evil in the world, but excuses the Author of the world by its not having been possible to be prevented; because it is grounded upon the limits of the nature of men, as finite beings.—But thereby that evil itself would be justified; and, as it cannot be imputed to men as their fault, one would need to cease to name it a moral evil.

c. The third vindication, that supposes that with respect to what we denominate moral evil men are actually guilty, [but] no guilt must be imputed to God, as he has from wise causes merely permitted, as a fact of men, but by no means approved and willed or prepared, that evil, [this vindication] tends (if no difficulty shall be found in the conception of the mere *permitting* of a Being, who is the sole Author of the world) to the same consequence with the foregoing apology (b), namely, that, as it was impossible for God himself to hinder this bad, without derogating from other higher and even moral ends, the ground of this evil (for it must now be properly named thus) must be unavoidably to be looked for in the essence of things, namely, the necessary limits of humanity as finite nature, and consequently cannot be imputed to it. [I.e., To accept either (b) or (c) is to deny the existence of moral evil, not to explain it. Eds.]

II. The justification of the Divine goodness for the [physical] evils, namely, pains, which are complained of in the world, consists herein.

a. That in the fates of men a preponderance of evil over the agreeable enjoyment of life is falsely supposed, because every one, however badly he may fare, chooses rather to live, than to be dead, and those few, who resolve on the latter, so long as they themselves delay it, thereby allow that preponderance still and, when they are insane enough to destroy themselves, merely pass to the state of insensibility, in which no pain can be felt.—But the answer to this sophistry may surely be left to the decision of every man of a sound understanding, who has lived and reflected long enough on the value of life to be able to pronounce a judgment on this, when the question is proposed to him, Whether, I will not say on the same, but on any other conditions he pleases (only not of a fairy, but of this our terrestrial world), he would not wish to act the play of life over again.

b. To the second justification, that the preponderancy of the painful feelings over the agreeable cannot be separated from the nature of an animal creature, like man, (as count Veri maintains in his book On the Nature of Pleasure)— one would reply, that, if it is so, there occurs another query. Why the Author of our existence has called us into life, when, according to our just calculation, it is not worthy of being wished for by us? Ill-humour here, as the Indian woman said to Dschingiskhan, who could neither give her satisfaction for the violence suffered, nor afford her security against the future, would answer, 'If thou will'st not protect us, why dost thou conquer us?'

c. The third solution of the knot is that for the sake of a future felicity God hath placed us out of goodness in the world, but that that beatitude which may be hoped for must be preceded by a state of thorough trouble and misery of the present life, where we must by the struggle with difficulties become worthy of that future glory.—But, that this time of probation (in which the most succumb, and the best have no proper satisfaction in their life) shall absolutely be the condition by the Supreme Wisdom of the pleasure that one day or other may be enjoyed by us, and that it was not feasible to let the creature become contented with every epoch of his life, may indeed be pretended, but absolutely cannot be perspected, and by an appeal to the Supreme Wisdom, who hath so willed it, the knot may be cut, to be sure, but not untied; to resolve which, however, the theodicée engages.

III. To the last charge preferred

against the justice of the Governour of the world,* is answered:

a. That the pretext of the impunity of the vicious in the world has no ground; because every crime, according to its nature, carries with itself here the punishment suitable to it, as the internal reproaches of conscience torment the vicious more than furies would.—But in this judgment there is evidently a misunderstanding. For the virtuous man herein lends his character of mind to the vicious, namely, conscientiousness in its whole strictness which, the more virtuous the man is, punishes the more rigorously on account of the smallest transgression, that the moral law in him disapproves. But, where this cast of mind and with it conscientiousness is wanting, there is likewise wanting the tormentor for crimes committed; and the vicious, if he can but escape the external chastisement for his crimes, laughs at the anxiety of the honest man to torment himself internally with his own rebukes; but the small reproaches, which he may sometimes make himself, he makes either not at all through conscience, or, if he has any, they are abundantly outweighed and requited by the sensual pleasure, for which only he has a taste.——If that charge shall be further refuted

b. by this, That it is indeed not to be denied that there is absolutely to be found no proportion conformable to justice between guilt and punishment in

* It is remarkable that among all the difficulties of uniting the course of the events of the world with the divinity of its Author, none forces itself so strongly on the mind, as that of the appearance of *justice* therein wanting. If it happens (though it is but seldom), that an unjust villain, especially one possessing power, does not escape out of the world unpunished, the impartial spectator, in a manner reconciled to heaven, rejoices. No other conformity-to-end in nature excites his affect to such a degree by the admiration of it, and so to speak lets the hand of God be so easily discerned. Why? It (the conformity-to-end) is here moral, and the only one of the sort, which one may hope to perceive in some measure in the world.

the world, and one must often perceive with indignation in the course of it a life led with crying injustice and yet happy to the very end; that this however lies in nature and is not intentionally prepared, consequently is not moral dissonance, because it is a property of virtue to struggle with adversity, (to which belongs the pain that the virtuous must suffer by the comparison of his own misfortune with the good fortune of the vicious, and sufferings serve but to enhance the value of virtue, therefore in the eye of reason this dissonance of the undeserved evils of life is resolved into the most glorious moral concord;—this solution is opposed by this, that, though these evils, when they, as the whetstone of virtue, either *precede* or accompany it, may, it is true, be represented as in a moral harmony with it, when at least the end of life crowns the latter and punishes vice; but that, when even this end falls out nonsensically, of which experience gives many examples, suffering seems to have fallen to the lot of the virtuous, not *in order* that his virtue shall be pure, but *because* it has been so (but on the other hand was contrary to the rules of prudent self-love): which is directly the contrary to justice, as man is able to form a conception of it to himself. For as to the possibility that the end of this terrestrial life may not perhaps be the end of all life, this possibility cannot be valid as a *vindication* of Providence, but is merely an authoritative decision of the morally faithful reason, by which the sceptic is referred to patience, but [is] not satisfied.

c. If finally the third solution of this unharmonious proportion between the moral value of men and the lot that falls to them, shall be attempted, by saying that, In this world must be judged all weal or ill, as a consequence of the use of the faculties of men merely according to laws of nature, proportioned to their applied address and prudence, at the same time to the circumstances also, into which they accidentally fall, but not according to their agreement with supersensible ends; whereas in a future world another order of things will subsist, and every one will obtain what his deeds here below are worth according to a moral judgment;—thus is this presupposition arbitrable. Reason, if it does not as a morally legislative faculty give an authoritative decision conformable to its interest, must rather find it probable according to mere rules of theoretical cognition, That the course of the world according to the order of nature, as here, so for the future, will determine our fate. For what other clue has reason for its theoretical presumption, than the law of nature? and, though it allowed itself, as was required of it (no. b.), to be referred to patience and the hope of a better future world; how can it expect that, as the course of things here according to the order of nature is of itself wise, it would according to the same laws in a future world be unwise? As, according to them, there is no comprehensible relation at all between the internal determining grounds of the will (namely, the moral cast of mind) according to laws of liberty, and between the (for the most part external) causes of our well-being independent of our will according to laws of nature; so the presumption remains, that the agreement of the fate of men with a Divine justice, according to the conceptions we form of it, is as little to be expected there as here. [I.e., if in this world punishment and evil are not proportioned, we are not entitled to infer from this fact that there will be a just proportionment of punishment and evil in a next life. This is the central idea in both (b) and (c). Eds.]

The issue of this process before the *forum* of philosophy is, that all theodicée has hitherto not performed what it promises, namely, to justify the moral wisdom in the government of the world against the doubts, which are entertained of it from what experience gives to cognise in this world; though indeed these doubts as objections, as far as our insight into the nature of our reason reaches with regard to the latter, cannot prove the contrary. But whether in progress of time more proper grounds of its vindication may not be found, not

to absolve the arraigned wisdom (as hitherto) merely *ab instantia*, remains still undetermined, if we do not succeed in shewing with certainty that our reason is absolutely unable for *the introspection of the relation, which a world, as we may always know it by experience bears to the Supreme Wisdom;* for then all farther essays of opiniative human wisdom to perspect the ways of Divine wisdom are totally rejected. That at least a negative wisdom, the insight of the necessary limitation of our pretensions with regard to what is beyond our reach, is attainable by us, must, in order to put an end *for ever* to this lawsuit, yet be proved; and this may be easily done.

We have a conception of a *wisdom of art* in the arrangement of this world, to which for our speculative faculty of reason objective reality is not wanting, for the purpose of arriving at a physico-theology. In like manner have we a conception of a *moral wisdom*, which may be placed in a world in general by a most perfect Author, in the moral idea of our own practical reason.—But of the *unity in the agreement* of that wisdom of art with the moral wisdom in a sensible world we have no conception, and can never hope to reach it, For, to be a creature, and as a being of nature, to follow the will of its Author merely; but yet, as a free agent (who has his will independent on external influence, which may be very contrary to the former), to be capable of imputation; and nevertheless to consider his own fact at the same time as the effect of a Supreme Being; are an association of conceptions, which we must conceive, it is true, in the idea of a world, as the chief good; but which he only, who penetrates to the knowledge of the supersensible (intelligible) world, and perspects the manner, in which it forms the basis of the sensible one, can introspect: upon which insight only the proof of the moral wisdom of the Author of the world can be grounded in the latter, as this presents but the phenomenon of the former world,—an insight which no mortal can attain.

All theodicée ought, properly speaking, to be an *explication* of nature, so far as God makes known by it the design of his will. Now every explication of the declared will of a legislator is either *doctrinal* or *authentic*. The former is what discovers by reasoning that will from the expressions, which it has used, in conjunction with the designs of the lawgiver otherwise known; the latter the legislator himself gives.

The world, as a work of God, may be contemplated by us as a divine publication of the *designs* of his will. In this however it is *frequently* for us a shut book; but it is *always* this, when, to conclude from it, though an object of experience, even the *final* end of God (which is always moral), is aimed at. The philosophical essays of this sort of explanation are doctrinal, and constitute the proper theodicée, which may therefore be termed the doctrinal one.—Yet the mere obviating of all objections to the Divine wisdom cannot be refused the name of a theodicée, when it is a *divine authoritative decision*, or (which in this case is to the same purpose) when it is a judgment of the same reason, by which we form to ourselves of necessity and before all experience the conception of God as a moral and wise Being. For there God is by our reason the very expounder of his own will announced by the creation; and this exposition we may denominate an *authentic* theodicée. Then, however, that is not the exposition of a *reasoning* (speculative) practical reason, but of a practical reason *possessing potency*, which, as it is without farther grounds absolutely commanding in legislating, may be considered as the immediate declaration and voice of God, by which he giveth a meaning to the letter of his creation. Such an authentic interpretation, now, I find in an ancient sacred book allegorically expressed.

JOB is represented as a man, to the enjoyment of whose life every thing possible to be conceived was united, in order to render it perfect. Healthy, opulent, free, a commander of others whom he may make happy, surrounded by a happy family, among beloved friends; and above all (what is the most essential), contented with himself in a good conscience.

All these riches, the latter excepted, a hard fate hung over him for a trial suddenly tore away from him. From the astonishment at this unexpected overthrow come by degrees to recollection, he gave vent to complaints against his disaster; on which between him and his friends who are present under a pretext to console themselves is soon begun a disputation, wherein both parties, every one according to his own way of thinking (but chiefly according to his situation), set forth their particular theodicée, for the moral interpretation of that bad fate. Job's friends declare themselves for the system of the interpretation of all evil in the world from Divine *justice*, as so many *punishments* for crimes perpetrated; and, though they could not name any, with which they could charge the unfortunate man, they believed to be able to judge *à priori* that he must needs be guilty of some, else it would not be possible according to the Divine justice that he should be unhappy. Whereas Job —who protests, with emotion, that his conscience does not reproach him in the least on account of his whole life; but as to inevitable human faults, God himself knoweth that he made him as a frail creature,—declares himself for the system of the *inconditional decree of God. He is of one mind*, continues Job, *and who can turn him?*

In what both parties reason or, if I may be allowed the word, overreason there is nothing remarkable; but the character, in which they do so, merits the more attention. Job speaks as he thinks, and every man in his situation would be of the same mind; his friends, on the other hand, speak as if the Almighty, on whose affair they decide, and to gain whose favour by their judgment they have more at heart than the truth, listened to them in secret. These their tricks, for the sake of appearance to maintain things, which they must allow they do not perspect, and to feign a conviction, which in fact they have not, contrast well with Job's plain sincerity, which is so far from false flattery as almost to border on temerity, greatly to his advantage. *Will you*, says he, *speak wickedly for God? and talk deceitfully for him? Will ye accept his person?* will ye *contend for God? He will surely reprove you, if ye do secretly accept persons!—for an hypocrite shall not come before him.*

The latter actually confirms the issue of the history. For God deigned to discover to Job the wisdom of his creation, chiefly on the side of its inscrutableness. He let him view the beautiful side of the creation where ends comprehensible to man set the wisdom and bountiful care of the Author of the world in an unambiguous light; but on the other hand the frightful side too, by naming to him productions of his potency and among these even pernicious dreadful things, every one of which, it is true, seems to be adjusted for itself and for its species conformably-to-end, but with regard to others and even to men destructive, contrary-to-end, and not harmonizing with an universal plan arranged by goodness and wisdom; whereby however he showeth the disposition and preservation of the whole announcing the wise Author of the world, though at the same time his ways, inscrutable to us, must be hidden even in the physical order of things, how much more then in their connexion with the moral (which is yet more impenetrable to our reason)?—The conclusion is, that, as Job acknowledges to have judged, not maliciously, for he is conscious to himself of his probity, but only imprudently, on things, which are too high for him, and which he does not understand, God pronounceth the condemnation of Job's friends, because they did not speak of him (God) so well (in point of conscientiousness), as his servant Job. If now the theory, which every one on both sides maintains, be contemplated, that of his friends may carry with it rather the appearance of more speculative reason and pious humility: and Job in all probability would have experienced a bad fate before every tribunal of dogmatical theologians, before a synod, an inquisition, a reverend classis, or every chief consistory of our time (one only excepted). Therefore, only the sincerity of the heart, not the preference

of knowledge, the honesty to acknowledge his doubts openly, and the aversion to feign conviction, where it is not felt, chiefly before God (where this craft besides is absurd), are the properties, which in the Divine judgment have decided the preference of the man of probity, in the person of Job, over the religious flatterer.

But the belief, which arose to him by so strange a solution of his doubts, namely, merely the conviction of his ignorance, could enter into the mind of none but him, who in the midst of his greatest doubts could say, *till I die I will not remove my integrity from me*, &c. For by this mindedness he proved that he did not ground his morality upon the belief, but the belief upon the morality: in which case this belief only, however weak it may be, is of a pure and genuine sort, that is, of that sort, which grounds a religion, not of courting favour, but of the good life.

CONCLUDING OBSERVATION

The theodicée, as has been shown, has not so much to do with a problem for the advantage of science, as rather with an affair of belief. From the authentic theodicée we saw that in such things it does not depend so much upon reasoning, as upon sincerity in the observation of the inability of our reason, and upon the honesty not to falsify one's thoughts in the utterance, let them be falsified with ever so pious a view.—This occasions the following short contemplation on a rich fund of matter, namely, sincerity, as the chief requisite in affairs of faith, in collision with the propension to falsity and impurity, as the principle defects in human nature.

That what one says either to himself or to another, is *true*, he cannot always be answerable (for he may err); but he can and must be answerable for his profession or his acknowledgment's being *veracious*, for of it he is immediately conscious to himself. In the former case he compares his asseveration with the object in the logical judgment (by the understanding); but in the latter, as he professes his holding-true, with the subject (before conscience). Does he make the profession relating to the former, without being conscious to himself of the latter? he lies, as he gives out something else than what he is conscious of.—The observation that there is such an impurity in the human heart, is not new (for Job made it); but one would almost think that the attention to it is new to teachers of morals and religion: so little is it found, that they, notwithstanding the difficulty which a purifying of the minds of men, even if they *would* act conformably to duty, carries with it, have made sufficient use of that observation.—This veracity may be named the *formal conscientiousness*, the *material* consists in the circumspection to venture nothing on the risk of its being wrong: as on the contrary that consists in the consciousness of having employed this circumspection in the given case.—Moralists speak of an erring conscience. But an erring conscience is a nonentity; and, were there such a thing, one could never be sure to have acted right, because the judge himself in the last instance might err. I may err, it is true, in the judgment, *in which I believe* to be in the right: for that belongs to the understanding, which only judges objectively (whether true or false); but in the consciousness, *Whether in fact I believe* to be in the right (or merely pretend it), I absolutely cannot err, as this judgment or rather this position says nothing but that I thus judge the object.

In the carefulness to be conscious to one's self of this belief (or unbelief), and not to give out any holding-true, of which one is not conscious, consists just the formal conscientiousness, which is the ground of veracity. Therefore, who says to himself (and, what is the same in the confessions of religion, before God) that *he believes*, without perhaps having examined himself, whether he is in fact conscious to himself of this holding-true or even of such a degree of it,* lies not

* The mean of extorting veracity in external deposing, *the oath* (*tortura spiritualis*) is held before a human tribunal not only allowed, but indispensable: a sad proof of the little reverence of men for truth, even in the

only in the most absurd manner (before a knower of hearts), but in the most wicked, because it saps the very foundation of every virtuous resolution, sin-

temple of public justice, where the mere idea of it ought of itself to inspire the greatest reverence! But men lie with regard to conviction, which they have not, at least of the sort, or in the degree, they pretend, even in their internal professions; and, as this improbity (since it tends by little and little to actual persuasion) may also have external pernicious consequents, to, that mean of extorting veracity, the oath, (but indeed only an internal one, that is, the essay, whether the holding-true stand the test of an internal *juratory* examining of the profession) may too be very well used to make the audaciousness more daring, at last, however, if not to restrain externally violent assertions, at least to stupify.—By an human tribunal nothing more is demanded of the conscience of him that makes oath, than the engaging that, if there is a future Judge of the world (therefore a God and a life to come), he will be answerable to him for the truth of his external profession; *that there is such a Judge of the world*, is a profession not necessary to be demanded of him, because, if the former protestation cannot withhold the lie, the latter false profession would create just as little scruple. After this internal delation of an oath one would ask himself, Wouldest thou take upon thee, by all that is dear and sacred to thee, to answer for the truth of that weighty tenet of faith or another holden so? At such a demand conscience would be suddenly roused by the danger, to which one exposes himself by pretending more, than he can maintain with certainty, where the believing concerns an object that is not at all attainable by the way of knowing [theoretical introspection], but whose assuming, by its only rendering possible the connexion of the chief practical principle of reason with that of the theoretical cognition of nature in one system (and thus reason agreeing with itself), is above all recommendable, but yet always free.—But professions of faith, whose source is historical, when they are enjoined others as precepts, must still more be subjected to this proof-by-fire of veracity: because here the impurity and feigned conviction is extended to move persons, and their guilt becomes a burden on him, who in a manner answers for the conscience of others (for men are willingly passive with their conscience).

cerity. It is easily conceived how soon such blind and external *confessions* (which are easily united with an internal confession just as false), when they furnish *means of acquisition*, may gradually occasion a certain falsehood in the cast of mind of even the commonwealth.— While this public purifying of the way of thinking in all probability remains deferred to a distant period, till it perhaps one day becomes an universal principle of education and doctrine under the protection of the liberty of thinking; a few lines still may be here bestowed on the contemplation of that vice, which seems to be deeply rooted in human nature.

There is something touching and which moves the soul in displaying a sincere character, divested of all falsehood and positive dissimulation; as integrity, however, a mere simplicity and rectitude of the way of thinking (especially when its ingenuity is excused) is the least that is requisite to a good character, and therefore it is not to be conceived upon what is grounded that admiration, with which we are impressed by such an object: it must then be, that sincerity is the property, with which human nature is the least endowed. A melancholy observation! As by that only all the other properties, so far as they rest upon principles, can have an intrinsic true value. None but a contemplative misanthrope (who wishes ill to nobody, but is inclined to believe every thing bad of men) can be doubtful whether to find men *worthy* of *hatred* or of *contempt.* The properties, on whose account he would judge them to be qualified for the former treatment, are those, by which they designedly do harm. That property, however, which seems rather to expose them to the latter degradation, can be no other, than a propensity, which is *in itself bad*, though it hurts nobody, a propensity to what can be used as a mean to no end whatever; which is therefore objectively good for nothing. The former evil is nothing but that of *enmity* (more mildly expressed, unkindness); the latter can be nothing else than a *lying disposi-*

tion (falsehood, even without any design to do hurt). The *one* inclination has a view, which may in certain other references be allowed and good, for instance, enmity against incorrigible disturbers of the peace. The *other* propensity, however, is that to the use of a mean (the lie) that, whatever be the view, is good for nothing, because it is in itself bad and blameable. In the quality of man of the former species there is *wickedness*, yet with which there may be combined a fitness for good ends in certain external relations and it sins but in the means, which are not rejectable in every view. The evil of the latter sort is *naughtiness (Nichtswürdigkeit)*, by which all character is refused to man. Here I chiefly insist on the impurity lying deeply concealed, as man knows to falsify even the internal declaration in presence of his own conscience. The less ought to surprise the external inclination to fraud; it must then be this, that, though every one knows the falseness of the coin, with which he trades, it can maintain itself equally well in circulation.

In de-Luec's letters on the mountains, the history of the earth and of men, I remember to have read the following result of his in part anthropological journey. The philanthropic author set out with the good quality of our species, and sought the confirmation of it, where city luxury cannot have such influence to corrupt the minds, in the mountains, from Switzerland to the Harze; and, after his belief in disinterested helping (*Hülfleistende*) inclination began somewhat to stagger by an experience in the former, he at last infers this conclusion, *That man, as to benevolence, is good enough* (no wonder! for this rests upon implanted inclination, of which God is the Author); *if a bad* propensity to fine deceit were but not inherent in him*

* In the very intermixture of the bad with the good lie the great springs, which rouse into action the dormant powers of humanity, and necessitate men to develop all their talents and to approach towards the perfection of their destination.

(which is likewise not astonishing; for to withhold this depends upon the character, which man himself must form in himself)!—A result of the inquiry that every

body, even without having travelled in the mountains, might have met with among his fellow-citizens, nay, yet nearer, in his own breast.

Evil and Omnipotence
J. L. MACKIE

The traditional arguments for the existence of God have been fairly thoroughly criticized by philosophers. But the theologian can, if he wishes, accept this criticism. He can admit that no rational proof of God's existence is possible. And he can still retain all that is essential to his position, by holding that God's existence is known in some other, nonrational way. I think, however, that a more telling criticism can be made by way of the traditional problem of evil. Here it can be shown, not that religious beliefs lack rational support, but that they are positively irrational, that the several parts of the essential theological doctrine are inconsistent with one another, so that the theologian can maintain his position as a whole only by a much more extreme rejection of reason than in the former case. He must now be prepared to believe, not merely what cannot be proved, but what can be *disproved* from other beliefs that he also holds.

The problem of evil, in the sense in which I shall be using the phrase, is a problem only for someone who believes that there is a God who is both omnipotent and wholly good. And it is a logical problem, the problem of clarifying and reconciling a number of beliefs: it is not a scientific problem that might be solved by further observations, or a practical problem that might be solved by a decision or an action. These points are obvious; I mention them only because they are sometimes ignored by theologians, who sometimes parry a statement of the problem with such remarks as

"Well, can you solve the problem yourself?" or "This is a mystery which may be revealed to us later" or "Evil is something to be faced and overcome, not to be merely discussed."

In its simplest form the problem is this: God is omnipotent; God is wholly good; and yet evil exists. There seems to be some contradiction between these three propositions, so that if any two of them were true the third would be false. But at the same time all three are essential parts of most theological positions: the theologian, it seems, at once *must* adhere and *cannot consistently* adhere to all three. (The problem does not arise only for theists, but I shall discuss it in the form in which it presents itself for ordinary theism.)

However, the contradiction does not arise immediately; to show it we need some additional premises, or perhaps some quasi-logical rules connecting the terms "good," "evil," and "omnipotent." These additional principles are that good is opposed to evil, in such a way that a good thing always eliminates evil as far as it can, and that there are no limits to what an omnipotent thing can do. From these it follows that a good omnipotent thing eliminates evil completely, and then the propositions that a good omnipotent thing exists, and that evil exists, are incompatible.

ADEQUATE SOLUTIONS
Now once the problem is fully stated it is clear that it can be solved, in the sense that the problem will not arise if

FROM: *Mind*, Vol. LXIV, No. 254 (1955). Reprinted by permission of the editor of *Mind* and the author.

one gives up at least one of the propositions that constitute it. If you are prepared to say that God is not wholly good, or not quite omnipotent, or that evil does not exist, or that good is not opposed to the kind of evil that exists, or that there are limits to what an omnipotent thing can do, then the problem of evil will not arise for you.

There are, then, quite a number of adequate solutions of the problem of evil, and some of these have been adopted, or almost adopted, by various thinkers. For example, a few have been prepared to deny God's omnipotence, and rather more have been prepared to keep the term "omnipotence" but severely to restrict its meaning, recording quite a number of things that an omnipotent being cannot do. Some have said that evil is an illusion, perhaps because they held that the whole world of temporal, changing things is an illusion, and that what we call evil belongs only to this world, or perhaps because they held that although temporal things *are* much as we see them, those that we call evil are not really evil. Some have said that what we call evil is merely the privation of good, that evil in a positive sense, evil that would really be opposed to good, does not exist. Many have agreed with Pope that disorder is harmony not understood, and that partial evil is universal good. Whether any of these views is *true* is, of course, another question But each of them gives an adequate solution of the problem of evil in the sense that if you accept it this problem does not arise for you, though you may, of course, have *other* problems to face

But often enough these adequate solutions are only *almost* adopted. The thinkers who restrict God's power, but keep the term "omnipotence," may reasonably be suspected of thinking, in other contexts, that his power is really unlimited. Those who say that evil is an illusion may also be thinking, inconsistently, that this illusion is itself an evil. Those who say that "evil" is merely privation of good may also be thinking,

inconsistently, that privation of good is an evil. (The fallacy here is akin to some forms of the "naturalistic fallacy" in ethics, where some think, for example, that "good" is just what contributes to evolutionary progress, and that evolutionary progress is itself good.) If Pope meant what he said in the first line of his couplet, that "disorder" is only harmony not understood, the "partial evil" of the second line must, for consistency, mean "that which, taken in isolation, falsely appears to be evil," but it would more naturally mean "that which, in isolation, really is evil." The second line, in fact, hesitates between two views, that "partial evil" isn't really evil, since only the universal quality is real, and that "partial evil" is really an evil, but only a little one.

In addition, therefore, to adequate solutions, we must recognize unsatisfactory inconsistent solutions, in which there is only a half-hearted or temporary rejection of one of the propositions which together constitute the problem. In these, one of the constituent propositions is explicitly rejected, but it is covertly reasserted or assumed elsewhere in the system.

FALLACIOUS SOLUTIONS

Besides these half-hearted solutions, which explicitly reject but implicitly assert one of the constituent propositions, there are definitely fallacious solutions which explicitly maintain all the constituent propositions, but implicitly reject at least one of them in the course of the argument that explains away the problem of evil.

There are, in fact, many so-called solutions which purport to remove the contradiction without abandoning any of its constituent propositions. These must be fallacious, as we can see from the very statement of the problem, but it is not so easy to see in each case precisely where the fallacy lies. I suggest that in all cases the fallacy has the general form suggested above: in order to solve the problem one (or perhaps more) of its constituent propositions is given up, but in such a way that it appears to have been retained, and can therefore be asserted without qualification in other contexts. Sometimes there is a further complication: the supposed solution moves to and fro between, say two of the constituent propositions, at one point asserting the first of these but covertly abandoning the second, at another point asserting the second but covertly abandoning the first. These fallacious solutions often turn upon some equivocation with the words "good" and "evil," or upon some vagueness about the way in which good and evil are opposed to one another, or about how much is meant by "omnipotence." I propose to examine some of these so-called solutions, and to exhibit their fallacies in detail. Incidentally, I shall also be considering whether an adequate solution could be reached by a minor modification of one or more of the constituent propositions, which would, however, still satisfy all the essential requirements of ordinary theism.

1. "Good cannot exist without evil" or "Evil is necessary as a counterpart to good."

It is sometimes suggested that evil is necessary as a counterpart to good, that if there were no evil there could be no good either, and that this solves the problem of evil. It is true that it points to an answer to the question "Why should there be evil?" But it does so only by qualifying some of the propositions that constitute the problem.

First, it sets a limit to what God can do, saying that God *cannot* create good without simultaneously creating evil, and this means either that God is not omnipotent or that there are *some* limits to what an omnipotent thing can do. It may be replied that these limits are always presupposed, that omnipotence has never meant the power to do what is logically impossible, and on the present view the existence of good without evil would be a logical impossibility. This

interpretation of omnipotence may, indeed, be accepted as a modification of our original account which does not reject anything that is essential to theism, and I shall in general assume it in the subsequent discussion. It is, perhaps, the most common theistic view, but I think that some theists at least have maintained that God can do what is logically impossible. Many theists, at any rate, have held that logic itself is created or laid down by God, that logic is the way in which God arbitrarily chooses to think. (This is, of course, parallel to the ethical view that morally right actions are those which God arbitrarily chooses to command, and the two views encounter similar difficulties.) And *this* account of logic is clearly inconsistent with the view that God is bound by logical necessities—unless it is possible for an omnipotent being to bind himself, an issue which we shall consider later, when we come to the Paradox of Omnipotence. This solution of the problem of evil cannot, therefore, be consistently adopted along with the view that logic is itself created by God.

But, secondly, this solution denies that evil is opposed to good in our original sense. If good and evil are counterparts, a good thing will not "eliminate evil as far as it can." Indeed, this view suggests that good and evil are not strictly qualities of things at all. Perhaps the suggestion is that good and evil are related in much the same way as great and small. Certainly, when the term "great" is used relatively as a condensation of "greater than so-and-so," and "small" is used correspondingly, greatness and smallness are counterparts and cannot exist without each other. But in this sense greatness is not a quality, not an intrinsic feature of anything; and it would be absurd to think of a movement in favor of greatness and against smallness in this sense. Such a movement would be self-defeating, since relative greatness can be promoted only by a simultaneous promotion of relative smallness. I feel sure that no theists would be content to regard God's goodness as analogous to this—as if what he supports were not the *good* but the *better*, and as if he had the paradoxical aim all things should be better than other things.

This point is obscured by the fact that "great" and "small" seem to have an absolute as well as a relative sense. I cannot discuss here whether there is absolute magnitude or not, but if there is, there could be an absolute sense for "great," it could mean of at least a certain size, and it would make sense to speak of all things getting bigger, of a universe that was expanding all over, and therefore it would make sense to speak of promoting greatness. But in *this* sense great and small are not logically necessary counterparts: either quality could exist without the other. There would be no logical impossibility in everything's being small or in everything's being great.

Neither in the absolute nor in the relative sense, then, of "great" and "small" do these terms provide an analogy of the sort that would be needed to support this solution of the problem of evil. In neither case are greatness and smallness *both* necessary counterparts *and* mutually opposed forces or possible objects for support and attack.

It may be replied that good and evil are necessary counterparts in the same way as any quality and its logical opposite: redness can occur, it is suggested, only if nonredness also occurs. But unless evil is merely the privation of good, they are not logical opposites, and some further argument would be needed to show that they are counterparts in the same way as genuine logical opposites. Let us assume that this could be given. There is still doubt of the correctness of the metaphysical principle that a quality must have a real opposite: I suggest that it is not really impossible that everything should be, say, red, that the truth is merely that if everything were red we should not notice redness, and so we should have no word "red"; we observe and give names to qualities only if they have real opposites. If so, the prin-

ciple that a term must have an opposite would belong only to our language or to our thought, and would not be an ontological principle, and, correspondingly, the rule that good cannot exist without evil would not state a logical necessity of a sort that God would just have to put up with. God might have made everything good, though *we* should not have noticed it if he had.

But, finally, even if we concede that this *is* an ontological principle, it will provide a solution for the problem of evil only if one is prepared to say, "Evil exists, but only just enough evil to serve as the counterpart of good." I doubt whether any theist will accept this. After all, the *ontological* requirement that non-redness should occur would be satisfied even if all the universe, except for a minute speck, were red, and, if there were a corresponding requirement for evil as a counterpart to good, a minute dose of evil would presumably do. But theists are not usually willing to say, in all contexts, that all the evil that occurs is a minute and necessary dose.

2. "Evil is necessary as a means to good."

It is sometimes suggested that evil is necessary for good not as a counterpart but as a means. In its simple form this has little plausibility as a solution of the problem of evil, since it obviously implies a severe restriction of God's power. It would be a *causal* law that you cannot have a certain end without a certain means, so that if God has to introduce evil as a means to good, he must be subject to at least some causal laws. This certainly conflicts with what a theist normally means by omnipotence. This view of God as limited by causal laws also conflicts with the view that causal laws are themselves made by God, which is more widely held than the corresponding view about the laws of logic. This conflict would, indeed, be resolved if it were possible for an omnipotent being to bind himself, and this possibility has still to be considered. Unless a favorable answer can be given to this question, the suggestion that evil is necessary as a means to good solves the problem of evil only by denying one of its constituent propositions, either that God is omnipotent or that "omnipotent" means what it says.

3. "The universe is better with some evil in it than it could be if there were no evil."

Much more important is a solution which at first seems to be a mere variant of the previous one, that evil may contribute to the goodness of a whole in which it is found, so that the universe as a whole is better as it is, with some evil in it, than it would be if there were no evil. This solution may be developed in either of two ways. It may be supported by an aesthetic analogy, by the fact that contrasts heighten beauty, that in a musical work, for example, there may occur discords which somehow add to the beauty of the work as a whole. Alternatively, it may be worked out in connection with the notion of progress, that the best possible organization of the universe will not be static, but progressive, that the gradual overcoming of evil by good is really a finer thing than would be the eternal unchallenged supremacy of good.

In either case, this solution usually starts from the assumption that the evil whose existence gives rise to the problem of evil is primarily what is called physical evil, that is to say, pain. In Hume's rather half-hearted presentation of the problem of evil, the evils that he stresses are pain and disease, and those who reply to him argue that the existence of pain and disease makes possible the existence of sympathy, benevolence, heroism, and the gradually successful struggle of doctors and reformers to overcome these evils. In fact, theists often seize the opportunity to accuse those who stress the problem of evil of taking a low, materialistic view of good and evil, equating these

with pleasure and pain, and of ignoring the more spiritual goods which can arise in the struggle against evils.

But let us see exactly what is being done here. Let us call pain and misery "first order evil" or "evil (1)." What contrasts with this, namely, pleasure and happiness, will be called "first order good" or "good (1)." Distinct from this is "second order good" or "good (2)" which somehow emerges in a complex situation in which evil (1) is a necessary component—logically, not merely causally, necessary. (Exactly *how* it emerges does not matter: in the crudest version of this solution good [2] is simply the heightening of happiness by the contrast with misery, in other versions it includes sympathy with suffering, heroism in facing danger, and the gradual decrease of first order evil and increase of first order good.) It is also being assumed that second order good is more important than first order good or evil, in particular that it more than outweighs the first order evil it involves.

Now this is a particularly subtle attempt to solve the problem of evil. It defends God's goodness and omnipotence on the ground that (on a sufficiently long view) this is the best of all logically possible worlds, because it includes the important second order goods, and yet it admits that real evils, namely first order evils, exist. But does it still hold that good and evil are opposed? Not, clearly, in the sense that we set out originally: good does not tend to eliminate evil in general. Instead, we have a modified, a more complex pattern. First order good (e.g., happiness) *contrasts with* first order evil (e.g., misery): these two are opposed in a fairly mechanical way; some second order goods (e.g., benevolence) try to maximize first order good and minimize first order evil; but God's goodness is not this, it is rather the will to maximize *second* order good. We might, therefore, call God's goodness an example of a third order goodness, or good (3). While this account is different from our original one, it might well be held to be an improvement on it, to give a more accurate description of the way in which good is opposed to evil, and to be consistent with the essential theist position.

There might, however, be several objections to this solution.

First, some might argue that such qualities as benevolence—and a fortiori the third order goodness which promotes benevolence—have a merely derivative value, that they are not higher sorts of good, but merely means to good (1), that is, to happiness, so that it would be absurd for God to keep misery in existence in order to make possible the virtues of benevolence, heroism, etc. The theist who adopts the present solution must, of course, deny this, but he can do so with some plausibility, so I should not press this objection.

Secondly, it follows from this solution that God is not in our sense benevolent or sympathetic: he is not concerned to minimize evil (1), but only to promote good (2); and this might be a disturbing conclusion for some theists.

But, thirdly, the fatal objection is this. Our analysis shows clearly the possibility of the existence of a *second* order evil, an evil (2) contrasting with good (2) as evil (1) contrasts with good (1). This would include malevolence, cruelty, callousness, cowardice, and states in which good (1) is decreasing and evil (1) increasing. And just as good (2) is held to be the important kind of good, the kind that God is concerned to promote, so evil (2) will, by analogy, be the important kind of evil, the kind which God, if he were wholly good and omnipotent, would eliminate. And yet evil (2) plainly exists, and indeed most theists (in other contexts) stress its existence more than that of evil (1). We should, therefore, state the problem of evil in terms of second order evil, and against this form of the problem the present solution is useless.

An attempt might be made to use this solution again, at a higher level, to explain the occurrence of evil (2): indeed the next main solution that we

shall examine does just this, with the help of some new notions. Without any fresh notions, such a solution would have little plausibility: for example, we could hardly say that the really important good was a good (3), such as the increase of benevolence in proportion to cruelty, which logically required for its occurrence the occurrence of some second order evil. But even if evil (2) could be explained in this way, it is fairly clear that there would be third order evils contrasting with this third order good: and we should be well on the way to an infinite regress, where the solution of a problem of evil, stated in terms of evil (n), indicated the existence of an evil $(n + 1)$, and a further problem to be solved.

4. "Evil is due to human free will."

Perhaps the most important proposed solution of the problem of evil is that evil is not to be ascribed to God at all, but to the independent actions of human beings, supposed to have been endowed by God with freedom of the will. This solution may be combined with the preceding one: first order evil (e.g., pain) may be justified as a logically necessary component in second order good (e.g., sympathy) while second order evil (e.g., cruelty) is not *justified*, but is so ascribed to human beings that God cannot be held responsible for it. This combination evades my third criticism of the preceding solution.

The free-will solution also involves the preceding solution at a higher level. To explain why a wholly good God gave men free will although it would lead to some important evils, it must be argued that it is better on the whole that men should act freely, and sometimes err, than that they should be innocent automata, acting rightly in a wholly determined way. Freedom, that is to say, is now treated as a third order good, and as being more valuable than second order goods (such as sympathy and heroism) would be if they were deterministically produced, and it is being assumed that second order evils, such as cruelty, are logically necessary accompaniments of freedom, just as pain is a logically necessary precondition of sympathy.

I think that this solution is unsatisfactory primarily because of the incoherence of the notion of freedom of the will: but I cannot discuss this topic adequately here, although some of my criticisms will touch upon it.

First I should query the assumption that second order evils are logically necessary accompaniments of freedom. I should ask this: if God has made men such that in their free choices they sometimes prefer what is good and sometimes what is evil, why could he not have made men such that they always freely choose the good? If there is no logical impossibility in a man's freely choosing the good on one, or on several, occasions, there cannot be a logical impossibility in his freely choosing the good on every occasion. God was not, then, faced with a choice between making innocent automata and making beings who, in acting freely, would sometimes go wrong: there was open to him the obviously better possibility of making beings who would act freely but always go right. Clearly, his failure to avail himself of this possibility is inconsistent with his being both omnipotent and wholly good.

If it is replied that this objection is absurd, that the making of some wrong choices is logically necessary for freedom, it would seem that "freedom" must here mean complete randomness or indeterminacy, including randomness with regard to the alternatives good and evil, in other words that men's choices and consequent actions can be "free" only if they are not determined by their characters. Only on this assumption can God escape the responsibility for men's actions; for if he made them as they are, but did not determine their wrong choices, this can only be because the wrong choices are not determined by men as they are. But then if freedom is randomness, how can it be a characteristic of *will?* And, still more, how can it be

the most important good? What value or merit would there be in free choices if these were random actions which were not determined by the nature of the agent?

I conclude that to make this solution plausible two different senses of "freedom" must be confused, one sense which will justify the view that freedom is a third order good, more valuable than other goods would be without it, and another sense, sheer randomness, to prevent us from ascribing to God a decision to make men such that they sometimes go wrong when he might have made them such that they would always freely go right.

This criticism is sufficient to dispose of this solution. But besides this there is a fundamental difficulty in the notion of an omnipotent God creating men with free will, for if men's wills are really free this must mean that even God cannot control them, that is, that God is no longer omnipotent. It may be objected that God's gift of freedom to men does not mean that he *cannot* control their wills, but that he always *refrains* from controlling their wills. But why, we may ask, should God refrain from controlling evil wills? Why should he not leave men free to will rightly, but intervene when he sees them beginning to will wrongly? If God could do this, but does not, and if he is wholly good, the only explanation could be that even a wrong free act of will is not really evil, that its freedom is a value which outweighs its wrongness, so that there would be a loss of value if God took away the wrongness and the freedom together. But this is utterly opposed to what theists say about sin in other contexts. The present solution of the problem of evil, then, can be maintained only in the form that God has made men so free that he *cannot* control their wills.

This leads us to what I call the "Paradox of Omnipotence": can an omnipotent being make things which he cannot subsequently control? Or, what is practically equivalent to this, can an omnipotent being make rules which then bind himself? (These are practically equivalent because any such rules could be regarded as setting certain things beyond his control, and vice versa.) The second of these formulations is relevant to the suggestions that we have already met, that an omnipotent God creates the rules of logic or causal laws, and is then bound by them.

It is clear that this is a paradox: the questions cannot be answered satisfactorily either in the affirmative or in the negative. If we answer "Yes," it follows that if God actually makes things which he cannot control, or makes rules which bind himself, he is not omnipotent once he has made them: there are *then* things which he cannot do. But if we answer "No," we are immediately asserting that there are things which he cannot do, that is to say that he is already not omnipotent.

It cannot be replied that the question which sets this paradox is not a proper question. It would make perfectly good sense to say that a human mechanic has made a machine which he cannot control: if there is any difficulty about the question it lies in the notion of omnipotence itself.

This, incidentally, shows that although we have approached this paradox from the free-will theory, it is equally a problem for a theological determinist. No one thinks that machines have free will, yet they may well be beyond the control of their makers. The determinist might reply that anyone who makes anything determines its ways of acting, and so determines its subsequent behavior: even the human mechanic does this by his *choice* of materials and structure for his machine, though he does not know all about either of these: the mechanic thus determines, though he may not foresee, his machine's actions. And since God is omniscient, and since his creation of things is total, he both determines and foresees the ways in which his creatures will act. We may grant this, but it is beside the point. The question is not whether God *originally* determined the future actions of his creatures, but

whether he can *subsequently* control their actions, or whether he was able in his original creation to put things beyond his subsequent control. Even on determinist principles the answers "Yes" and "No" are equally irreconcilable with God's omnipotence.

Before suggesting a solution of this paradox, I would point out that there is a parallel Paradox of Sovereignty. Can a legal sovereign make a law restricting its own future legislative power? For example, could the British parliament make a law forbidding any future parliament to socialize banking, and also forbidding the future repeal of this law itself? Or could the British parliament, which was legally sovereign in Australia in, say, 1899, pass a valid law, or series of laws, which made it no longer sovereign in 1933? Again, neither the affirmative nor the negative answer is really satisfactory. If we were to answer "Yes," we should be admitting the validity of a law which, if it were actually made, would mean that parliament was no longer sovereign. If we were to answer "No," we should be admitting that there is a law, not logically absurd, which parliament cannot validly make, that is, that parliament is not now a legal sovereign. This paradox can be solved in the following way. We should distinguish between first order laws, that is laws governing the actions of individuals and bodies other than the legislature, and second order laws, that is laws about laws, laws governing the actions of the legislature itself. Correspondingly, we should distinguish two orders of sovereignty, first order sovereignty (sovereignty [1]) which is unlimited authority to make first order laws, and second order sovereignty (sovereignty [2]) which is unlimited authority to make second order laws. If we say that parliament is sovereign we might mean that any parliament at any time has sovereignty (1), or we might mean that parliament has both sovereignty (1) and sovereignty (2) at present, but we cannot without contradiction mean both that the present parliament has sovereignty (2) and that every parliament at every time has sovereignty (1), for if the present parliament has sovereignty (2) it may use it to take away the sovereignty (1) of later parliaments. What the paradox shows is that we cannot ascribe to any continuing institution legal sovereignty in an inclusive sense.

The analogy between omnipotence and sovereignty shows that the paradox of omnipotence can be solved in a similar way. We must distinguish between first order omnipotence (omnipotence [1]), that is unlimited power to act, and second order omnipotence (omnipotence [2]), that is unlimited power to determine what powers to act things shall have. Then we could consistently say that God all the time has omnipotence (1), but if so no beings at any time have powers to act independently of God. Or we could say that God at one time had omnipotence (2), and used it to assign independent powers to act to certain things, so that God thereafter did not have omnipotence (1). But what the paradox shows is that we cannot consistently ascribe to any continuing being omnipotence in an inclusive sense.

An alternative solution of this paradox would be simply to deny that God is a continuing being, that any times can be assigned to his actions at all. But on this assumption (which also has difficulties of its own) no meaning can be given to the assertion that God made men with wills so free that he could not control them. The paradox of omnipotence can be avoided by putting God outside time, but the free-will solution of the problem of evil cannot be saved in this way, and equally it remains impossible to hold that an omnipotent God *binds himself* by causal or logical laws.

CONCLUSION

Of the proposed solutions of the problem of evil which we have examined, none has stood up to criticism. There may be other solutions which require examination, but this study strongly suggests that there is no valid solution of the problem which does not modify at least one of the constituent propositions in a way which would seriously affect the essential core of the theistic position.

Quite apart from the problem of evil, the paradox of omnipotence has shown that God's omnipotence must in any case be restricted in one way or another, that unqualified omnipotence cannot be ascribed to any being that continues through time. And if God and his actions are not in time, can omnipotence, or power of any sort, be meaningfully ascribed to him?

Omnipotence, Evil, and Supermen
NINIAN SMART

It has in recent years been argued, by Professors Antony Flew and J. L. Mackie;[1] that God could have created men wholly good. For, causal determi-

[1] See Antony Flew, "Divine Omnipotence and Human Freedom," in *New Essays in Philosophical Theology,* A. Flew and A. MacIntyre, eds. (New York: The Macmillan Company, 1955), Chap. 8, and J. L. Mackie, "Evil and Omnipotence." (See above.)

nism being compatible with free will, men could have been made in such a way that, without loss of freedom, they would never have fallen (and would never fall) into sin. This if true would constitute a weighty antitheistic argument. And yet intuitively it seems unconvincing. I wish here to uncover the roots of this intuitive suspicion.

There are in the argument two as-

FROM: *Philosophy,* Vol. XXXVI, No. 137 (1961). Reprinted by permission of the editors of *Philosophy* and the author.

sertions to be distinguished. First, that causal determinism (i.e., the claim that all human actions are the results of prior causes) is compatible with free will.[2] I call this the Compatibility Thesis. Second, there is the assertion that God could have created men wholly good. This I shall call the Utopia Thesis. An apparent inference from the latter is that God cannot be both omnipotent and wholly good, since men are in fact wicked.

In the present discussion I shall concentrate on the Utopia Thesis. Clearly, of course, if the Compatibility Thesis is not established the Utopia Thesis loses its principal basis and becomes altogether doubtful. But I shall here merely try to show that the Utopia Thesis does not follow from the Compatibility Thesis, despite appearances. This may well indicate that there is something queer about the latter (and the Paradigm Case Argument, on which perhaps it principally rests, has lately come in for perspicacious criticism).[3] In the discussion I shall be assuming the truth of determinism; for if it is false, the Compatibility Thesis becomes irrelevant and the Utopia Thesis totters. The chief points in my reasoning are as follows:

The concept *good* as applied to humans connects with other concepts such as *temptation, courage, generosity*, etc. These concepts have no clear application if men were built wholly good. I bring this out by a piece of anthropological fiction, i.e., (1) let us conjure up a universe like ours, only where men are supposed to be wholly good; or (2) let us consider the possibility of Utopian universes quite unlike ours. Under (1), I try to show that it is unclear whether the "men" in such a universe are to be called wholly good or even good, and that it

[2] See Flew, *op. cit.*, p. 151.

[3] See the article "Farewell to the Paradigm-Case Argument" by J. W. N. Watkins, and Flew's comment and Watkins' reply to the comment, all in *Analysis*, Vol. XVIII, No. 2 (1957), and the articles by R. Harré and H. G. Alexander in *Analysis*, Vol. XVIII, Nos. 4–5 (1958), respectively.

is unclear whether they should be called men. And under (2), I try to show that we have even stronger reasons for saying that these things are unclear. Thus the abstract possibility that men might have been created wholly good has no clearly assignable content. Hence, it is rational to be quite agnostic about such a possibility. It follows that it will be quite unclear whether a Utopian universe will be superior (in respect of moral goodness) to ours. So the Utopia Thesis cannot constitute an antitheistic argument.

I

When we say that a man is good, we are liable to render an account of why we say this by giving reasons. For example, it might be because he has been heroic in resisting temptations, courageous in the fact of difficulties, generous to his friends, etc. Thus *good* normally connects with concepts like *courage* and so forth.

Let us look first at *temptation*. It is clear (at least on the determinist assumption) that if two identical twins were in otherwise similar situations but where one has a temptation not to do what is right, while no such temptation is presented to the other twin, and other things being equal, the tempted twin will be less likely to do what is right than the untempted one. It is this fact that temptations are empirically discovered to affect conduct that doubtless makes it relevant to consider them when appraising character and encouraging virtue. Moreover, unless we were built in a certain way there would be no temptations: for example, unless we were built so that sexual gratification is normally very pleasant there would be no serious temptations to commit adultery, etc. It would appear then that the only way to ensure that people were wholly good would be to build them in such a way that they were never tempted or only tempted to a negligible extent. True, there are two other peculiar possibilities, which I shall go on to deal with, namely (1) through lucky combination of circumstances men might never sin; (2)

frequent miraculous intervention might keep them on the straight and narrow path. However, for the moment, I consider the main possibility, that to ensure that *all* men were *always* good, men would have to possess a built-in resistance to all temptations.

Similar remarks apply to courage, generosity, etc., although in some cases the situation may be rather complex. It will, I think, be conceded that we credit people with courage on such grounds as that they have faced adverse situations with calm and disregard for danger. But the adversities arise because there are fears, desires for comfort, disinclinations to offend people, and so on. And it will be generally agreed, at least by determinists, that one twin faced with a situation where doing right inspires fear will be less likely to do what is right than the other twin not so faced with adversity, and similarly with regard to desires for comfort and so forth. Thus to ensure that men would never panic, never wilt, etc., it would be necessary, as the main possibility, to build them differently.

Perhaps generosity is a trickier case. But it is clear that a person is praised for generosity because very often there is a conflict of generosity and self-interest. Indeed, if there were not some such conflict, or thought to be, however remote, an action would not really count as generosity, perhaps; the slight qualification here is due to the possibility of situations where a person has so much money, say, that it makes no psychological difference whether he gives away a certain sum or not, but he does it out of sympathy—I shall deal with such cases below. And to say that generosity conflicts with self-interest is a shorthand way of saying that one's inclinations for comfort, etc., are liable to have a more restricted fulfilment than would otherwise be the case.

Then there are actions which exhibit such dispositions as pride, which seem remote from simple inclinations such as likings for certain sorts of food or for sexual gratification and from fairly simple impulses such as fear. But though the springs of pride are hard to fathom, it is doubtless true that people would not display pride, in the ordinary sense, if they did not live in a socially competitive atmosphere, if they did not have desires to assert themselves, etc. One would not be sure quite how men would have to be rebuilt to immunize them from pride, but rebuilding would surely be necessary, on the determinist view.

As for the peculiar cases mentioned above—generosity not involving sacrifice and similar examples—I do not think that such instances are at all serious ones, inasmuch as (1) virtues are dispositions, and so there is a point in calling such nonsacrificial generosity generosity, in that it exhibits a disposition whose basic exercise involves sacrifice; (2) without the occasions for basic exercise of the disposition it is obscure as to what could be meant by calling the nonbasic instances of generosity instances of generosity.

These examples, then, are meant to indicate that the concept *goodness* is applied to beings of a certain sort, beings who are liable to temptations, possess inclinations, have fears, tend to assert themselves and so forth; and that if they were to be immunized from evil they would have to be built in a different way. But it soon becomes apparent that to rebuild them would mean that the ascription of goodness would become unintelligible, for the reasons why men are called good and bad have a connection with human nature as it is empirically discovered to be. Moral utterance is embedded in the cosmic status quo.

II

Of course, God is not bound by synthetic necessities: He is in no way shackled by the causal laws of our universe, for example. But in a backhanded way, He is confined by meaninglessness. For to say that God might do such-and-such where the "such-and-such" is meaningless or completely obscure is not to assert that God can *do* anything. I therefore hope to show that "God might have created men wholly good" is without intelligible content, and hence that this alleged possibility has no force as an antitheistic argument.

"God might have created men wholly good" *appears* to have content because at least it does not seem self-contradictory and because we think we can imagine such a situation. But I shall bring out its emptiness by in fact trying to do this, by imagining other possible universes. Now it may well be objected that in doing this I am showing nothing. For example, one will be wanting to make imaginative causal inferences like "If men are never to panic they must be built in such-and-such a way." But since God is not bound by causal principles the inferences have no legitimacy.

But this objection misses the point of my procedure. For my argument is based on the following dilemma. *Either* we can hope to assign a reasonably clear meaning to the possibility that men might have been created wholly good by imagining a Utopia—in which case the paradox arises that it would be quite unclear as to whether such "men" could reasonably be called wholly good. *Or* we can refuse to assign such a reasonably clear meaning to the possibility by simply postulating an unimaginable alternative universe—in which case there are even stronger reasons for doubting whether the possibility has content. Or, to make the matter *ad hominem* as against Flew, I am saying that alleged possibilities as well as alleged facts can die the Death by a Thousand Qualifications.*

I proceed then to imagine possible universes. In line with the above dilemma, I divide such universes into two classes. First, those which are cosmomorphic, i.e., those which are governed by physical laws at least roughly comparable to those found in our cosmos. Second, I consider noncosmomorphic universes, i.e., ones with a quite different set-up from ours.

1. *Cosmomorphic Utopia A*—The

first and main type of cosmomorphic utopia, where men are wholly good, can be described perhaps as follows, in line with the earlier remarks about temptations, etc.

Men will never be seriously tempted to harm or injure each other. For this reason: that no one has any serious desires liable to conflict with those of others. For instance, they would be so built that one and only one woman would attract any one man and conversely. Say: one would have an over-riding infatuation for the first uninfatuated woman one met and vice versa. As for property: men might arrive in the world with an automatic supply of necessities and comforts, and the individual would have a built-in mechanism to ensure that the supplies of others were mysteriously distasteful (the other man's passion-fruit smells like dung). And what of danger? During, say, a thunderstorm no one would be so seriously perturbed that he would be likely to panic and harm others. Let us suppose that a signal would (so to speak) flash in the individual's brain, telling him to take cover. What if he was in the middle of an *al fresco* dinner? Perhaps the signal flashing would dry up the juices in his mouth. And so forth. (Admittedly this picture is not elaborated with much scientific expertize: of this I shall say more later.)

I think that none of the usual reasons for calling men good would apply in such a Utopia. Consider one of these harmless beings. He is wholly good, you say? Really? Has he been courageous? No, you reply, not exactly, for such creatures do not feel fear. Then he is generous to his friends perhaps? Not precisely, you respond, for there is no question of his being ungenerous. Has he resisted temptations? No, not really, for there are no temptations (nothing you could really *call* temptations). Then why call them good? Well, you say, these creatures never harm each other. . . . Yes, but the inhabitants of Alpha Centauri never harm *us*. Ah, you reply, Centaurians do not harm us because there

* For Flews' use of this phrase, see below, first essay in the section *Is Religious Language Meaningful?*

are as yet no ways for them to impinge upon us. Quite so, I say; it is causally impossible for them to harm us. Similarly the set-up of the Cosmomorphic Utopians makes it causally impossible for them to harm each other. The fact that it is distance in the one case and inner structure in the other makes no odds.

Now admittedly in such a conversation we are not brought face to face with the Death by a Thousand Qualifications in the form described by Flew in regard to such statements as "God loves His children." For there the criticism of the theologian is that when counterevidence is presented he takes refuge in increasingly recondite senses of "love." But in the present case one who claims that the inhabitants of Cosmomorphic Utopia A are wholly good is not precisely resisting counterevidence (that is, he is not resisting evidence that these creatures are not good and so possibly bad). Rather he is failing to give the usual reasons for calling them bad. And the positive moves are up to him. It is not sufficient airily and vaguely to say that in such an alternative universe men can be said to be wholly good. Similarly the traveller from Jupiter who tells us that unicorns are to be found there, though queer unicorns for they possess neither horns nor feet, leaves us at a justifiable loss.

Hence it is so far obscure as to what is meant by the possibility that men might have been created wholly good. For the usual criteria, at least in Cosmomorphic Utopia A, do not seem to apply. And so, even if the Compatibility Thesis is correct, it does not appear so far evident that men might have been created wholly good. For an unintelligible assertion cannot either be said to follow or not to follow from some other. And in any case, are the Utopians described above properly to be called *men?* Perhaps we ought to invent a new name: let us dub them "sapients." The question for the theist now becomes: "Why did God create men rather than sapients?" I shall return to this question later.

2. *Cosmomorphic Utopia B*—Circumstances here combine always to make men good. Adolf Hitler would never in fact be foul. He might have incipient impulses of hatred towards Jews, but these would luckily never overwhelm him, because circumstances would prevent this: he would fall in love with a Jewess, he would never get into anti-Semitic company, he would not meet with miseries in his youth, and so forth. Whenever on the point of falling for some temptation, his attention would be distracted. The whole thing would be a very, very long story. And everyone, not just the Führer, would be consistently lucky with regard to virtue and vice.

The trouble about this Utopia is that it is more like a dream than a fantasy. A corresponding meteorological dream would be: since circumstances occasionally combine to make the sun shine, let us suppose that the sky would never be overcast. This does not seem self-contradictory, to say "The sky might never be overcast." But what would a cosmomorphic universe have to be like for this to happen? Clearly it is not just luck that makes the sun shine sometimes: it is because the weather operates in a certain way. For the weather so to operate that it was never cloudy meteorological laws would have to be rewritten (and physics and biology too)—unless you are thinking of a place like the moon. Similarly, in a cosmomorphic utopia where circumstances forever combined in favor of virtue, the set-up would, according to the determinist, have to be different. Thus Cosmomorphic Utopia B is either a version of A (or of some other) or it is a mere dream masquerading as an alternative universe.

3. *Cosmomorphic Utopia C*—Suppose men were always virtuous, not because of the set-up (which would be as now) but because of frequent miraculous intervention.

It is hard to make sense of the supposition. But observationally in such a world we might discover situations like this. Causal factors C usually give rise to actions of a certain empirical type, type-A. But in some circumstances type-

A actions are wrong, and in these cases C will not have type-A effects. But it will not be that some other empirical factor will be present in such exceptions, for *ex hypothesi* the nonoccurrence of the type-A action is due to miraculous intervention. Hence either we have to count rightness and wrongness as empirical differences in order to formulate a causal law here or we must confess that no strict causal laws of human behavior could be formulated in this cosmos. The former alternative is baffling and unacceptable, while the latter is incompatible with determinism. Hence Cosmomorphic Utopia C provides no support for the Utopia Thesis.

4. I now turn to the thought of a *Noncosmomorphic Utopia.* As has been insisted, God is not limited to a cosmomorphic alternative. My anthropological fictions are feeble in comparison with the possibilities contained in God's thoughts. He might have produced a cosmos utterly unlike ours.

But as we have no notion what sapients in such a world would be like, it is even unclearer in this case what would be meant by calling them good. We would have to remain completely agnostic about such a world; and all the difficulties there are in knowing what is meant by calling God a person and good would recur with *extra* force when we try to understand what "wholly good men" could mean here. *Extra* force, because whereas God's nature is perhaps revealed to a limited extent in the *actual* cosmos, the nature of an alternative *possible* and *noncosmomorphic* universe can in no way be so revealed. Hence it follows that it is totally unclear what the possibility that God might have created a noncosmomorphic utopia amounts to.

It is therefore also unclear as to whether it would be superior to this universe. Moreover, it is most doubtful as to whether the sapients of Cosmomorphic Utopia A are superior to ourselves. I am not sure, of course, how one judges such matters; but if we rely on native wit, in default of some new method of evaluating alternative universes, it seems

by no means clear that such a utopia is a better place than ours here.

III

It may be complained that I have been unfair. My anthropological fiction has been crude and possibly biased. And the thing has not been worked out with any scientific expertize. But no one, so far as I know, with the requisite physiological, psychological and biological knowledge has attempted to work out such a fictional alternative anthropology, doubtless there are enough problems in the real-life biological sciences without our going off into subtle fantasies. But until someone were to do so, it remains obscure as to what a determinist cosmomorphic utopia would amount to.

Again it may be objected that writers have occasionally dreamed of utopias and described them. Surely these descriptions are not empty or self-contradictory? But first, fictions are no good guide unless systematically elaborated. For example, and notoriously, there are situations in science fiction which are revealed on reflection to be unintelligible or self-contradictory (e.g., in regard to "going back in time"). Again, fiction writers may not have any clearly formulated views about determinism. And it might turn out that what is allowable on a hard free will theory is not so on a determinist view. For example, an indeterminist may simply say that it might have been the case that men were always wholly good. But the determinist can only make sense of this possibility on the assumption that wholly good men would have a causal difference from men as they are. In order to imagine a man's always overcoming his harmful inclinations, he must surely imagine some change in the way his personality is built. But we have no assurance that some *unspecified* causal change would leave men more or less human and yet produce the consequence of complete goodness. Hence the change has to be specified. I have tried out a plausible fiction or two here, to show that so far one can assign no clear content to the possibility of men's being built wholly good. But maybe some determinist will dream up a plausible fantasy to establish his point. But let him do so: for so far the Utopia Thesis is wrapped in cloud.

Again it might be argued, from the side of theism, that this discussion works against angels just as much as it works against the possibility of wholly good men. If we cannot make sense of noncosmomorphic worlds we cannot make sense of angelic worlds. Maybe so: though angels, qua messengers of God, could share in the intelligibility of God. But that takes us too far afield.

Conclusion — My anthropological fiction seems to bring out the point that moral discourse is embedded in the cosmic status quo (or even more narrowly, in the planetary status quo). For it is applied to a situation where men are beings of a certain sort. Thus the abstract possibility that men might have been created wholly good loses its clarity as soon as we begin to imagine alternative possible universes. If then the Utopia Thesis is quite unclear, it cannot assert anything intelligible about God. And so it cannot serve as part of an antitheistic argument. There remains of course many serious difficulties for the theist in regard to human evil. But the Utopia Thesis is not one of them.

Or not yet. We shall see how the science fiction goes.

Is
Man
Immortal?

Is
Personal Survival
Possible and Provable?

*I*n the dialogue "Phaedo," Plato offers an argument by analogy for the claim that man's soul (the principle of life in man and the source of his rational and moral capacities) is immortal. Strato, of the Peripatetic School, replies to this argument. What is the argument Plato offers, and what difficulty does Strato find with it?

Cebes, a character in the "Phaedo," is concerned that at death man's soul disperses (as dust is dispersed by the wind). In other words, he fears that man's capacity for thought, choice, inference, and the like vanishes when he dies. Socrates offers an argument intended to show that this does not occur.

Only certain *sorts* of things can disperse, or "come apart." It is "most probable that the incomposite things are those that are always constant and unchanging, while the composite ones are those that are different at different times and never constant." *If*, then, the soul is simple (incomposite, not composed of parts), then it is most probable that it does not change. But *is* the soul simple?

Socrates endeavors to answer this question by comparing the soul with "the equal itself, the beautiful itself, the being itself whatever it may be."

The reference here is to the Forms. These are unchanging, eternal entities that provide the reference for general terms and in virtue of which everyday objects possess the qualities that they have. There is, for example, the Form of the Good (the highest of the Forms). The word 'good' denotes this Form, and if Jones, Smith, and Brown are all good men, then each has the quality of being good. This quality they possess in virtue of "participating in" the Form of the Good. Exactly how "participating in" is to be explained is one of the perennial problems of Platonic interpretation, but whatever is good is so because it stands in this relation to the Form of the Good. Every Form, then, is non-physical, "real . . ., uniform and independent": Forms "remain unchanging and constant, never admitting any sort of change whatever." Suppose, for the sake of argument, that Plato has proved that there are Forms. Will this help to prove that the soul is immortal?

Consider, in contrast to Forms, everyday objects—chairs, tables, human bodies, and the like. These are composite, visible, changing, divisible. The soul is not visible, and, not being spatial, it can have no physical parts.

Further, the soul is what *knows*, and the Forms are the objects of knowledge. All genuine knowledge is certain, and we can know with certainty only that which is unchanging. There must be some resemblance between what is known and the knower.

The soul therefore is like the Forms, which do not change, in that it is invisible and has no physical parts. It is unlike objects, which do change and come into and go out of existence, because they are visible and composed of physical parts. Also the soul knows the Forms and so must be like them. This—plus the *value* of knowledge and of that which can know (compare the reference to the soul "ruling" and so being "divine")—give probability to the claim that the soul (conceived as distinguishable from the body) is unchanging and simple; and so the dispersal of the body does not entail the dispersal of the soul. While the force of the argument no doubt increases when it is put into the context of more of Plato's philosophy, the above account seems fair to Socrates' claims.

Now what objection did Strato have? To find out, let us fill out the Socratic argument a bit by noting some other premises to which he appeals. Being alive is essential to being a soul; as Strato puts it, "soul, so long as it exists, cannot be dead." Socrates had appealed to this premise (compare 103B):

(1) If having a property *P* is essential to *X* (that is, if being an *X* entails having *P*—as, for example, "being a mammal" entails "having vertebrae")—then *X* can never become not-*P*.

As an instantiation of (1), he offered:

(2) Being alive is essential to being a soul (or having a soul), so a soul can never lose life (become not-alive).

Socrates then inferred:

(3) The soul is immortal.

Strato questions this inference. He notes that another instantiation of (1) is:

(4) Being hot is essential to being a fire.

But this does not entail

(5) A fire cannot burn out.

We need to supplement (2) and (4) by adding "so long as it exists." But then neither (3) nor (5) can be inferred from their respective premises.

This issue is related to the portion of Socrates' argument contained in the selection that follows. We saw above that Socrates argued, by analogy, that we have better reason to accept than to deny:

(6) The soul is simple.

And we could perhaps add:

(7) Being simple is essential to being a soul.

Thus we could claim:

(8) The soul will always be simple.

But, as in previous cases, all we are entitled to claim is that so long as a soul exists, it is simple. This of course does not show that any soul always will exist.

Strato challenges Socrates' argument in yet another way. Why must something simple be therefore eternal? It cannot, of course, undergo a change in its parts—it has none. But it can simply cease to exist. In a passage that points out several of Socrates' theses, Strato puts the point forcefully:

May it not be that, even if we escape all the rest [of the objections], we cannot rebut the objection that soul is limited and has (only) a limited power? Let us grant that it brings us life, that it can exist as a separate substance, that it cannot admit the death that is opposite to the life which it brings up: nevertheless it will wear itself out one day, will be extinguished and perish of its own accord, without any attack from outside.

Cebes raises the same issue (at 87C) when he wonders if the soul may not be related to the body like a weaver to his coats—he outlasts many but is himself outlasted by his final coat. To put the problem in another way, the soul perhaps continues the same throughout many replacements of all of the cells of its body, and in that sense has many bodies. But when the last "body" ceases to function, the soul ceases to exist.

A crucial portion of Socrates' reply to Cebes depends not only on the likeness of the soul to the Forms but also on further applications of (1) (see

103A–105B); and the new applications seem, given Strato's objection, to be no sounder than the others we have considered.

H. H. Price approaches the question of imortality in a very different manner than Plato did. Offering no proof of immortality in his essay, he asks instead what is *meant* by "surviving one's death". He analyzes this notion by dealing with objections raised by those who suspect that the phrase in question has no meaning at all. A useful way of introducing Price's contentions is to list the most important objections and note his responses.

The first objection is that a disembodied mind will have no sense organs, so no sense experience, and so perhaps no experience at all. Price does not challenge the assumption that surviving one's death and being disembodied are necessarily connected. They are not, and in this regard John Hick's essay included under "Is religious language meaningful?" is a useful supplement to Price's essay. Nor does Price challenge the further claim, also implicit in the objection, that a logically necessary condition of having sense experience is having sense organs, although this claim is not self-evident. Instead he develops a conception of postmortem experience as *imaging*, or having visual, tactile, or auditory images. ("Images" here means, roughly, "experiences private to those who have them.") These images are mind-dependent; they have no existence independent of human experience. But they obey causal laws (more like the laws of Freud's psychology than those of physics, perhaps) and so allow prediction and retrodiction. Further, memory is a feature of the envisioned postmortem experience. An individual with such experiences would not, of course, be "alive" in any biochemical sense but would be quite alive in the psychological sense of "having experiences." Such images could even contain feelings of warmth, cold, dizziness, and the like, visual experiences similar to those one has of the surface of his own nose and cheeks, and a wide range of other quasi-sensory experiences.

Against this backdrop Price responds to other possible objections. If "persons are what you meet," how could any such center of experience be *met* and so be a person? Although it is not clear that this is a correct account of what persons are, one could meet others in the context Price describes if those who have image-experiences also have telepathic powers (that is, can produce images for others as well as for themselves), perhaps including the power to produce images in others that resemble a human body (similar, perhaps, to one's own body—the one he previously possessed). So persons can, in one sense, "meet" each other in the afterlife Price envisions or meet a person "there" whom one had known "here."

Reference to "here" and "there" raises another question. *Where* is the next world conceived as being? Price contends that the question is, strictly speaking, nonsense. I dream that I see, say, a tiger in a cage. The cage and the tiger are spatially related to one another. But neither is any number of feet from the head of my bed or any other material object. Price depends here on there being a distinction between perceptual space and physical space and (implicitly) claims that the former can exist without the latter.

Price continues by explaining in what senses his "next world" can, and cannot, be said to be (a) delusory, (b) unreal, and (c) subjective, contending that there are perfectly clear and respectable senses in which it is real and objective. He concludes by considering how the notion of a "next world," elaborated along the lines indicated, can be connected with the desires and character that men have in this life and how the concept of punishment could be applied to such a world.

Price is certainly correct in suggesting that the question as to how continued existence after death is to be conceived is logically prior to (its answer is presupposed by) the question as to whether there is any reason to suppose that such continued existence occurs. If his analysis of this notion is coherent, then survival is a meaningful or intelligible hypothesis. This is not unimportant; as Price notes, one cannot have evidence for an unintelligible thesis. There are other conceptions of continued existence after death than the one Price discusses. But his analysis is certainly interesting and seems to provide one sense in which a man could be said to have postmortem existence.

An Argument for Human Immortality
PLATO

Socrates now takes up the point raised by Cebes, that the soul may be dispersed at death. He urges that dispersal can only be suffered by composite objects, whereas the soul is not composite but of a single nature, like 'the beautiful itself', 'the equal itself' and Forms in general. Souls are akin to Forms, for both belong to the unseen order, whose attributes are changelessness and indestructibility, whereas body belongs to the visible order, whose attributes are the opposite of these. We may therefore believe that soul is 'altogether indestructible or nearly so'.

S*ocrates then* resumed: 'Now the sort of question that we ought to put to ourselves is this: what kind of thing is in fact liable to undergo this dispersal that you speak of? For what kind of thing should we fear that it may be dispersed, and for what kind should we not? And next we should consider to which kind the soul belongs, and so find

some ground for confidence or for apprehension about our own souls. Am I right?'

'Yes, you are.'

'Well now, isn't anything that has been compounded or has a composite nature liable to be split up into its component parts? Isn't it incomposite things alone that can possibly be exempt from that?'

'I agree that that is so', replied Cebes.

'And isn't it most probable that the incomposite things are those that are always constant and unchanging, while the composite ones are those that are different at different times and never constant?'

'I agree.'

'Then let us revert to those objects which we spoke of earlier. What of that very reality of whose existence we give an account when we question and answer each other?[1] Is that always un-

[1] I.e. in philosophical discussions; cf. 75 D 2.

FROM: *Plato's Phaedo*, R. Hackforth, trans. (New York: The Cambridge University Press, pp. 79–87), 78B–80C. Reprinted by permission of the Cambridge University Press.

changing and constant, or is it different at different times? Can the equal itself, the beautiful itself, the being itself whatever it may be, ever admit any sort of change? Or does each of these real beings, uniform[2] and independent, remain unchanging and constant, never admitting any sort of alteration whatever?'

'They must be unchanging and constant', Cebes replied.

'But what about the many beautiful things, beautiful human beings, say, or horses or garments or anything else you like? What about the many equal things? What about all the things that are called by the same name as those real beings? Are *they* constant, or in contrast to those is it too much to say that they are never identical with themselves nor identically related to one another?'[3]

'You are right about them too,' said Cebes, 'they are never constant.'

'Then again, you can touch them and see them or otherwise perceive them with your senses, whereas those unchanging objects cannot be apprehended save by the mind's reasoning. Things of that sort are invisible, are they not?'[4]

'That is perfectly true.'

'Then shall we say there are two kinds[5] of thing, the visible and the invisible?'

'Very well.'

'The invisible being always constant, the visible never?'

'We may agree to that too.'

'To proceed: we ourselves are partly body, partly soul, are we not?'

'Just so.'

'Well, which kind of thing shall we say the body tends to resemble and be akin to?'

'The visible kind; anyone can see that.'

'And the soul? Is that visible or invisible?'

'Not visible to the human eye, at all events, Socrates.'

'Oh well, we were speaking of what is or is not visible to mankind: or are you thinking of some other sort of being?'

'No: of a human being.'

'Then what is our decision about the soul, that it can be seen, or cannot?'

'That it cannot.'

'In fact it is invisible?'

'Yes.'

'Hence soul rather than body is like the invisible, while body rather than soul is like the visible.'

'Unquestionably, Socrates.'

'Now were we not saying some time ago that when the soul makes use of the body to investigate something through vision or hearing or some other sense—of course investigating by means of the body is the same as investigating by sense—it is dragged by the body towards objects that are never constant, and itself wanders in a sort of dizzy drunken confusion, inasmuch as it is apprehending confused objects?'

'Just so.'

'But when it investigates by itself alone, it passes to that other world of pure, everlasting, immortal, constant

[2] The term μονοειδές recurs at 80B in close conjunction with ἀδ ἄλυτον, and it is used of the Form of beauty at *Symp.* 211B. It has the same force as πᾶν ὅμοιον which Parmenides asserts of his ἓν ὄν, viz. the denial of internal difference or distinction of unlike parts.

[3] Of two things called beautiful one may be to-day more beautiful, to-morrow less so, than the other; of two things called equal one may come to be greater, or smaller, than the other. But it seems possible that οὔτε ἀλλήλοις may be added simply because equality involves two terms. I do not see how ἀλλήλοις can, as Burnet supposes, refer to things appearing beautiful or ugly, equal or unequal *to different people*, as they were said to do at 74B8.

[4] The pleonasm ἀιδῆ καὶ οὐχ ὁρατά, though of a sort common enough in Greek, would be intolerable in English.

[5] As Prof. Grube has pointed out, the words εἶδος and ιδέα are not used in a technical sense until 103E, and thereafter become common. It is possible that this is due, or partly due, to the need to use εἶδος in its ordinary sense of 'class' or 'kind' here.

being, and by reason of its kinship thereto abides ever therewith, whensoever it has come to be by itself and is suffered to do so; and then it has rest from wandering and ever keeps close to that being, unchanged and constant, inasmuch as it is apprehending unchanging objects. And is not the experience which it then has called intelligence?'

'All you have said, Socrates, is true and admirably put.'

'Once again, then, on the strength of our previous arguments as well as of this last, which of the two kinds of thing do you find that soul resembles and is more akin to?'

'On the strength of our present line of inquiry, Socrates, I should think that the veriest dullard would agree that the soul has a far and away greater resemblance to everlasting, unchanging being than to its opposite.'

'And what does the body resemble?'

'The other kind.'

'Now consider a further point. When soul and body are conjoined, Nature prescribes that the latter should be slave and subject, the former master and ruler. Which of the two, in your judgement, does that suggest as being like the divine, and which like the mortal? Don't you think it naturally belongs to the divine to rule and lead,

and to the mortal to be ruled and subjected?'

'Yes, I do.'

'Then which is soul like?'

'Of course it is obvious, Socrates, that soul is like the divine, and body like the mortal.'

'Would you say then, Cebes, that the result of our whole discussion amounts to this: on the one hand we have that which is divine, immortal, indestructible, of a single form, accessible to thought, ever constant and abiding true to itself; and the soul is very like it: on the other hand we have that which is human, mortal, destructible, of many forms, inaccessible to thought,[6] never constant nor abiding true to itself; and the body is very like that. Is there anything to be said against that, dear Cebes?'

'Nothing.'

'Well then, that being so, isn't it right and proper for the body to be quickly destroyed, but for the soul to be altogether indestructible, or nearly so?'

'Certainly.'

[6] The word ἀνόητος usually means 'foolish', but for using it to mean 'not the object of thought' Plato has the precedent of Parmenides 8, 17 DK. Burnet speaks of a 'play on words', but it is hardly that.

A Critique of Plato
STRATO

*O*lympiodorus, the sixth-century Neoplatonist, has preserved in his commentary on the *Phaedo* some criticism made by Strato, known as ὁ φυσικός, the third head of the Peripatetic school, who succeeded Theophrastu sabout 287 B.C. These may most conveniently be found in Fritz Wehrli, *Die Schule des Aristoteles*, Heft V, *Strato von Lampsakos*

(1950). I have attempted a translation, following Wehrli's numbering of the fragments, and giving the pages of Norvin's edition of Olympiodorus. The meaning is usually clear enough; but two, viz. 123 (i) and (l), are unintelligible to me. I leave readers to decide for themselves on their cogency, but it may be remarked that W. Capelle, who gives a

FROM: *Plato's Phaedo*, R. Hackforth, trans. (New York: The Cambridge University Press, pp. 195–198). Reprinted by permission of Cambridge University Press.

good account of their general purport in Pauly-Wissowa, *RE* iv, i (1931), s.v. Strato 13, speaks of them as 'bündig'. (R. Hackforth)

OBJECTIONS TO

γένεσις ἐξ ἐναντίων O R ἀνταπόδοσις

(OBJECTIONS TO
COMING-TO-BE
FROM OPPOSITES OR
RECIPROCAL CHANGE
[OF OPPOSITES])
122 (D63, p. 221 N.):

(*a*) What has perished arises from what existed; yet inasmuch as the reverse is not true, what reason is there to believe in the cogency of an argument of this type?

(*b*) If a dead part of a body, e.g. a finger or a gouged-out eye, does not come back to life, then neither, plainly, can the whole [creature].

(*c*) It may be suggested that the identity between things arise out of one another is not numerical, but only specific.

(*d*) Flesh may come from food, but food does not come from flesh; rust may come from bronze, and charcoal from wood, but not *vice versa*.

(*e*) The old come from the young; but the reverse does not happen.

(*f*) Opposites may come from opposites if a substratum persists, but not if it is destroyed.

(*g*) It may be suggested that the continuance of coming-to-be is no more than the constant renewal of a species or type, as we find even in man-made objects.

OBJECTIONS TO THE
PRINCIPLE OF EXCLUSION
OF OPPOSITES
123 (C11 178–90, p. 183 N.):

(*a*) On this showing, is not every living creature deathless? For it cannot 'admit' death: that is to say, there could never be a dead living creature, any more than a dead soul.

(*b*) On this showing, are not even the souls of irrational creatures deathless, inasmuch as they 'bring up' life and cannot 'admit' the opposite of that which they bring up?

(*c*) And presumably, on this showing, the souls of plants too, for they too make their bodies into living bodies.

(*d*) Is not everything that comes-to-be imperishable? For they are all, equally with souls, incapable of admitting their opposites: a thing that comes-to-be could never be a thing that has perished.

(*e*) Would not this apply to every natural object? Any such object exhibits a development according to its nature, and therefore cannot admit of development contrary thereto; and *qua* incapable of admitting that, it can never perish.

(*f*) On this showing it will be equally true that a composite object will never be broken up: for it cannot admit its opposite: that is to say, while remaining a composite it can never be a broken-up object.

(*g*) If we grant that a negation can have more senses than one, the soul may be 'undying' (ἀθάνατος) not in the sense that it is, or possesses, inextinguishable life, but in the sense that it can only admit one of a pair of opposites, and must either exist together with that opposite or not exist at all.

(*h*) Is it not too readily assumed that, if the soul is incapable of admitting death, and in that sense deathless, it is therefore indestructible? A stone is deathless in the sense of this argument, but a stone is not indestructible.

(*i*) What is the ground for saying that the soul 'brings up' life as a concomitant, with the purpose of arguing that it cannot admit the opposite of what is brought up? In some cases the soul is brought up [itself].

(*k*) May it not be that a thing is alive, yet the life it has is imported from without, so that it can one day lose it?

(*l*) May it not be that the soul, while not admitting the death that is the opposite of that life which soul brings up, nevertheless does admit another death, that namely which is opposite to the life which brings up soul?

(*m*) May it not be that just as fire, so long as it exists, cannot be cold, so soul, so long as it exists, cannot be dead? For it brings up life so long [only] as it exists.

(*n*) May it not be that, even if we escape all the rest, we cannot rebut the objection that soul is limited and has [only] a limited power? Let us grant that it brings up life, that it can exist as a separate substance, that it cannot admit the death that is opposite to the life which it brings up: nevertheless it will wear itself out one day, will be extinguished and perish of its own accord, without any attack from outside.

124 (D 78, p. 226 N):

But on this showing even life in a substrate cannot admit its opposite; for it cannot admit death and yet continue to exist, any more than cold can admit heat and yet continue to exist. Hence life in a substrate is incapable of being dead in the same sense as cold is incapable of being hot; nevertheless life does come to an end.

Secondly, the perishing of a thing is not the reception by it of death; if it were, a living creature would never perish; the fact is that a creature does not persist, having admitted death; rather it is dead because it has lost life; for death is loss of life.

[*The second part of this may be condensed as follows: to be dead is not to possess a positive attribute which the soul cannot in fact possess: it is the body's having lost an attribute, viz. life, which it previously possessed.*] (R. Hackforth)

(*Note by Olympiodorus.*) To this argument of Strato's Proclus adds that the extinction of a soul is its dying, and dying, in Strato's own words, is the losing by the substrate [or body] of life.

OBJECTIONS TO THE
THEORY OF RECOLLECTION
125 (D25, p. 211 N.). Why can one not 'recollect' without demonstration?

126 (II41, p. 158 N.). If there is such a thing as 'recollection', how is it

that we do not attain scientific knowledge without demonstration? Or how is it that no one has ever become a wind-player or string-player without practice?

127 (D65, p. 223 N.). The mind's possession of scientific knowledge is either (*a*) antecedent to time, in which case it has no need of time and is unaffected by time, so that men are eternally possessed of it; or (*b*) subsequent to time, in which case either the mind possesses it without 'recollection', learning [what it learns in this life] for the first time, or else what it recollects is knowledge immanent in it before its incarnation; [I say knowledge] for its maker presumably makes it a perfect, and therefore a *knowing* mind; yet on entering into this world minds need to learn, that is to 'recollect'.

[*This seems tantamount to complaining that Plato's assumption of a loss of knowledge at birth is arbitrary.*] R. Hackforth

(*Note by Olympiodorus.*) Furthermore Strato in his division eliminates 'everlasting time'; the thing which [supposedly] has everlasting existence in time is, he argues, something that falls between that which exists before time was and that which exists at some point in time.

[*The argument seems to be that all existence must be either timeless (outside time) and external or temporal (in time) and impermanent.*] R. Hackforth

And why, he asks, cannot we *readily* employ 'recollection'? Or is it the fact that some of us can, but most need training for it?

OBJECTION TO THE
REFUTATION OF THE [SOUL AS A
HARMONY] ψυχὴ ἁρμονία THEORY
118 (II 134, p. 174 N.). As one attunement is sharper (ὀξυτέρα) or flatter than another, so one soul is sharper or more sluggish than another.

Survival and the Idea of "Another World"
H. H. PRICE

As you all know, this year is the seventieth anniversary of the foundation of the Society for Psychical Research. From the very beginning, the problem of survival has been one of the main interests of the Society; and that is my excuse, if any excuse is needed, for discussing some aspects of the problem this evening. I shall not, however, talk about the evidence for survival. In this lecture I am concerned only with the conception of survival; with the *meaning* of the Survival Hypothesis, and not with its truth or falsity. When we consider the Survival Hypothesis, whether we believe it or disbelieve it, what is it that we have in mind? Can we form any idea, even a rough and provisional one, of what a disembodied human life might be like? Supposing we cannot, it will follow that what is called the Survival Hypothesis is a mere set of words and not a hypothesis at all. The evidence adduced in favour of it might still be evidence for something, and perhaps for something important, but we should no longer have the right to claim that it is evidence for survival. There cannot be evidence for something which is completely unintelligible to us.

Now let us consider the situation in which we find ourselves after seventy years of psychical research. A very great deal of work has been done on the problem of survival, and much of the best work by members of our Society. Yet there are the widest differences of opinion about the results. A number of intelligent persons would maintain that we now have a very large mass of evidence in favour of survival; that some of it is of very good quality indeed, and cannot be explained away unless we suppose that the supernormal cognitive powers of some embodied human minds are vastly more extensive and more accurate than we can easily believe them to be; in short, that on the evidence available the Survival Hypothesis is more probable than not. Some people—and not all of them are silly or credulous—would even maintain that the Survival Hypothesis is proved, or as near to being so as my empirical hypothesis can be. On the other hand, there are also many intelligent persons who entirely reject these conclusions. Some of them, no doubt, have not taken the trouble to examine the evidence. But others of them have; they may even have given years of study to it. They would agree that the evidence is evidence of *something*, and very likely of something important. But, they would say, it cannot be evidence of survival; there *must* be some alternative explanation of it, however difficult it may be to find out. Why do they take this line? I think it is because they find the very conception of survival unintelligible. The very idea of a "discarnate human personality" seems to them a muddled or absurd one; indeed not an idea at all, but just a phrase—an emotionally exciting one, no doubt—to which no clear meaning can be given.

Moreover, we cannot just ignore the people who have not examined the evidence. Some of our most intelligent and most highly educated contemporaries are among them. These men are well aware, by this time, that the evidence does exist, even if their predecessors fifty years ago were not. If you asked them why they do not trouble to examine it in detail, they would be able to offer reasons for their attitude. And one of their reasons, and not the least weighty in their eyes, is the contention

FROM: "Survival and the Idea of 'Another World,'" *Proceedings of the Society for Psychical Research*, Vol. L, Part 182 (January 1953), 1–25. Reprinted by permission of editor and author.

I mentioned just now, that the very idea of survival is a muddled or absurd one. To borrow an example from Whately Carington, we know pretty well what we mean by asking whether Jones has survived a shipwreck. We are asking whether he continues to live after the shipwreck has occurred. Similarly it makes sense to ask whether he survived a railway accident, or the bombing of London. But if we substitute "his own death" for "a shipwreck," and ask whether he has survived it, our question (it will be urged) becomes unintelligible. Indeed, it *looks* self-contradictory, as if we were asking whether Jones is still alive at a time when he is no longer alive—whether Jones is both alive and not alive at the same time. We may try to escape from this logical absurdity by using phrases like "discarnate existence," "alive, but disembodied." But such phrases, it will be said, have no clear meaning. No amount of facts, however well established, can have the slightest tendency to support a meaningless hypothesis, or to answer an unintelligible question. It would therefore be a waste of time to examine such facts in detail. There are other and more important things to do.

If I am right so far, questions about the meaning of the word "survival" or of the phrase "life after death" are not quite so arid and academic as they may appear. Anyone who wants to maintain that there is empirical evidence for survival ought to consider these questions, whether he thinks the evidence strong or weak. Indeed, anyone who thinks there is a *problem* of survival at all should ask himself what his conception of survival is.

Now why should it be thought that the very idea of life after death is unintelligible? Surely it is easy enough to conceive (whether or not it is true) that experiences might occur after Jones's death which are linked with experiences which he had before his death, in such a way that his personal identity is preserved? But, it will be said, the idea of after-death *experiences* is just the difficulty. What kind of experiences could

they conceivably be? In a disembodied state, the supply of sensory stimuli is perforce cut off, because the supposed experient has no sense organs and no nervous system. There can therefore be no sense-perception. One has no means of being aware of material objects any longer; and if one has not, it is hard to see how one could have any emotions or wishes either. For all the emotions and wishes we have in this present life are concerned directly or indirectly with material objects, including of course our own organisms and other organisms, especially other human ones. In short, one could only be said to have experiences at all, if one is aware of some sort of a *world*. In this way, the idea of survival is bound up with the idea of "another world" or a "next world." Anyone who maintains that the idea of survival is after all intelligible must also be claiming that we can form some conception, however rough and provisional, of what "the next world" or "other world" might be like. The skeptics I have in mind would say that we can form no such conception at all; and this, I think, is one of the main reasons why they hold that the conception of survival itself is unintelligible. I wish to suggest, on the contrary, that we *can* form some conception, in outline at any rate, of what a "next world" or "another world" might be like, and consequently of the kind of experiences which disembodied minds, if indeed there are such, might be supposed to have.

The thoughts which I wish to put before you on this subject are not at all original. Something very like them is to be found in the chapter on survival in Whately Carington's book *Telepathy*,[1] and in the concluding chapter of Professor C. J. Ducasse's book *Nature, Mind and Death*.[2] Moreover, if I am not mistaken, the Hindu conception of *Kama*

[1] Whately Carington, *Telepathy* (London: Methuen & Co., Ltd., 1945).

[2] C. J. Ducasse, *Nature, Mind and Death* (La Salle, Ill.: Open Court Publishing Co. 1951).

Loka (literally, "the world of desire") is essentially the same as the one I wish to discuss; and something very similar is to be found in Mahayana Buddhism. In these two religions, of course, there is not just one "other world" but several different "other worlds," which we are supposed to experience in succession; not merely the next world, but the next but one, and another after that. But I think it will be quite enough for us to consider just the next world, without troubling ourselves about any additional other worlds which there might be. It is a sufficiently difficult task, for us Western people, to convince ourselves that it makes sense to speak of any sort of after-death world at all. Accordingly, with your permission, I shall use the expressions "next world" and "other world" interchangeably. If anyone thinks this is an oversimplification, it will be easy for him to make the necessary corrections.

The next world, I think, might be conceived as a kind of dream-world. When we are asleep, sensory stimuli are cut off, or at any rate are prevented from having their normal effects upon our brain-centres. But we still manage to have experiences. It is true that sense-perception no longer occurs, but something sufficiently like it does. In sleep, our image-producing powers, which are more or less inhibited in waking life by a continuous bombardment of sensory stimuli, are released from this inhibition. And then we are provided with a multitude of objects of awareness, about which we employ our thoughts and towards which we have desires and emotions. These objects which we are aware of behave in a way which seems very queer to us when we wake up. The laws of their behaviour are not the laws of physics. But however queer their behaviour is, it does not at all disconcert us at the time and our personal identity is not broken.

In other words, my suggestion is that the next world, if there is one, might be a world of mental images. Nor need such a world be so "thin and insubstantial" as you might think. Paradoxical as it may sound, there is nothing imaginary about a mental image. It is an actual entity, as real as anything can be. The seeming paradox arises from the ambiguity of the verb "to imagine." It does sometimes mean "to have mental images." But more usually it means "to entertain propositions without believing them"; and very often they are false propositions, and moreover we *dis*believe them in the act of entertaining them. This is what happens, for example, when we read Shakespeare's play *The Tempest*, and that is why we say that Prospero and Ariel are "imaginary characters." Mental images are not in this sense imaginary at all. We do actually experience them, and they are no more imaginary than sensations. To avoid the paradox, though at the cost of some pedantry, it would be well to distinguish between *imagining* and *imaging*, and to have two different adjectives "imaginary" and "imagy." In this terminology, it is imaging, and not imagining, that I wish to talk about; and the next world, as I am trying to conceive of it, is an *imagy* world, but not on that account an imaginary one.

Indeed, to those who experienced it an image-world would be just as "real" as this present world is; perhaps so like it, that they would have considerable difficulty in realizing that they were dead. We are, of course, sometimes told in mediumistic communications that quite a lot of people do find it difficult to realize that they are dead; and this is just what we should expect if the next world is an image-world. Lord Russell and other philosophers have maintained that a material object in this present physical world is nothing more nor less than a complicated system of *appearances*. So far as I can see, there might be a set of visual images related to each other perspectivally, with front views and side views and back views all fitting neatly together in the way that ordinary visual appearances do now. Such a group of images might contain tactual images too. Similarly it might contain auditory images and smell images. Such a family of interrelated images would make a pretty good object. It would be quite a satisfactory substitute for the material objects which we perceive in this present life. And a whole world composed of such families of mental images would make a perfectly good world.

It is possible, however, and indeed likely, that some of those images would be what Francis Galton called *generic* images. An image representing a dog or a tree need not necessarily be an exact replica of some individual dog or tree one has perceived. It might rather be a representation of a *typical* dog or tree. Our memories are more specific on some subjects than on others. How specific they are depends probably on the degree of interest we had in the individual objects or events at the time when we perceived them. An event which moved us deeply is likely to be remembered specifically and in detail; and so is an individual object to which we were much attached (for example, the home of our childhood). But with other objects which interested us less and were less attended to, we retain only a "general impression" of a whole class of objects collectively. Left to our own resources, as we should be in the other world, with nothing but our memories to depend on, we should probably be able to form only generic images of such objects. In this respect, an image-world would not be an exact replica of this one, not even of those parts of this one which we have actually perceived. To some extent it would be, so to speak, a generalized picture, rather than a detailed reproduction.

Let us now put our question in another way, and ask what kind of experience a disembodied human mind might be supposed to have. We can then answer that it might be an experience in which *imaging* replaces sense-perception; "replaces" it, in the sense that imaging would perform much the same function as sense-perception performs now, by providing us with objects about which we could have thoughts, emotions and wishes. There is no reason why we should not be "as much alive," or at any rate *feel* as much alive, in an image-world as

we do now in this present material world, which we perceive by means of our sense-organs and nervous systems. And so the use of the word "survival" ("life after death") would be perfectly justifiable.

It will be objected, perhaps, that one cannot be said to be alive unless one has a body. But what is meant here by "alive"? It is surely conceivable (whether or not it is true) that *experiences* should occur which are not causally connected with a physical organism. If they did, should we or should we not say that "life" was occurring. I do not think it matters much whether we answer Yes or No. It is purely a question of definition. If you define "life" in terms of certain very complicated physico-chemical processes, as some people would, then of course life after death is by definition impossible, because there is no longer anything to be alive. In that case, the problem of survival (*life after bodily death*) is misnamed. Instead, it ought to be called the problem of after-death *experiences*. And this is in fact the problem with which all investigators of the subject have been concerned. After all, what people want to know, when they ask whether we survive death, is simply whether experiences occur after death, or what likelihood, if any, there is that they do; and whether such experiences, if they do occur, are linked with each other and with *ante mortem* ones in such a way that personal identity is preserved. It is not physico-chemical processes which interest us, when we ask such questions. But there is another sense of the words "life" and "alive" which may be called the psychological sense; and in this sense "being alive" just *means* "having experiences of certain sorts." In this psychological sense of the word "life," it is perfectly intelligible to ask whether there is life after death, even though life in the physiological sense does *ex hypothesi* come to an end when someone dies. Or, if you like, the question is whether one could feel alive after bodily death, even though (by hypothesis) one would not *be* alive at the time. It will be just enough to satisfy most of us if the *feel-*

ing of being alive continues after death. It will not make a halfpennyworth of difference that one will not then *be* alive in the physiological or biochemical sense of the word.

It may be said, however, that "feeling alive" (life in the psychological sense) cannot just be equated with having experiences in general. Feeling alive, surely, consists in having experiences of a special sort, namely *organic sensations*— bodily feelings of various sorts. In our present experience, these bodily feelings are not as a rule separately attended to unless they are unusually intense or unusually painful. They are a kind of undifferentiated mass in the background of consciousness. All the same, it would be said, they constitute our feeling of being alive; and if they were absent (as surely they must be when the body is dead) the feeling of being alive could not be there.

I am not at all sure that this argument is as strong as it looks. I think we should still feel alive—or alive enough —provided we experienced emotions and wishes, even if no organic sensations accompanied these experiences, as they do now. But in case I am wrong here, I would suggest that *images* of organic sensations could perfectly well provide what is needed. We can quite well image to ourselves what it feels like to be in a warm bath, even when we are not actually in one; and a person who has been crippled can image what it felt like to climb a mountain. Moreover, I would ask whether we do not feel alive when we are dreaming. It seems to me that we obviously do—or at any rate quite alive enough to go on with.

This is not all. In an image-world, a dream-like world such as I am trying to describe, there is no reason at all why there should not be *visual* images resembling the body which one had in this present world. In this present life (for all who are not blind) visual percepts of one's own body form as it were the constant centre of one's perceptual world. It is perfectly possible that visual images of one's own body might perform the same function in the next. They might form the continuing centre or nucleus of one's image world, remaining more or less constant while other images altered. If this were so, we should have an additional reason for expecting that recently dead people would find it difficult to realize that they were dead, that is, disembodied. To all appearances they *would* have bodies just as they had before, and pretty much the same ones. But, of course, they might discover in time that these image-bodies were subject to rather peculiar causal laws. For example, it might be found that in an image-world our wishes tend *ipso facto* to fulfil themselves in a way they do not now. A wish to go to Oxford might be immediately followed by the occurrence of a vivid and detailed set of Oxfordlike images; even though, at the moment before, one's images had resembled Piccadilly Circus or the palace of the Dalai Lama in Tibet. In that case, one would realize that "going somewhere"— transferring one's body from one place to another—was a rather different process from what it had been in the physical world. Reflecting on such experiences, one might come to the conclusion that one's body was not after all the same as the physical body one had before death. One might conclude perhaps that it must be a "spiritual" or "psychical" body, closely resembling the old body in appearance, but possessed of rather different causal properties. It has been said, of course, that phrases like "spiritual body" or "psychical body" are utterly unintelligible, and that no conceivable empirical meaning could be given to such expressions. But I would rather suggest that they might be a way (rather a misleading way perhaps) of referring to a set of body-like images. If our supposed dead empiricist continued his investigations, he might discover that his whole world—not only his own body, but everything else he was aware of—had different causal properties from the physical world, even though everything in it had shape, size, colour, and other qualities which material objects have now. And so eventually, by the exercise of ordinary inductive good sense, he could draw the conclusion that he was in "the next world" or "the other world" and no longer in this one. If, however, he were a very dogmatic philosopher, who distrusted inductive good sense and preferred a priori reasoning, I do not know what condition he would be in. Probably he would never discover that he was dead at all. Being persuaded, on a priori grounds, that life after death was impossible, he might insist on thinking that he must still be in this world, and refuse to pay attention to the new and strange causal laws which more empirical thinkers would notice.

I think, then, that there is no difficulty in conceiving that the experience of feeling alive could occur in the absence of a physical organism; or, if you prefer to put it so, a disembodied personality could *be* alive in the psychological sense, even though by definition it would not be alive in the physiological or biochemical sense.

Moreover, I do not see why disembodiment need involve the destruction of personal identity. It is, of course, sometimes supposed that personal identity depends on the continuance of a background of organic sensation—the "mass of bodily feeling" mentioned before. (This may be called the somato-centric analysis of personal identity.) We must notice, however, that this background of organic sensation is not literally the same from one period of time to another. The very most that can happen is that the organic sensations which form the background of my experience now should be *exactly similar* to those which were the background of my experience a minute ago. And as a matter of fact, the present ones need not *all* be exactly similar to the previous ones. I might have a twinge of toothache now which I did not have then. I may even have an overall feeling of lassitude now which I did not have a minute ago, so that the whole mass of bodily feeling, and not merely part of it, is rather different; and this would not interrupt my personal identity at all. The most that is required is only that the majority (not all) of my organic sensations should be closely (not exactly) similar to those I previously

had. And even this is only needed if the two occasions are close together in my private time series; the organic sensations I have now might well be very unlike those I used to have when I was one year old. I say "in my private times series." For when I wake up after eight hours of dreamless sleep my personal identity is not broken, though in the physical or public time series there has been a long interval between the last organic sensations I experienced before falling asleep, and the first ones I experience when I wake up. But if similarity, and not literal sameness, is all that is required of this "continuing organic background," it seems to me that the continuity of it could be perfectly well preserved if there were organic *images* after death very like the organic *sensations* which occurred before death.

As a matter of fact, this whole "somato-centric" analysis of personal identity appears to me highly disputable. I should have thought that Locke was much nearer the truth when he said that personal identity depends on memory. But I have tried to show that even if the "somato-centric" theory of personal identity is right, there is no reason why personal identity need be broken by bodily death, provided there are images after death which sufficiently resemble the organic sensations one had before; and this is very like what happens when one falls asleep and begins dreaming.

There is, however, another argument against the conceivability of a disembodied person, to which some present-day linguistic philosophers would attach great weight. It is neatly expressed by Mr. A. G. N. Flew when he says, "people are what you meet."[3] By a "per-

---

[3] *University*, Vol. II, No. 2, 38, in a symposium on "Death" with Professor D. M. Mackinnon. Mr. Flew obviously uses "people" as the plural of "person"; but if we are to be linguistic, I am inclined to think that the nuances of "people" are not quite the same as those of "person." When we used the word "person," in the singular or the plural, the notion of consciousness is more prominently before our minds than it is when we use the word "people."

son" we are supposed to mean a human organism which behaves in certain ways, and especially one which speaks and can be spoken to. And when we say, "this is the same person whom I saw yesterday," we are supposed to mean just that it is the same human organism which I saw yesterday, and also that it behaves in a recognizably similar way.

"People are what you meet." With all respect to Mr. Flew, I would suggest that he does not in this sense "meet" *himself*. He might indeed have had one of those curious out-of-body experiences which are occasionally mentioned in our records, and he might have seen his body from outside (if he has, I heartily congratulate him); but I do not think we should call this "meeting." And surely the important question is, what constitutes my personal identity *for myself*. It certainly does not consist in the fact that other people can "meet" me. It might be that I was for myself the same person as before, even at a time when it was quite impossible for others to meet me. No one can "meet" me when I am dreaming. They can, of course, come and look at my body lying in bed; but this is not "meeting," because no sort of social relations are possible between them and me. Yet, although temporarily "unmeetable," during my dreams I am still, for myself, the same person that I was. And if I went on dreaming *in perpetuum*, and could never be "met" again, this need not prevent me from continuing to be, for myself, the same person.

As a matter of fact, however, we can quite easily conceive that "meeting" of a kind might still be possible between discarnate experients. And therefore, even if we do make it part of the definition of "a person," that he is capable of being met by others, it will still make sense to speak of "discarnate persons," provided we allow that telepathy is possible between them. It is true that a special sort of telepathy would be needed; the sort which in life produces *telepathic apparitions*. It would not be sufficient that *A*'s thoughts or emotions should be telepathically affected by *B*'s. If such telepathy were sufficiently prolonged and

continuous, and especially if it were reciprocal, it would indeed have some of the characteristics of social intercourse; but I do not think we should call it "meeting," at any rate in Mr. Flew's sense of the word. It would be necessary, in addition, that *A* should be aware of something which could be called "*B*'s body," or should have an experience not too unlike the experience of *seeing* another person in this life. This additional condition would be satisfied if *A* experienced a telepathic apparition of *B*. It would be necessary, further, that the telepathic apparition by means of which *B* "announces himself" (if one may put it so) should be recognizably similar on different occasions. And if it were a case of meeting some person *again* whom one had previously known in this world, the telepathic apparition would have to be recognizably similar to the physical body which that person had when he was still alive.

There is no reason why an image-world should not contain a number of images which are telepathic apparitions; and if it did, one could quite intelligently speak of "meeting other persons" in such a world. All the experiences I have when I meet another person in this present life could still occur, with only this difference, that percepts would be replaced by images. It would also be possible for another person to "meet" me in the same manner, if I, as a telepathic agent could cause him to experience a suitable telepathic apparition, sufficiently resembling the body I used to have when he formerly "met" me in this life.

I now turn to another problem which may have troubled some of you. If there be a next world, *where* is it? Surely it must be somewhere. But there does not seem to be any room for it. We can hardly suppose that it is up in the sky (i.e., outside the earth's atmosphere) or under the surface of the earth, as Homer and Vergil seemed to think. Such suggestions may have contented our ancestors, and the Ptolemaic astronomy may have made them acceptable, for some ages, even to the learned; but they will hardly content us. Surely the next world, if it exists, must be somewhere; and yet, it seems, there is nowhere for it to be.

The answer to this difficulty is easy if we conceive of the next world in the way I have suggested, as a dream-like world of mental images. Mental images, including dream images, are in a space of their own. They do have spatial properties. Visual images, for instance, have extension and shape, and they have spatial relations to one another. But they have no spatial relation to objects in the physical world. If I dream of a tiger, my tiger-image has extension and shape. The dark stripes have spatial relation to the yellow parts, and to each other; the nose has a spatial relation to the tail. Again, the tiger image as a whole may have spatial relations to another image in my dream, for example to an image resembling a palm tree. But suppose we have to ask how far it is from the foot of my bed, whether it is three inches long, or longer or shorter; is it not obvious that these questions are absurd ones? We cannot answer them, not because we lack the necessary information or find it impracticable to make the necessary measurements, but because the questions themselves have no meaning. In the space of the physical world these images are nowhere at all. But in relation to other images of mine, each of them is somewhere. Each of them is extended, and its parts are in spatial relations to one another. There is no a priori reason why all extended entities must be in physical space.

If we now apply these considerations to the next world, as I am conceiving of it, we see that the question "where is it?" simply does not arise. An image-world would have a space of its own. We could not find it anywhere in the space of the physical world, but this would not in the least prevent it from being a spatial world all the same. If you like, it would be its own "where."[4]

I am tempted to illustrate this point by referring to the fairy-tale of Jack and the Beanstalk. I am not of course suggesting that we should take the story seriously. But if we were asked to try to make sense of it, how should we set about it? Obviously the queer world which Jack found was not at the top of the beanstalk in the literal, spatial sense of the words "at the top of." Perhaps he found some very large pole rather like a beanstalk, and climbed up it. But (we shall say) when he got to the top he suffered an abrupt change of consciousness, and began to have a dream or waking vision of a strange country with a giant in it. To choose another and more respectable illustration: In Book VI of Vergil's *Aeneid*, we are told how Aeneas descended into the Cave of Avernus with the Sibyl and walked from there into the other world. If we wished to make the narrative of the illustrious poet intelligible, how should we set about it? We should suppose that Aeneas did go down into the cave, but that once he was there he suffered a change of consciousness, and all the strange experiences which happened afterwards—seeing the River Styx, the Elysian Fields and the rest—were part of a dream or vision which he had. The space he passed through in his journey was an image space, and the River Styx was not three Roman miles, or any other number of miles, from the cave in which his body was.

It follows that when we speak of "passing" from this world to the next, this passage is not to be thought of as any sort of movement in space. It should rather be thought of as a change of consciousness, analogous to the change which occurs when we "pass" from waking experience to dreaming. It would be a change from the perceptual type of consciousness to another type of consciousness in which perception ceases and

---

[4] Conceivably its geometrical structure might also be different from the geometrical structure of the physical world. In that case the space of the next world would not only be other than the space of the physical world, but would also be a different *sort* of space.

imaging replaces it, but unlike the change from waking consciousness to dreaming in being irreversible. I suppose that nearly everyone nowadays who talks of "passing" from this world to the other does think of the transition in this way, as some kind of irreversible change of consciousness, and not as a literal spatial transition in which one goes from one place to another place.

So much for the question "where the next world is," if there be one. I have tried to show that if the next world is conceived of as a world of mental images, the question simply does not arise. I now turn to another difficulty. It may be felt that an image-world is somehow a deception and a sham, not a real world at all. I have said that it would be a kind of dream-world. Now when one has a dream in this life, surely the things one is aware of in the dream are not *real* things. No doubt the dreamer really does have various mental images. These images do actually occur. But this is not all that happens. As a result of having these images, the dreamer believes, or takes for granted, that various material objects exist and various physical events occur; and these beliefs are mistaken. For example, he believes that there is a wall in front of him and that by a mere effort of will he succeeds in flying over the top of it. But the wall did not really exist, and he did not really fly over the top of it. He was in a state of delusion. Because of the images which he really did have, there *seemed* to him to be various objects and events which did not really exist at all. Similarly, you may argue, it may *seem* to discarnate minds (if indeed there are such) that there is a world in which they live, and a world not unlike this one. If they have mental images of the appropriate sort, it may even *seem* to them that they have bodies not unlike the ones they had in this life. But surely they will be mistaken. It is all very well to say, with the poet, that "dreams are real while they last"—that dream-objects are only called "unreal" when one wakes up, and normal sense-perceptions begin to occur with which

the dream experiences can be contrasted. And it is all very well to conclude from this that if one did *not* wake up, if the change from sense-perception to imaging were irreversible, one would not call one's dream-objects unreal, because there would then be nothing with which to contrast them. But would they not still *be* unreal for all that? Surely discarnate minds, according to my account of them, would be in a state of permanent delusion; whereas a dreamer in this life (fortunately for him) is only in a temporary one. And the fact that a delusion goes on for a long time, even forever and ever, does not make it any less delusive. Delusions do not turn themselves into realities just by going on and on. Nor are they turned into realities by the fact that their victim is deprived of the power of detecting their delusiveness.

Now, of course, if it were true that the next life (supposing there is one) is a condition of permanent delusion, we should just have to put up with it. We might not like it; we might think that a state of permanent delusion is a bad state to be in. But our likes and dislikes are irrelevant to the question. I would suggest, however, that this argument about the "delusiveness" or "unreality" of an image-world is based on confusion.

One may doubt whether there is any clear meaning in using the words "real" and "unreal" *tout court*, in this perfectly general and unspecified way. One may properly say, "this is real silver, and that is not," "this is a real pearl and that is not," or again "this is a real pool of water, and that is only a mirage." The point here is that something X is mistakenly believed to be something else Y, because it does resemble Y in some respects. It makes perfectly good sense, then, to say that X is not really Y. This piece of plated brass is not real silver, true enough. It only looks like silver. But for all that, it cannot be called "unreal" in the unqualified sense, in the sense of not existing at all. Even the mirage is something, though it is not the pool of water you took it to be. It is a perfectly good set of visual appearances, though it is not related to other appearances in the way you thought it was; for example, it does not have the relations to tactual appearances, or to visual appearances from other places, which you expected it to have. You may properly say that the mirage is not a real pool of water, or even that it is not a real physical object, and that anyone who thinks it is must be in a state of delusion. But there is no clear meaning in saying that it is just "unreal" *tout court*, without any further specification or explanation. In short, when the word "unreal" is applied to something, one means that it is different from something else, with which it might be mistakenly identified; what that something else is may not be explicitly stated, but it can be gathered from the context.

What, then, could people mean by saying that a next world such as I have described would be "unreal"? If they are saying anything intelligible, they must mean that it is different from something else, something else which it does resemble in some respects, and might therefore be confused with. And what is that something else? It is the present physical world in which we now live. An image-world, then, is only "unreal" in the sense that it is not really physical, though it might be mistakenly thought to be physical by some of those who experience it. But this only amounts to saying that the world I am describing would be an *other* world, other than this present physical world, which is just what it ought to be; other than this present physical world, and yet sufficiently like it to be possibly confused with it, because images do resemble percepts. And what would this otherness consist in? First, in the fact that it is a *space* which is other than physical space; secondly, and still more important, in the fact that the *causal laws* of an image-world would be different from the laws of physics. And this is also our ground for saying that the events we experience in dreams are "unreal," that is, not really physical, though mistakenly believed by the dreamer to be so. They do in some ways closely resemble physical events,

and that is why the mistake is possible. But the causal laws of their occurrence are quite different, as we recognize when we wake up; and just occasionally we recognize it even while we are still asleep.

Now let us consider the argument that the inhabitants of the other world, as I have described it, would be in a state of delusion. I admit that some of them might be. That would be the condition of the people described in the mediumistic communications already referred to—the people who "do not realize that they are dead." Because their images are so like the normal percepts they were accustomed to in this life, they believe mistakenly that they are still living in the physical world. But, as I already tried to explain, their state of delusion need not be permanent and irremediable. By attending to the relations between one image and another, and applying the ordinary inductive methods by which we ourselves have discovered the casual laws of this present world in which *we* live, they too could discover in time what the causal laws of *their* world are. These laws, we may suppose, would be more like the laws of Freudian psychology than the laws of physics. And once the discovery was made, they would be cured of their delusion. They would find out, perhaps with surprise, that the world they were experiencing was *other* than the physical world which they experienced before, even though like it in some respects.

Let us now try to explore the conception of a world of mental images a little more fully. Would it not be a *"subjective"* world? And surely there would be many *different* next worlds, not just one; and each of them would be private. Indeed, would there not be as many next worlds as there are discarnate minds, and each of them wholly private to the mind which experiences it? In short, it may seem that each of us, when dead, would have his own dream-world, and there would be no common or public next world at all.

"Subjective," perhaps, is a rather slippery word. Certainly, an image-world would have to be subjective in the sense of being mind-dependent, dependent for its existence upon mental processes of one sort or another; images, after all, are mental entities. But I do not think that such a world need be completely private, if telepathy occurs in the next life. I have already mentioned the part which telepathic apparitions might play in it in connection with Mr. Flew's contention that "people are what you meet." But there is more to be said. It is reasonable to suppose that in a disembodied state telepathy would occur more frequently than it does now. It seems likely that in this present life our telepathic powers are constantly being inhibited by our need to adjust ourselves to our physical environment. It even seems likely that many telepathic "impressions" which we receive at the unconscious level are shut out from consciousness by a kind of biologically motivated censorship. Once the pressure of biological needs is removed, we might expect that telepathy would occur continually, and manifest itself in consciousness by modifying and adding to the images which one experiences. (Even in this life, after all, some dreams are telepathic.)

If this is right, an image-world such as I am describing would not be the product of one single mind only, nor would it be purely private. It would be the joint product of a group of telepathically interacting minds and public to all of them. Nevertheless, one would not expect it to have unrestricted publicity. It is likely that there would still be *many* next worlds, a different one for each group of like-minded personalities. I admit I am not quite sure what might be meant by "like-minded" and "unlike-minded" in this connection. Perhaps we could say that two personalities are like-minded if their memories or their characters are sufficiently similar. It might be that Nero and Marcus Aurelius do not have a world in common, but Socrates and Marcus Aurelius do.

So far, we have a picture of many "semi-public" next worlds, if one may put it so; each of them composed of mental images, and yet not wholly private

for all that, but public to a limited group of telepathically interacting minds. Or, if you like, after death everyone does have his own dream, but there is still some overlap between one person's dream and another's because of telepathy.

I have said that such a world would be mind-dependent, even though dependent on a group of minds rather than a single mind. In what way would it be mind-dependent? Presumably in the same way as dreams are now. It would be dependent on the *memories* and the *desires* of the persons who experienced it. Their memories and their desires would determine what sort of images they had. If I may put it so, the "stuff" or "material" of such a world would come in the end from one's memories, and the "form" of it from one's desires. To use another analogy, memory would provide the pigments, and desire would paint the picture. One might expect, I think, that desires which had been unsatisfied in one's earthly life would play a specially important part in the process. That may seem an agreeable prospect. But there is another which is less agreeable. Desires which had been *repressed* in one's earthly life, because it was too painful or too disgraceful to admit that one had them, might also play a part, and perhaps an important part, in determining what images one would have in the next. And the same might be true of repressed memories. It may be suggested that what Freud (in one stage of his thought) called "the censor"—the force or barrier or mechanism which keeps some of our desires and memories out of consciousness, or only lets them in when they disguise themselves in symbolic and distorted forms—operates only in this present life and not in the next. However we conceive of "the censor," it does seem to be a device for enabling us to adapt ourselves to our environment. And when we no longer have an environment, one would expect that the barrier would come down.

We can now see that an after-death world of mental images can also be quite reasonably described in the terminology of the Hindu thinkers as "a world of desire" (Rama Loka). Indeed, this is just what we should expect if we assume that dreams, in this present life, are the best available clue to what the next life might be like. Such a world could also be described as "a world of memories"; because imaging, in the end, is a function of memory, one of the ways in which our memory-dispositions manifest themselves. But this description would be less apt, even though correct as far as it goes. To use the same rather inadequate language as before, the "materials" out of which an image-world is composed would have to come from the memories of the mind or group of minds whose world it is. But it would be their desires (including those repressed in earthly life) which determined the way in which these memories were used, the precise kind of dream which was built up out of them or on the basis of them.

It will, of course, be objected that memories cannot exist in the absence of a physical brain, nor yet desires, nor images either. But this proposition, however plausible, is after all just an empirical hypothesis, not a necessary truth. Certainly there is empirical evidence in favour of it. But there is also empirical evidence against it. Broadly speaking one might say, perhaps, that the "normal" evidence tends to support this materialistic or epiphenomenalist theory of memories, images, and desires, whereas the "supernormal" evidence on the whole tends to weaken the materialist or epiphenomenalist theory of human personality (of which this hypothesis about the brain-dependent character of memories, images, and desires is a part). Moreover, any evidence which directly supports the Survival Hypothesis (and there is quite a lot of evidence which does, provided we are prepared to admit that the Survival Hypothesis is intelligible at all) is *pro tanto* evidence against the materialistic conception of human personality.

In this lecture, I am not trying to argue in favour of the Survival Hypothesis. I am only concerned with the more modest task of trying to make it intelligible. All I want to maintain, then, is that there is nothing self-contradictory or logically absurd in the hypothesis that memories, desires, and images can exist in the absence of a physical brain. The hypothesis may, of course, be false. My point is only that it is not absurd; or if you like, that it is at any rate intelligible, whether true or not. To put the question in another way, when we are trying to work out for ourselves what sort of thing a discarnate life might conceivably be (if there is one) we have to ask what kind of *equipment*, so to speak, a discarnate mind might be supposed to have. It cannot have the power of sense-perception, nor the power of acting on the physical world by means of efferent nerves, muscles, and limbs. What would it have left? What could we take out with us, as it were, when we pass from this life to the next? What we take out with us, I suggest, can only be our memories and desires, and the power of constructing out of them an image world to suit us. Obviously we cannot take our material possessions out with us; but I do not think this is any great loss, for if we remember them well enough and are sufficiently attached to them, we shall be able to construct image-replicas of them which will be just as good, and perhaps better.

In this connection I should like to mention a point which has been made several times before. Both Whately Carington and Professor Ducasse have referred to it, and no doubt other writers have. But I believe it is of some importance and worth repeating. Ecclesiastically minded critics sometimes speak rather scathingly of the "materialistic" character of mediumistic communications. They are not at all edified by these descriptions of agreeable houses, beautiful landscapes, gardens, and the rest. And then, of course, there is Raymond Lodge's notorious cigar.[5] These critics

[5] See: Sir Oliver Lodge, *Raymond Revised* (London: Methuen & Co., Ltd., 1922), p. 113.

complain that the next world as described in these communications is no more than a reproduction of this one, slightly improved perhaps. And the argument apparently is that the "materialistic" character of the communications is evidence against their genuineness. On the contrary, as far as it goes, it is evidence *for* their genuineness. Most people in this life do like material objects and are deeply interested in them. This may be deplorable, but there it is. If so, the image-world they would create for themselves in the next life might be expected to have just the "materialistic" character of which these critics complain. If one had been fond of nice houses and pleasant gardens in this life, the image-world one would create for himself in the next might be expected to contain image-replicas of such objects, and one would make these replicas as like "the real thing" as one's memories permitted; with the help, perhaps, of telepathic influences from other minds whose tastes were similar. This would be all the more likely to happen if one had not been able to enjoy such things in this present life as much as one could wish.

But possibly I have misunderstood the objection which these ecclesiastical critics are making. Perhaps they are saying that if the next world is like this, life after death is not worth having. Well and good. If they would prefer a different sort of next world, and find the one described in these communications insipid and unsatisfying to their aspirations, then they can expect to get a different one—in fact, just the sort of next world they want. They have overlooked a crucial point which seems almost obvious; that if there is an after-death life at all, there must surely be many next worlds, separate from and as it were impenetrable to one another, corresponding to the *different* desires which different groups of discarnate personalities have.

The belief in life after death is often dismissed as "mere wish-fulfilment." Now it will be noticed that the next world as I have been trying to con-

ceive of it is precisely a wish-fulfilment world, in much the same sense in which some dreams are described as wish-fulfilments. Should not this make a rational man very suspicious of the ideas I am putting before you? Surely this account of the other world is "too good to be true"? I think not. Here we must distinguish two different questions. The question whether human personality continues to exist after death is a question of fact, and wishes have nothing to do with it one way or the other. But *if* the answer to this factual question were "Yes" (and I emphasise the "if"), wishes might have a very great deal to do with the kind of world which discarnate beings would live in. Perhaps it may be helpful to consider a parallel case. It is a question of fact whether dreams occur in this present life. It has been settled by empirical investigation, and the wishes of the investigators have nothing to do with it. It is just a question of what the empirical facts are, whether one likes them or not. Nevertheless, granting that dreams do occur, a man's wishes might well have a very great deal to do with determining what the content of his dreams is to be; especially unconscious wishes on the one hand, and on the other, conscious wishes which are not satisfied in waking life. Of course the parallel is not exact. There is one very important difference between the two cases. With dreams, the question of fact is settled. It is quite certain that many people do have dreams. But in the case of survival, the question of fact is not settled, or not at present. It is still true, however, that though wishes have nothing to do with it, they have a very great deal to do with the kind of world we should live in after death, *if* we survive death at all.

But perhaps this does not altogether dispose of the objection that my account of the other world is "too good to be true." Surely a sober-minded and cautious person would be very shy of believing that there is, or even could be, a world in which all our wishes are fulfilled? How very suspicious we are about travellers' tales of Eldorado or descriptions of idyllic South Sea islands! Certainly we are, and on good empirical grounds. For they are tales about this present material world; and we know that matter is very often recalcitrant to human wishes. But in a dream-world Desire is king. This objection would only hold good if the world I am describing were supposed to be some part of the *material* world—another planet perhaps, or the Earthly Paradise of which some poets have written. But the next world as I am trying to conceive of it (or rather next worlds, for we have seen that there would be many different ones) is not of course supposed to be part of the material world at all. It is a dream-like world of mental images. True enough, some of these images might be expected to resemble some of the material objects with which we are familiar now; but only if, and to the extent that, their percipients *wanted* this resemblance to exist. There is every reason, then, for being suspicious about descriptions of this present material world, or alleged parts of it, on the ground that they are "too good to be true"; but when it is a "country of the mind" (if one may say so) which is being described, these suspicions are groundless. A purely mind-dependent world, if such a world there be, would *have* to be a wish-fulfilment world.

Nevertheless, likes and dislikes, however irrelevant they may be, do of course have a powerful psychological influence upon us when we consider the problem of survival; not only when we consider the factual evidence for or against, but also when we are merely considering the theoretical implications of the Survival Hypothesis itself, as I am doing now. It is therefore worthwhile to point out that the next world as I am conceiving of it need not necessarily be an agreeable place at all. If arguments about what is good or what is bad did have any relevance, a case could be made out for saying that this conception of the next world is "too bad to be true," rather than too good. As we have seen, we should have to reckon with

many different next worlds, not just with one. The world you experience after death would depend upon the kind of person you are. And if what I have said so far has any sense in it, we can easily conceive that some people's next worlds would be much more like purgatories than paradises—and pretty unpleasant purgatories too.

This is because there are *conflicting* desires within the same person. Few people, if any, are completely integrated personalities, though some people come nearer to it than others. And sometimes when a man's desires appear (even to himself) to be more or less harmonious with one another, the appearance is deceptive. His conscious desires do not conflict with one another or not much; but this harmony has only been achieved at the cost of repression. He has unconscious desires which conflict with the neatly organized pattern of his conscious life. If I was right in suggesting that repression is a biological phenomenon, if the "threshold" between conscious and unconscious no longer operates in a disembodied state, or operates much less effectively, this seeming harmony will vanish after the man is dead. To use scriptural language, the secrets of his heart will be revealed—at any rate to himself. These formerly repressed desires will manifest themselves by appropriate images, and these images might be exceedingly horrifying—as some dream-images are in this present life, and for the same reason. True enough, they will be "wish-fulfilment" images, like everything else that he experiences in the next world as I am conceiving it. But the wishes they fulfil will conflict with other wishes which he also has. And the emotional state which results might be worse than the worst nightmare; worse, because the dreamer cannot wake up from it. For example, in his after-death dream world he finds himself doing appallingly cruel actions. He never did them in his earthly life. Yet the desire to do them was there, even though repressed and unacknowledged. And now the lid is off, and this cruel desire fulfils itself by creating appropriate images. But unfortunately for his comfort, he has benevolent desires as well, perhaps quite strong ones; and so he is distressed and even horrified by these images, even though there is also a sense in which they are just the ones he wanted. Of course his benevolent desires too may be expected to manifest themselves by appropriate wish-fulfilment images. But because there is this conflict in his nature, they will not wholly satisfy him either. There will be something in him which rejects them as tedious and insipid. It is a question of the point of view, if one cares to put it so. Suppose a person has two conflicting desires A and B. Then from the point of view of desire A, the images which fulfil desire B will be unsatisfying, or unpleasant, or even horrifying; and vice versa from the point of view of desire B. And unfortunately, both points of view belong to the same person. He occupies them both at once.

This is not all. If psychoanalysts are right, there is such a thing as a desire to be punished. Most people, we are told, have guilt-feelings which are more or less repressed; we have desires, unacknowledged or only half-acknowledged, to suffer for the wrongs we have done. These desires too will have their way in the next world, if my picture of it is right, and will manifest themselves by images which fulfil them. It is not a very pleasant prospect, and I need not elaborate it. But it looks as if everyone would experience an image-purgatory which exactly suits him. It is true that his unpleasant experiences would not literally be punishments, any more than terrifying dreams are in this present life. They would not be inflicted upon him by an external judge; though, of course, if we are theists, we shall hold that the laws of nature, in other worlds as in this one, are in the end dependent on the will of a Divine Creator. Each man's purgatory would be just the automatic consequence of his own desires; if you like, he would punish himself by having just those images which his own good

feelings demand. But, if there is any consolation in it, he would have these unpleasant experiences because he *wanted* to have them; exceedingly unpleasant as they might be, there would still be something in him which was satisfied by them.

There is another aspect of the conflict of desires. Every adult person has what we call "a character"; a set of more or less settled and permanent desires, with the corresponding emotional dispositions, expressing themselves in a more or less predictable pattern of thoughts, feelings, and actions. But it is perfectly possible to desire that one's character should be different, perhaps very different, from what it is at present. This is what philosophers call a "second-order" desire, a desire that some of one's own desires should be altered. Such second-order desires are not necessarily ineffective, as New Year resolutions are supposed to be. People can within limits alter their own characters, and sometimes do; and if they succeed in doing so, it is in the end because they *want* to. But these "second-order" desires—desires to alter one's own character—are seldom effective immediately; and even when they appear to be, as in some cases of religious conversion, there has probably been a long period of subconscious or unconscious preparation first. To be effective, desires of this sort must occur again and again. I must go on wishing to be more generous or less timid, and not just wish it on New Year's day; I must train myself to act habitually—and think too—in the way that I should act and think if I possessed the altered character for which I wish. From the point of view of the present moment, however, one's character is something fixed and given. The wish I have at half-past twelve today will do nothing, or almost nothing, to alter it.

These remarks may seem very remote from the topic I am supposed to be discussing. But they have a direct bearing on a question which has been mentioned before: whether, or in what sense, the next world as I am conceiving of it should be called a "subjective" world. As I have already said, a next world such as I have described *would* be subjective, in the sense of mind-dependent. The minds which experience it would also have created it. It would just be the manifestation of their own memories and desires, even though it might be the joint creation of a number of telepathically interacting minds, and therefore not wholly private. But there is a sense in which it might have a certain objectivity all the same. One thing we mean by calling something "objective" is that it is so whether we like it or not, and even if we dislike it. This is also what we mean by talking about "hard facts" or "stubborn facts."

At first sight it may seem that in an image-world such as I have described there could be no hard facts or stubborn facts, and nothing objective in this sense of the word "objective." How could there be, if the world we experience is itself a wish-fulfilment world? But a man's character *is* in this sense "objective"; objective in the sense that he has it whether he likes it or not. And facts about his character are as "hard" or "stubborn" as any. Whether I like it or not, and even though I dislike it, it is a hard fact about me that I am timid or spiteful, that I am fond of eating oysters or averse from talking French. I may wish sometimes that these habitual desires and aversions of mine were different, but at any particular moment this wish will do little or nothing to alter them. In the short run, a man's permanent and habitual desires are something "given" which he must accept and put up with as best he can, even though in the very long run they are alterable.

Now in the next life, according to my picture of it, it would be these permanent and habitual desires which would determine the nature of the world in which a person has to live. His world would be, so to speak, the outgrowth of his character; it would be his own character represented before him in the form of dream-like images. There is therefore a sense in which he gets exactly the sort of world he wants, whatever internal conflicts there may be between one of these wants and another. Yet he may very well dislike having the sort of character he does have. In the short run, as I have said, his character is something fixed and given, and objective in the sense that he has that character whether he likes it or not. Accordingly his image-world is also objective in the same sense. It is objective in the sense that it insists on presenting itself to him whether he likes it or not.

To look at the same point in another way: the next world as I am picturing it may be a very queer sort of world, but still it would be subject to causal laws. The laws would not, of course, be the laws of physics. As I have suggested already, they might be expected to be more like the laws of Freudian psychology. But they would be laws all the same, and objective in the sense that they hold good whether one liked it or not. And if we do dislike the image-world which our desires and memories create for us—if, when we get what we want, we are horrified to discover what things they were which we wanted—we shall have to set about altering our characters, which might be a very long and painful process.

Some people tell us, of course, that all desires, even the most permanent and habitual ones, will wear themselves out in time by the mere process of being satisfied. It may be so, and perhaps there is comfort in the thought. In that case the dream-like world of which I have been speaking would only be temporary, and we should have to ask whether after the next world there is a next but one. The problem of survival would then arise again in a new form. We should have to ask whether personal identity could still be preserved when we were no longer even dreaming. It could, I think, be preserved through the transition from this present, perceptible world to a dream-like image world of the kind I have been describing. But if even imaging were to cease, would there be anything left of human personality at all? Or would the state of existence—if any—which followed be one to which the notion of personality, at any rate our present notion, no longer had any application? I think that these are questions upon which it is unprofitable and perhaps impossible to speculate. (If anyone wishes to make the attempt, I can only advise him to consult the writings of the mystics, both Western and Oriental.) It is quite enough for us to consider what the *next* world might conceivably be like, and some of you may think that even this is too much.

Before I end, I should like to make one concluding remark. You may have noticed that the next world, according to my account of it, is not at all unlike what some metaphysicians say *this* world is. In the philosophy of Schopenhauer, this present world itself, in which we now live, is a world of "will and idea." And so it is in Berkeley's philosophy too; material objects are just collections of "ideas," though according to Berkeley the will which presents these ideas to us is the will of God, acting directly upon us in a way which is in effect telepathic. Could it be that these idealist metaphysicians have given us a substantially correct picture of the next world, though a mistaken picture of this one? The study of metaphysical theories is out of question nowadays. But perhaps students of psychical research would do well to pay some attention to them. *If* there are other worlds than this (again I emphasize the "if") who knows whether with some stratum of our personalities we are not living in them now, as well as in this present one which conscious sense-perception discloses? Such a repressed and unconscious awareness of a world different from this one might be expected to break through into consciousness occasionally in the course of human history, very likely in a distorted form, and this might be the source of those very queer ideas which we read of with so much incredulity and astonishment in the writings of some speculative metaphysicians. Not knowing their source, they mistakenly applied these ideas to this world in which we now live, embellishing them sometimes with an elaborate façade of deductive reasoning. Viewed in cold blood and with a skeptical eye, their attempts may appear extremely unconvincing and their deductive reasoning fallacious. But perhaps, without knowing it, they may have valuable hints to give us if we are trying to form some conception, however tentative, of "another world." And this is something we must try to do if we take the problem of survival seriously.

Is Religious
Language
Meaningful?

Is Being Testable
a Condition of Being Intelligible?

*A*ntony *Flew* lays down a challenge to the religious believer who accepts "God exists" as true. This statement cannot be true unless it is also meaningful. For any meaningful statement that is not true or false simply by definition, there must be some conceivable state of affairs which, if it occurred and were known, would count as evidence that the statement was false. Thus even though we have good evidence that George Washington was the first U.S. President, we can at least conceive of finding evidence that he was not. In so doing, we admit that it is conceivable that Washington was not the first President; we know what, for example, "Thomas Jefferson was the first U.S. President" *means*. But in the case of "God exists," what evidence would count against its being true? For the theist, Flew suggests, no evidence could possibly count against God's existence. Therefore "God exists" is not a genuine assertion at all and cannot possibly be false; if it cannot be false, it cannot be true either; as far as truth and falsity are concerned, it is meaningless.

R. M. Hare grants the thrust of Flew's argument and offers a flanking movement. He introduces the concept of a "blik." While not the most lucid concept ever formulated, the notion of a blik does clarify certain things about

what Hare intends. Bliks are to be classified as beliefs that are not empirically verifiable or falsifiable. (Hare contrasts them to "more normal beliefs").
Though bliks are neither true nor false, they are presupposed by explanations,
and at least some of them can be (in some sense) wrong (*see* Hare's example
of the man who believes he is in danger from Oxford dons or instructors).
Still the examples Hare gives of bliks provide a pretty mixed bag, and it
seems clear that if the concept of a blik is to be of help in understanding
theological statements, it must first be clarified far beyond anything that Hare
offers. As it is, it provides a point of departure rather than a destination.

Basil Mitchell's response is apparently straightforward. The existence of
evil counts as evidence against "God loves us," but not as conclusive evidence.
Mitchell adds, however, that no believer can admit that any evidence *could*
count decisively against his religious beliefs. This is altogether dubious. A
man may admit the conceivability of conclusive evidence that he is not married
but know perfectly well that there is in fact no such evidence. Analogously
a believer may admit the conceivability of a world in which men *only* suffer
and in which it would be clear that no God existed who loved them but
may know that in fact there is no such evidence and (since God does love
us) never will be. Nonetheless the response from Flew elicited by Mitchell's
remarks is revealing and important.

Mitchell, we have seen, agrees with Flew that theological propositions
must be viewed (if possible) as assertions and that one could conceive of
evidence that would prove them false. Indeed, there is at least apparent evidence
that "God loves us," for example, is false—namely, the fact of evil. For
Mitchell the evidence is *only* an apparent disproof of God's existence. For
Flew the existence of evil is incompatible with the existence of God. (Flew
thus assumes a thesis that, as we saw in the section on the problem of evil,
is quite complex and disputable.) In reply to Mitchell, Flew admits that he
can offer only a disjunction: either "God exists" is meaningless or "God exists"
is (due to the existence of evil) false. The latter half of the disjunction depends
for its plausibility on an issue that is not clearly to be decided in Flew's favor.
So perhaps, even on Flew's ground, "God exists" is meaningful, but not
falsified by the existence of evil.

Flew's response to Hare is brief and pointed. Bliks, Hare says, are not
assertions. For any view rightly called Christian (and Flew could have added
"or Jewish"), "God loves us" is an assertion. So Hare's analysis works only
for a quite heterodox theology. Second, bliks cannot serve as *reasons* for
beliefs or actions as theological statements do, in the reflections of believers.
So the analysis Hare offers is again not successful for theological statements
as normally used.

John Hick also responds to Flew's challenge but in a way markedly different from Hare's and Mitchell's. He appeals to the notion of "eschatological
verification"—verification in terms of events that occur after the death of the
individual who experiences those events. (Hick's article is therefore also relevant
to the topic dealt with by Price under the question "Is man immortal?")

Hick agrees that assertions must be empirically testable. (It is worth
mentioning that not all philosophers grant this claim. He thus asks: what empirical evidence would in fact verify "God exists"? For Hick, to verify means to

remove ignorance or uncertainty concerning the truth or falsity of some statement. He suggests that ignorance or uncertainty concerning whether "God exists" is true could be removed by a man's surviving his death and discovering that his new environment has certain properties. He describes these properties.

There are, I suggest, two possible developments of our experience such that, if they occurred in conjunction with one another (whether in this life or in another life to come) they would assure us beyond rational doubt of the reality of God, as conceived in the Christian faith. These are, first, an experience of the fulfillment of God's purpose for ourselves, as this has been disclosed in the Christian revelation; in conjunction, second, with an experience of God as he has revealed himself in the person of Christ.

Several remarks may help in clarifying Hick's program and appraising its chances for success. First, it might seem that one could only *verify* the claim that "God exists" along the lines Hick suggests. For if no one survived his death, no one could have the "developments of experience" Hick mentions. But of course one could survive and have other sorts of experience that might falsify the claim in question. So while there is no doubt an asymmetry between verification and falsification (see Hick's examples), it does not, on Hick's account, apply in the case of "God exists." Second, as Hick himself notes in the parenthetic comment in the quotation above, there is nothing *logically* impossible about verification occurring in *this* life. So, if Hick requires only that the claim "God exists" be, under *conceivable* conditions, empirically verified or falsified, reference to empirical evidence attained *after one's death* is superfluous. Third, perhaps only *some* people could, even after death, have the "developments of experience" which, according to Hick, would verify "God exists." Hick notes that these developments can perhaps "only be experienced by those who have . . . faith" in God now. This is not sufficient reason to discount such developments as positive evidence; that one can attain this evidence only by meeting specified conditions (making certain commitments) is also true for, as examples, "Parenthood has satisfactions that override its frustrations" and "Acting unselfishly is its own reward." Fourth, even when such phrases as "The fulfillment of God's purpose for ourselves" receive the clarification they obviously require (what exactly will *count* as fulfillment?), and if it is clear how postmortem experiences will be *less* ambiguous with respect to providing evidence of God's existence than present experience is, postmortem experiences will still be somewhat ambiguous in the sense that they can (without contradiction) be interpreted in more than one way. This is compatible with there being only one *plausible* interpretation. Finally, as Hick intends, his account of what would verify the claim that God exists is developed quite explicitly within the context of Christian theology. (One could, of course, develop a similar account in the context of other religious systems.) But this means that the plausibility of the claim that were these experiences to occur, we *would* have verification of "God exists" depends squarely on the acceptability of Christian theology as a context of thought in which such experiences can be interpreted. This raises large and important issues, which cannot be discussed here; but this point remains clear: a given interpretation of an experience verifies a claim only if the conceptual context within which the interpretation occurs is acceptable. This shifts the issue from one of empirical confirmation or disconfirmation of a single statement to a more complex one of appraising conceptual schemes. As his book *Faith and Knowledge* reveals, Hick is well aware of (and sympathetic toward) this line of reasoning (compare his comment in footnote 6). This is, perhaps, the logical development of reflection upon Flew's original challenge, even though it may seem far removed from the apparent simplicity of that challenge.

Religious Language Is Not Meaningful
ANTONY FLEW

Let us begin with a parable. It is a parable developed from a tale told by John Wisdom in his haunting and revelatory article "Gods." Once upon a time two explorers came upon a clearing in the jungle. In the clearing were growing many flowers and many weeds. One explorer says, "Some gardener must tend this plot." The other disagrees, "There is no gardener." So they pitch their tents and set a watch. No gardener is ever seen. "But perhaps he is an invisible gardener." So they set up a barbed-wire fence. They electrify it. They patrol with bloodhounds. (For they remember how H. G. Wells's *The Invisible Man* could be both smelt and touched through he could not be seen.) But no shrieks ever suggest that some intruder has received a shock. No movements of the wire ever betray an invisible climber. The bloodhounds never give cry. Yet still the Believer is not convinced. "But there is a gardener, invisible, intangible, insensible to electric shocks, a gardener who has no scent and makes no sound, a gardener who comes secretly to look after the garden which he loves." At last the Skeptic despairs, "But what remains of your original assertion? Just how does what you call an invisible, intangible, eternally elusive gardener differ from an imaginary gardener or even from no gardener at all?"

In this parable we can see how what starts as an assertion, that something exists or that there is some analogy between certain complexes of phenomena, may be reduced step by step to an altogether different status, to an expression perhaps of a "picture preference."[1] The skeptic says there is no gardener. The Believer says there is a gardener (but invisible, etc.). One man talks about sexual behaviour. Another man prefers to talk of Aphrodite (but knows that there is not really a superhuman person additional to, and somehow responsible for, all sexual phenomena). The process of qualification may be checked at any point before the original assertion is completely withdrawn and something of that first assertion will remain (tautology). Mr. Wells's invisible man could not, admittedly, be seen, but in all other respects he was a man like the rest of us. But though the process of qualification may be, and of

[1] Cf. J. Wisdom, "Other Minds," *Mind* (1940), reprinted in his *Other Minds* (Oxford: Basil Blackwell, 1952).

FROM: *New Essays in Philosophical Theology*, Antony Flew and Alasdair MacIntyre, eds. (New York: The Macmillan Co.; and London: Student Christian Movement Press Limited, 1955), pp. 275–295. Reprinted by permission of the publishers and Professor R. M. Hare. This is the source of this essay and the following three, which form one symposium.

course usually is, checked in time, it is not always judiciously so halted. Someone may dissipate his assertion completely without noticing that he has done so. A fine brash hypothesis may thus be killed by inches, the death by a thousand qualifications.

And in this, it seems to me, lies the peculiar danger, the endemic evil, of theological utterance. Take such utterances as "God has a plan," "God created the world," "God loves us as a father loves his children." They look at first sight very much like assertions, vast cosmological assertions. Of course, this is no sure sign that they either are, or are intended to be, assertions. But let us confine ourselves to the cases where those who utter such sentences intend them to express assertions. (Merely remarking parenthetically that those who intend or interpret such utterances as crypto-commands, expressions of wishes, disguised ejaculations, concealed ethics, or as anything else but assertions are unlikely to succeed in making them either properly orthodox or practically effective.)

Now to assert that such and such is the case is necessarily equivalent to denying that such and such is not the case. Suppose then that we are in doubt as to what someone who gives vent to an utterance is asserting, or suppose that, more radically, we are skeptical as to whether he is really asserting anything at all, one way of trying to understand (or perhaps it will be to expose) his utterance is to attempt to find what he would regard as counting against, or as being incompatible with, its truth. For if the utterance is indeed an assertion, it will necessarily be equivalent to a denial of the negation of that assertion. And anything which would count against the assertion, or which would induce the speaker to withdraw it and to admit that it had been mistaken, must be part of (or the whole of) the meaning of the negation of that assertion. And to know

the meaning of the negation of an assertion is as near as makes no matter to know the meaning of that assertion. And if there is nothing which a putative assertion denies then there is nothing which it asserts either: and so it is not really an assertion. When the Skeptic in the parable asked the Believer, "Just how does what you call an invisible, intangible, eternally elusive gardener differ from an imaginary gardener or even from no gardener at all?" he was suggesting that the Believer's earlier statement had been so eroded by qualification that it was no longer an assertion at all.

Now it often seems to people who are not religious as if there was no conceivable event or series of events the occurrence of which would be admitted by sophisticated religious people to be a sufficient reason for conceding "There wasn't a God after all" or "God does not really love us then." Someone tells us that God loves us as a father loves his children. We are reassured. But then we see a child dying of inoperable cancer of the throat. His earthly father is driven frantic in his efforts to help, but his Heavenly Father reveals no obvious sign of concern. Some qualification is made—God's love is "not a merely human love" or it is "an inscrutable love," perhaps—and we realize that such sufferings are quite compatible with the truth of the assertion that "God loves us as a father (but, of course, . . .)." We are reassured again. But then perhaps we ask: what is this assurance of God's (appropriately qualified) love worth, what is this apparent guarantee really a guarantee against? Just what would have to happen not merely (morally and wrongly) to tempt but also (logically and rightly) to entitle us to say "God does not love us" or even "God does not exist"? I therefore put to the succeeding symposiasts the simple central questions, "What would have to occur or to have occurred to constitute for you a disproof of the love of, or of the existence of, God?"

A Reply to Flew (1)

R. M. HARE

I wish to make it clear that I shall not try to defend Christianity in particular, but religion in general—not because I do not believe in Christianity, but because you cannot understand what Christianity is, until you have understood what religion is.

I must begin by confessing that, on the ground marked out by Flew, he seems to me to be completely victorious. I therefore shift my ground by relating another parable. A certain lunatic is convinced that all dons want to murder him. His friends introduce him to all the mildest and most respectable dons that they can find, and after each of them has retired, they say, "You see, he doesn't really want to murder you; he spoke to you in a most cordial manner; surely you are convinced now?" But the lunatic replies "Yes, but that was only his diabolical cunning; he's really plotting against me the whole time, like the rest of them; I know it I tell you." However many kindly dons are produced, the reaction is still the same.

Now we say that such a person is deluded. But what is he deluded about? About the truth or falsity of an assertion? Let us apply Flew's test to him. There is no behaviour of dons that can be enacted which he will accept as counting against his theory; and therefore his theory, on this test, asserts nothing. But it does not follow that there is no difference between what he thinks about dons and what most of us think about them—otherwise we should not call him a lunatic and ourselves sane, and dons would have no reason to feel uneasy about his presence in Oxford.

Let us call that in which we differ from this lunatic, our respective *bliks*. He has an insane *blik* about dons; we have a sane one. It is important to realize that we save a sane one, not no *blik* at all; for there must be two sides to any argument—if he has a wrong *blik*, then those who are right about dons must

have a right one. Flew has shown that a *blik* does not consist in an assertion or system of them; but nevertheless it is very important to have the right *blik*.

Let us try to imagine what it would be like to have different *bliks* about other things than dons. When I am driving my car, it sometimes occurs to me to wonder whether my movements of the steering-wheel will always continue to be followed by corresponding alterations in the direction of the car. I have never had a steering failure, though I have had skids, which must be similar. Moreover, I know enough about how the steering of my car is made to know the sort of thing that would have to go wrong for the steering to fail—steel joints would have to part, or steel rods break, or something—but how do I know that this won't happen? The truth is, I don't know; I just have a *blik* about steel and its properties, so that normally I trust the steering of my car; but I find it not at all difficult to imagine what it would be like to lose this *blik* and acquire the opposite one. People would say I was silly about steel; but there would be no mistaking the reality of the difference between our respective *bliks*—for example, I should never go in a motor-car. Yet I should hesitate to say that the difference between us was the difference between contradictory assertions. No amount of safe arrivals or bench-tests will remove my *blik* and restore the normal one; for my *blik* is compatible with any finite number of such tests.

It was Hume who taught us that our whole commerce with the world depends upon our *blik* about the world; and that differences between *bliks* about the world cannot be settled by observation of what happens in the world. That was why, having performed the interesting experiment of doubting the ordinary man's *blik* about the world, and showing that no proof could be given to make us adopt one *blik* rather than another, he turned to backgammon to take his mind off the problem. It seems, indeed, to be impossible even to formulate as an assertion the normal *blik* about the world which makes me put my confidence in the future reliability of steel joints, in the continued ability of the road to support my car, and not gape beneath it revealing nothing below; in the general non-homicidal tendencies of dons; in my own continued well-being (in some sense of that word that I may not now fully understand) if I continue to do what is right according to my lights; in the general likelihood of people like Hitler coming to a bad end. But perhaps a formulation less inadequate than most is to be found in the Psalms: "The earth is weak and all the inhabiters thereof: I bear up the pillars of it."

The mistake of the position which Flew selects for attack is to regard this kind of talk as some sort of *explanation*, as scientists are accustomed to use the word. As such, it would obviously be ludicrous. We no longer believe in God as an Atlas—*nous n'avons pas besoin de cette hypothèse* [we have no need of that hypothesis]. But it is nevertheless true to say that, as Hume saw, without a *blik* there can be no explanation; for it is by our *bliks* that we decide what is and what is not an explanation. Suppose we believed that everything that happened, happened by pure chance. This would not of course be an assertion; for it is compatible with anything happening or not happening, and so, incidentally, is its contradictory. But if we had this belief, we should not be able to explain or predict or plan anything. Thus, although we should not be *asserting* anything different from those of a more normal belief, there would be a great difference between us; and this is the sort of difference that there is between those who really believe in God and those who really disbelieve in him.

The word "really" is important, and may excite suspicion. I put it in, because when people have had a good Christian upbringing, as have most of those who now profess not to believe in any sort of religion, it is very hard to discover what they really believe. The reason why they find it so easy to think that they are not religious is that they have never got into the frame of mind of one who suffers from the doubts to which religion is the answer. Not for them the terrors of the primitive jungle. Having abandoned some of the more picturesque fringes of religion, they think that they have abandoned the whole thing—whereas in fact they still have got, and could not live without, a religion of a comfortably substantial, albeit highly sophisticated, kind, which differs from that of many "religious people" in little more than this, that "religious people" like to sing Psalms about theirs—a very natural and proper thing to do. But nevertheless there may be a big difference lying behind—the difference between two people who, though side by side, are walking in different directions. I do not know in what direction Flew is walking; perhaps he does not know either. But we have had some examples recently of various ways in which one can walk away from Christianity, and there are any number of possibilities. After all, man has not changed biologically since primitive times; it is his religion that has changed, and it can easily change again. And if you do not think that such changes make a difference, get acquainted with some Sikhs and some Mussulmans of the same Punjabi stock; you will find them quite different sorts of people.

There is an important difference between Flew's parable and my own which we have not yet noticed. The explorers do not *mind* about their garden; they discuss it with interest, but not with concern. But my lunatic, poor fellow, minds about dons; and I mind about the steering of my car; it often has people in it that I care for. It is because I mind very much about what goes on in the garden in which I find myself, that I am unable to share the explorers' detachment.

A Reply to Flew (2)
BASIL MITCHELL

lew's article is searching and perceptive, but there is, I think, something odd about his conduct of the theologian's case. The theologian surely would not deny that the fact of pain counts against the assertion that God loves men. This very incompatibility generates the most intractable of theological problems—the problem of evil. So the theologian *does* recognize the fact of pain as counting against Christian doctrine. But it is true that he will not allow it—or anything—to count decisively against it; for he is committed by his faith to trust in God. His attitude is not that of the detached observer, but of the believer.

Perhaps this can be brought out by yet another parable. In time of war in an occupied country, a member of the resistance meets one night a stranger who deeply impresses him. They spend that night together in conversation. The Stranger tells the partisan that he himself is on the side of the resistance—indeed that he is in command of it, and urges the partisan to have faith in him no matter what happens. The partisan is utterly convinced at that meeting of the Stranger's sincerity and constancy and undertakes to trust him.

They never meet in conditions of intimacy again. But sometimes the Stranger is seen helping members of the resistance, and the partisan is grateful and says to his friends, "He is on our side."

Sometimes he is seen in the uniform of the police handing over patriots to the occupying power. On these occasions his friends murmur against him: but the partisan still says, "He is on our side." He still believes that, in spite of appearances, the Stranger did not deceive him. Sometimes he asks the Stranger for help and receives it. He is then thankful. Sometimes he asks and does not receive it. Then he says, "The Stranger knows best." Sometimes his friends, in exasperation, say "Well, what *would* he have to do for you to admit that you were wrong and that he is not on our side?" But the partisan refuses to answer. He will not consent to put the Stranger to the test. And sometimes his friends complain, "Well, if *that's* what you mean by his being on our side, the sooner he goes over to the other side the better."

The partisan of the parable does not allow anything to count decisively against the proposition "The Stranger is on our side." This is because he has committed himself to trust the Stranger. But he of course recognizes that the Stranger's ambiguous behaviour *does* count against what he believes about him. It is precisely this situation which constitutes the trial of his faith.

When the partisan asks for help and doesn't get it, what can he do? He can (*a*) conclude that the Stranger is not on our side; or (*b*) maintain that he is on our side, but that he has reasons for withholding help.

The first he will refuse to do. How long can he uphold the second position without its becoming just silly?

I don't think one can say in advance. It will depend on the nature of the impression created by the Stranger in the first place. It will depend, too, on the manner in which he takes the Stranger's behaviour. If he blandly dismisses it as of no consequence, as having no bearing upon his belief, it will be assumed that he is thoughtless or insane. And it quite obviously won't do for him to say easily, "Oh, when used of the Stranger the phrase 'is on our side' *means* ambiguous behaviour of this sort." In that case he would be like the religious man who says blandly of a terrible disaster "It is God's will." No, he will only be regarded as sane and reasonable in his belief, if he experiences in himself the full force of the conflict.

It is here that my parable differs

from Hare's. The partisan admits that many things may and do count against his belief: whereas Hare's lunatic who has a *blik* about dons doesn't admit that anything counts against his *blik*. Nothing *can* count against *bliks*. Also the partisan has a reason for having in the first instance committed himself, viz., the character of the Stranger; whereas the lunatic has no reason for his *blik* about dons—because, of course, you can't have reasons for *bliks*.

This means that I agree with Flew that theological utterances must be assertions. The partisan is making an assertion when he says, "The Stranger is on our side."

Do I want to say that the partisan's belief about the Stranger is, in any sense, an explanation? I think I do. It explains and makes sense of the Stranger's behaviour: it helps to explain also the resistance movement in the context of which he appears. In each case it differs from the interpretation which the others put upon the same facts.

"God loves men" resembles "the Stranger is on our side" (and many other significant statements, e.g., historical ones) in not being conclusively falsifiable. They can both be treated in at least three different ways: (1) as provisional hypotheses to be discarded if experience tells against them, (2) as significant articles of faith, (3) as vacuous formulae (expressing, perhaps, a desire for reassurance) to which experience makes no difference and which make no difference to life.

The Christian, once he has committed himself, is precluded by his faith from taking up the first attitude: "Thou shalt not tempt the Lord thy God." He is in constant danger, as Flew has observed, of slipping into the third. But he need not; and, if he does, it is a failure in faith as well as in logic.

A Response to Criticism
ANTONY FLEW

*I*t has been a good discussion; and I am glad to have helped to provoke it. But now . . . it must come to an end: and [I shall] make some concluding remarks. Since it is impossible to deal with all the issues raised or to comment separately upon each contribution, I will concentrate on Mitchell and Hare, as representative of two very different kinds of response to [my] challenge. . . .

The challenge, it will be remembered, ran like this. Some theological utterances seem to, and are intended to, provide explanations or express assertions. Now an assertion, to be an assertion at all, must claim that things stand thus and thus; *and not otherwise.* Similarly an explanation, to be an explanation at all, must explain why this particular thing occurs; *and not something else.* Those last clauses are crucial. And yet sophisticated religious people— or so it seemed to me—are apt to overlook this, and tend to refuse to allow, not merely that anything actually does occur, but that anything conceivably could occur, which would count against their theological assertions and explanations. But insofar as they do this their supposed explanations are actually bogus, and their seeming assertions are really vacuous.

Mitchell's response to this challenge is admirably direct, straightforward, and understanding. He agrees "that theological utterances must be assertions." He agrees that if they are to be assertions, there must be something that would count against their truth. He agrees, too, that believers are in constant danger of transforming their would-be assertions into "vacuous formulae." But he takes me to task for an oddity in my "conduct of the theologian's case. The theologian surely would not deny that the fact of pain counts against the assertion that God loves men. This very incompatibility generates the most intractable of theological problems, the problem of evil." I think he is right. I should have made a distinction between two very different ways of dealing with what looks like evidence against the love of God; the way I stressed was the expedient of qualifying the original assertion; the way the theologian usually takes, at first, is to admit that it looks bad but to insist that there is—there must be—some explanation which will show that, in spite of appearances, there really is a God who loves us. His difficulty, it seems to me, is that he has given God attributes which rule out all possible saving explanations. In Mitchell's parable of the Stranger it is easy for the believer to find plausible excuses for ambiguous behaviour; for the Stranger is a man. But suppose the Stranger is God. We cannot say that he would like to help but cannot; God is omnipotent. We cannot say that he would help if he only knew; God is omniscient. We cannot say that he is not responsible for the wickedness of others; God creates those others. Indeed an omnipotent, omniscient God must be an accessory before (and during) the fact to every human misdeed; as well as being responsible for every non-moral defect in the universe. So, though I entirely concede that Mitchell was absolutely right to insist against me that the theologian's first move is to look for an *explanation*, I still think that in the end, if relentlessly pursued, he will have to resort to the avoiding action of *qualification*. And there lies the danger of that death by a thousand qualifications, which would, I agree, constitute "a failure in faith as well as in logic."

Hare's approach is fresh and bold. He confesses that "on the ground marked out by Flew, he seems to me to be completely victorious." He therefore introduces the concept of *blik*. But while I think that there is room for some such concept in philosophy, and that philosophers should be grateful to Hare for

his invention, I nevertheless want to insist that any attempt to analyze Christian religious utterances as expressions or affirmations of a *blik* rather than as (at least would-be) assertions about the cosmos is fundamentally misguided. First, because thus interpreted they would be entirely unorthodox. If Hare's religion really is a *blik*, involving no cosmological assertions about the nature and activities of a supposed personal creator, then surely he is not a Christian at all? Second, because thus interpreted, they could scarcely do the job they do. If they were not even intended as assertions, then many religious activities would become fraudulent, or merely silly. If "You ought *because* it is God's will" asserts no more than "You ought," then the person who prefers the former phraseology is not really giving a reason, but a fraudulent substitute for one, a dialectical dud check. If "My soul must be immortal *because* God loves his children, etc." asserts no more than "My soul must be immortal," then the man who reassures himself with theological arguments for immortality is being as silly as the man who tries to clear his overdraft by writing his bank a check on the same account. (Of course neither of these utterances would be distinctively Christian; but this discussion never pretended to be so confined.) Religious utterances may indeed express false or even bogus assertions: but I simply do not believe that they are not both intended and interpreted to be or at any rate to presuppose assertions, at least in the context of religious practice, whatever shifts may be demanded, in another context, by the exigencies of theological apologetic.

One final suggestion. The philosophers of religion might well draw upon George Orwell's last appalling nightmare, *1984*, for the concept of *doublethink*. "*Doublethink* means the power of holding two contradictory beliefs simultaneously, and accepting both of them. The party intellectual knows that he is playing tricks with reality, but by the exercise of *doublethink* he also satisfies himself that reality is not violated." Perhaps religious intellectuals too are sometimes driven to doublethink in order to retain their faith in a loving God in face

of the reality of a heartless and indifferent world. But of this more another time, perhaps.

Religious Language Is Meaningful
JOHN HICK

To ask "Is the existence of God verifiable?" is to pose a question which is too imprecise to be capable of being answered. There are many different concepts of God, and it may be that statements employing some of them are open to verification or falsification while statements employing others of them are not. Again, the notion of verifying is itself by no means perfectly clear and fixed; and it may be that on some views of the nature of verification the existence of God is verifiable whereas on other views it is not.

Instead of seeking to compile a list of the various different concepts of God and the various possible senses of "verify," I wish to argue with regard to one particular concept of deity, namely the Christian concept, that divine existence is in principle verifiable; and as the first stage of this argument I must indicate what I mean by "verifiable."[1]

I

The central core of the concept of verification, I suggest, is the removal of ignorance or uncertainty concerning the truth of some proposition. That *p* is verified (whether *p* embodies a theory, hypothesis, prediction, or straightforward assertion) means that something happens which makes it clear that *p* is true. A question is settled so that there is no longer room for rational doubt concerning it. The way in which grounds for rational doubt are excluded varies of

[1] For the considerations that lead Hick to raise this question, see the preceding four essays.

course with the subject matter. But the general feature common to all cases of verification is the ascertaining of truth by the removal of grounds for rational doubt. Where such grounds are removed, we rightly speak of verification having taken place.

To characterize verification in this way is to raise the question whether the notion of verification is purely logical or is both logical and psychological. Is the statement that *p* is verified simply the statement that a certain state of affairs exists (or has existed), or is it the statement also that someone is aware that this state of affairs exists (or has existed) and notes that its existence establishes the truth of *p*? A geologist predicts that the earth's surface will be covered with ice in 15 million years time. Suppose that in 15 million years time the earth's surface *is* covered with ice, but that in the meantime the human race has perished, so that no one is left to observe the event or to draw any conclusion concerning the accuracy of the geologist's prediction. Do we now wish to say that his prediction has been verified, or shall we deny that it has been verified on the ground that there is no one left to do the verifying?

The use of "verify" and its cognates is sufficiently various to permit us to speak in either way. But the only sort of verification of theological propositions which is likely to interest us is one in which human beings participate. We may therefore, for our present purpose, treat verification as a logico-psychological rather than as a purely logical concept. I suggest then that "verify" be construed

FROM: *Theology Today*, "Eschatological Verification," April, 1960. Published by permission of editor and author.

as a verb which has its primary uses in the active voice: I verify, you verify, we verify, they verify or have verified. The impersonal passive, it is verified, now becomes logically secondary. To say that *p* has been verified is to say that (at least) someone has verified it, often with the implication that his or their report to this effect is generally accepted. But it is impossible, on this usage, for *p* to have been verified without someone having verified it. "Verification" is thus primarily the name for an event which takes place in human consciousness.[2] It refers to an experience, the experience of ascertaining that a given proposition or set of propositions is true. To this extent verification is a psychological notion. But of course it is also a logical notion. For needless to say, not *any* experience is rightly called an experience of verifying *p*. Both logical and psychological conditions must be fulfilled in order for verification to have taken place. In this respect, "verify" is like "know." Knowing is an experience which someone has or undergoes, or perhaps a dispositional state in which someone is, and it cannot take place without someone having or undergoing it or being in it; but not by any means every experience which people have, or every dispositional state in which they are, is rightly called knowing.

With regard to this logico-psychological concept of verification, such questions as the following arise. When *A*, but nobody else, has ascertained that *p* is true, can *p* be said to have been verified; or is it required that others also have undergone the same ascertainment? How public, in other words, must verification be? Is it necessary that *p* could in principle be verified by anyone without restriction even though perhaps only

A has in fact verified it? If so, what is meant here by "in principle"; does it signify, for example, that *p* must be verifiable by anyone who performs a certain operation; and does it imply that to do this is within everyone's power?

These questions cannot, I believe, be given any general answer applicable to all instances of the exclusion of rational doubt. The answers must be derived in each case from an investigation of the particular subject matter. It will be the object of subsequent sections of this article to undertake such an investigation in relation to the Christian concept of God.

Verification is often construed as the verification of a prediction. However verification, as the exclusion of grounds for rational doubt, does not necessarily consist in the proving correct of a prediction; a verifying experience does not always need to have been predicted in order to have the effect of excluding rational doubt. But when we are interested in the verifiability of propositions as the criterion for their having factual meaning, the notion of prediction becomes central. If a proposition contains or entails predictions which can be verified or falsified, its character as an assertion (though not of course its character as a true assertion) is thereby guaranteed.

Such predictions may be and often are conditional. For example, statements about the features of the dark side of the moon are rendered meaningful by the conditional predictions which they entail to the effect that if an observer comes to be in such a position in space, he will make such-and-such observations. It would in fact be more accurate to say that the prediction is always conditional, but that sometimes the conditions are so obvious and so likely to be fulfilled in any case that they require no special mention, while sometimes they require for their fulfillment some unusual expedition or operation. A prediction, for example, that the sun will rise within twenty-four hours is intended unconditionally, at least as concerns conditions to be fulfilled by the observer; he

[2] This suggestion is closely related to Carnap's insistence that, in contrast to "true," "confirmed" is time-dependent. To say that a statement is confirmed, or verified, is to say that it has been confirmed at a particular time—and, I would add, by a particular person. *See* Rudolf Carnap, "Truth and Confirmation," Feigl and Sellars, *Readings in Philosophical Analysis*, 1949, pp. 119 f.

is not required by the terms of the prediction to perform any special operation. Even in this case however there is an implied negative condition that he shall not put himself in a situation (such as immuring himself in the depths of a coal mine) from which a sunrise would not be perceptible. Other predictions however are explicitly conditional. In these cases it is true for any particular individual that in order to verify the statement in question he must go through some specified course of action. The prediction is to the effect that if you conduct such an experiment you will obtain such a result; for example, if you go into the next room you will have such-and-such visual experiences, and if you then touch the table which you see you will have such-and-such tactual experiences, and so on. The content of the "if" clause is always determined by the particular subject matter. The logic of "table" determines what you must do to verify statements about tables; the logic of "molecule" determines what you must do to verify statements about molecules; and the logic of "God" determines what you must do to verify statements about God.

In those cases in which the individual who is to verify a proposition must himself first perform some operation, it clearly cannot follow from the circumstances that the proposition is true that everybody has in fact verified it, or that everybody will at some future time verify it. For whether or not any particular person performs the requisite operation is a contingent matter.

II

What is the relation between verification and falsification? We are all familiar today with the phrase, "theology and falsification." Antony Flew[3] and others have raised instead of the question, "What possible experiences would verify 'God exists'?" the matching question

"What possible experiences would falsify 'God exists'? What conceivable state of affairs would be incompatible with the existence of God?" In posing the question in this way it was apparently assumed that verification and falsification are symmetrically related, and that the latter is apt to be the more accessible of the two.

In the most common cases, certainly, verification and falsification are symmetrically related. The logically simplest case of verification is provided by the crucial instance. Here it is integral to a given hypothesis that if, in specified circumstances, A occurs, the hypothesis is thereby shown to be true, whereas if B occurs the hypothesis is thereby shown to be false. Verification and falsification are also symmetrically related in the testing of such a proposition as "There is a table in the next room." The verifying experiences in this case are experiences of seeing and touching, predictions of which are entailed by the proposition in question, under the proviso that one goes into the next room; and the absence of such experience in those circumstances serves to falsify the proposition.

But it would be rash to assume, on this basis, that verification and falsification must always be related in this symmetrical fashion. They do not necessarily stand to one another as do the two sides of a coin, so that once the coin is spun it must fall on one side or the other. There are cases in which verification and falsification each correspond to a side on a different coin, so that one can fail to verify without this failure constituting falsification.

Consider, for example, the proposition that "there are three successive sevens in the decimal determination of π." So far as the value of π has been worked out, it does not contain a series of three sevens, but it will always be true that such a series may occur at a point not yet reached in anyone's calculations. Accordingly, the proposition may one day be verified if it is true, but can never be falsified if it is false.

The hypothesis of continued con-

[3] Antony Flew, "Theology and Falsification," reprinted above. On the philosophical antecedents of this change from the notion of verification to that of falsification, *see* Karl R. Popper, *The Logic of Scientific Discovery* (1934; E.T., 1959).

scious existence after bodily death provides an instance of a different kind of such asymmetry, and one which has a direct bearing upon the theistic problem. This hypothesis has built into it a prediction that one will after the date of one's bodily death have conscious experiences, including the experience of remembering that death. This is a prediction which will be verified in one's own experience if it is true, but which cannot be falsified if it is false. That is to say, it can be false, but *that* it is false can never be a fact which anyone has experientially verified. But this circumstance does not undermine the meaningfulness of the hypothesis, since it is also such that if it be true, it will be known to be true.

It is important to remember that we do not speak of verifying logically necessary truths, but only propositions concerning matters of fact. Accordingly verification is not to be identified with the concept of logical certification or proof. The exclusion of rational doubt concerning some matter of fact is not equivalent to the exclusion of the logical possibility of error or illusion. For truths concerning fact are not logically necessary. Their contrary is never self-contradictory. But at the same time the bare logical possibility of error does not constitute ground for rational doubt as to the veracity of our experience. If it did, no empirical proposition could ever be verified, and indeed the notion of empirical verification would be without use and therefore without sense. What we rightly seek, when we desire the verification of a factual proposition, is not a demonstration of the logical impossibility of the proposition being false (for this would be a self-contradictory demand), but such kind and degree of evidence as suffices, in the type of case in question, to exclude rational doubt.

III

These features of the concept of verification—that verification consists in the exclusion of grounds for rational doubt concerning the truth of some proposition; that this means its exclusion from particular minds; that the nature of the ex-

perience which serves to exclude grounds for rational doubt depends upon the particular subject matter; that verification is often related to predictions and that such predictions are often conditional; that verification and falsification may be asymmetrically related; and finally, that the verification of a factual proposition is not equivalent to logical certification— are all relevant to the verification of the central religious claim, "God exists." I wish now to apply these discriminations to the notion of eschatological verification, which has been briefly employed by Ian Crombie in his contribution to *New Essays in Philosophical Theology*,[4] and by myself in *Faith and Knowledge*.[5] This suggestion has on each occasion been greeted with disapproval by both philosophers and theologians. I am, however, still of the opinion that the notion of eschatological verification is sound; and further, that no viable alternative to it has been offered to establish the factual character of theism.

The strength of the notion of eschatological verification is that it is not an *ad hoc* invention but is based upon an actually operative religious concept of God. In the language of Christian faith, the word "God" stands at the center of a system of terms, such as Spirit, grace, Logos, incarnation, Kingdom of God, and many more; and the distinctly Christian conception of God can only be fully grasped in its connection with these related terms.[6] It belongs to a complex of notions which together constitute a picture of the universe in which we live, of man's place therein, of a comprehensive

[4] *Op. cit.*, p. 126.

[5] Ithaca: Cornell University Press and London: Oxford University Press. 1957, pp. 150–62.

[6] Its clear recognition of this fact, with regard not only to Christianity but to any religion, is one of the valuable features of Ninian Smart's *Reasons and Faiths* (1958). He remarks, for example, that "the claim that God exists can only be understood by reference to many, if not all, other propositions in the doctrinal scheme from which it is extrapolated" (p. 12).

divine purpose interacting with human purposes, and of the general nature of the eventual fulfillment of that divine purpose. This Christian picture of the universe, entailing as it does certain distinctive expectations concerning the future, is a very different picture from any that can be accepted by one who does not believe that the God of the New Testament exists. Further, these differences are such as to show themselves in human experience. The possibility of experiential confirmation is thus built into the Christian concept of God; and the notion of eschatological verification seeks to relate this fact to the problem of theological meaning.

Let me first give a general theological indication of this suggestion, by repeating a parable which I have related elsewhere,[7] and then try to make it more precise and eligible for discussion. Here, first, is the parable.

Two men are travelling together along a road. One of them believes that it leads to a Celestial City, the other that it leads nowhere; but since this is the only road there is, both must travel it. Neither has been this way before, and therefore neither is able to say what they will find around each next corner. During their journey they meet both with moments of refreshment and delight, and with moments of hardship and danger. All the time one of them thinks of his journey as a pilgrimage to the Celestial City and interprets the pleasant parts as encouragements and the obstacles as trials of his purpose and lessons in endurance, prepared by the king of that city and designed to make of him a worthy citizen of the place when at last he arrives there. The other, however, believes none of this and sees their journey as an unavoidable and aimless ramble. Since he has no choice in the matter, he enjoys the good and endures the bad. But for him there is no Celestial City to be reached, no all-encompassing purpose ordaining their journey; only the road itself and the luck of the road in good weather and in bad.

During the course of the journey the issue between them is not an experimental one. They do not entertain different expectations about the coming details of the road, but only about its ultimate destination. And yet when they do turn the last corner it will be apparent that one of them has been right all the time and the other wrong. Thus although the issue between them has not been experimental, it has nevertheless from the start been a real issue. They have not merely felt differently about the road; for one was feeling appropriately and the other inappropriately in relation to the actual state of affairs. Their opposed interpretations of the road constituted genuinely rival assertions, though assertions whose assertion-status has the peculiar characteristic of being guaranteed retrospectively by a future crux.

This parable has of course (like all parables) strict limitations. It is designed to make only one point: that Christian doctrine postulates an ultimate unambiguous state of existence *in patria* as well as our present ambiguous existence *in via*. There is a state of having arrived as well as a state of journeying, an eternal heavenly life as well as an earthly pilgrimage. The alleged future experience of this state cannot, of course, be appealed to as evidence for theism as a present interpretation of our experience; but it does suffice to render the choice between theism and atheism a real and not a merely empty or verbal choice. And although this does not affect the logic of the situation, it should be added that the alternative interpretations are more than theoretical, for they render different practical plans and policies appropriate now.

The universe as envisaged by the theist, then, differs as a totality from the universe as envisaged by the atheist. This difference does not, however, from our present standpoint within the universe, involve a difference in the objective content of each or even any of its passing moments. The theist and the atheist do not (or need not) expect different events to occur in the successive details of the temporal process. They do not (or need not) entertain divergent expectations of the course of history viewed from within. But the theist does and the atheist does not expect that when history is completed it will seem to have led to a particular end-state and to have fulfilled a specific purpose, namely that of creating "children of God."

IV

The idea of an eschatological verification of theism can make sense, however, only if the logically prior idea of continued personal existence after death is intelligible. A desultory debate on this topic has been going on for several years in some of the philosophical periodicals. C. I. Lewis has contended that the hypothesis of immortality "is an hypothesis about our own future experience. And our understanding of what would verify it has no lack of clarity."[8] And Morris Schlick agreed, adding. "We must conclude that immortality, in the sense defined [i.e. 'survival after death,' rather than 'never-ending life'], should not be regarded as a 'metaphysical problem,' but is an empirical hypothesis, because it possesses logical verifiability. It could be verified by following the prescription: 'Wait until you die!' "[9] However, others have challenged this conclusion, either on the ground that the phrase "surviving death" is self-contradictory in ordinary language or, more substantially, on the ground that the traditional distinction between soul and body cannot be sustained.[10] I should like to address myself to this latter view. The only self of which we know, it is said, is the empirical self, the walking, talking, acting, sleeping individual who lives, it may be, for some

sixty to eighty years and then dies. Mental events and mental characteristics are analyzed into the modes of behavior and behavioral dispositions of this empirical self. The human being is described as an organism capable of acting in the "high-level" ways which we characterize as intelligent, thoughtful, humorous, calculating, and the like. The concept of mind or soul is thus not the concept of a "ghost in the machine" (to use Gilbert Ryle's loaded phrase[11]) but of the more flexible and sophisticated ways in which human beings behave and have it in them to behave. On this view there is no room for the notion of soul in distinction from body; and if there is no soul in distinction from body there can be no question of the soul surviving the death of the body. Against this philosophical background the specifically Christian (and also Jewish) belief in the resurrection of the flesh or body, in contrast to the Hellenic notion of the survival of a disembodied soul, might be expected to have attracted more attention than it has. For it is consonant with the conception of man as an indissoluble psychophysical unity, and yet it also offers the possibility of an empirical meaning for the idea of "life after death."

Paul is the chief Biblical expositor of the idea of the resurrection of the body.[12] His view, as I understand it, is this. When someone has died he is, apart from any special divine action, extinct. A human being is by nature mortal and subject to annihilation by death. But in fact God, by an act of sovereign power, either sometimes or always resurrects or (better) reconstitutes or recreates him— not, however, as the identical physical organism that he was before death, but as a *soma pneumatikon* ("spiritual body") embodying the dispositional characteristics and memory traces of the deceased physical organism, and inhabiting an environment with which the *soma pneu-*

8 "Experience and Meaning," *Philosophical Review*, 1934, reprinted in Feigl and Sellars, *Readings in Philosophical Analysis,* 1949, p. 142.

9 "Meaning and Verification," *Philosophical Review,* 1936, reprinted in Feigl and Sellars, *op. cit.*, p. 160.

10 *See* e.g., A. G. N. Flew, "Death," *New Essays in Philosophical Theology*; "Can a Man Witness his own Funeral?" *Hibbert Journal,* 1956.

11 *The Concept of Mind,* 1949, which contains an important exposition of the interpretation of "mental" qualities as characteristics of behavior.

12 I Cor. 15.

matikon is continuous as the ante-mortem body was continuous with our present world. In discussing this notion we may well abandon the word "spiritual," as lacking today any precise established usage, and speak of "resurrection bodies" and of "the resurrection world." The principal questions to be asked concern the relation between the physical world and the resurrection world, and the criteria of personal identity which are operating when it is alleged that a certain inhabitant of the resurrection world is the same person as an individual who once inhabited this present world. The first of these questions turns out on investigation to be the more difficult of the two, and I shall take the easier one first.

Let me sketch a very odd possibility (concerning which, however, I wish to emphasize not so much its oddness as its possibility!), and then see how far it can be stretched in the direction of the notion of the resurrection body. In the process of stretching it will become even more odd than it was before; but my aim will be to show that, however odd, it remains within the bounds of the logically possible. This progression will be presented in three pictures, arranged in a self-explanatory order.

First picture: Suppose that at some learned gathering in this country one of the company were suddenly and inexplicably to disappear, and that at the same moment an exact replica of him were suddenly and inexplicably to appear at some comparable meeting in Australia. The person who appears in Australia is exactly similar, as to both bodily and mental characteristics, with the person who disappears in America. There is continuity of memory, complete similarity of bodily features, including even fingerprints, hair and eye coloration and stomach contents, and also of beliefs, habits, and mental propensities. In fact there is everything that would lead us to identify the one who appeared with the one who disappeared, except continuity of occupancy of space. We may suppose, for example, that a deputation of the colleagues of the man who

disappeared fly to Australia to interview the replica of him which is reported there, and find that he is in all respects but one exactly as though he had traveled from say, Princeton to Melbourne, by conventional means. The only difference is that he describes how, as he was sitting listening to Dr. Z. reading a paper, on blinking his eye he suddenly found himself sitting in a different room listening to a different paper by an Australian scholar. He asks his colleagues how the meeting had gone after he ceased to be there, and what they had made of his disappearance, and so on. He clearly thinks of himself as the one who was present with them at their meeting in the United States. I suggest that faced with all these circumstances his colleagues would soon, if not immediately, find themselves thinking of him and treating him as the individual who had so inexplicably disappeared from their midst. We should be extending our normal use of "same person" in a way which the postulated facts would both demand and justify if we said that the one who appears in Australia is the same person as the one who disappears in America. The factors inclining us to identify them would far outweigh the factors disinclining us to do this. We should have no reasonable alternative but to extend our usage of "the same person" to cover the strange new case.

Second picture: Now let us suppose that the event in America is not a sudden and inexplicable disappearance, and indeed not a disappearance at all but a sudden death. Only, at the moment when the individual dies, a replica of him as he was at the moment before his death, complete with memory up to that instant, appears in Australia. Even with the corpse on our hands, it would still, I suggest, be an extension of "same person" required and warranted by the postulated facts, to say that the same person who died has been miraculously re-created in Australia. The case would be considerably odder than in the previous picture, because of the existence of the corpse in America contemporaneously with the existence of the living person in Australia. But I submit that, although the oddness of this circumstance may be stated as strongly as you please, and can indeed hardly be overstated, yet it does not exceed the bounds of the logically possible. Once again we must imagine some of the deceased's colleagues going to Australia to interview the person who has suddenly appeared there. He would perfectly remember them and their meeting, be interested in what had happened, and be as amazed and dumbfounded about it as anyone else; and he would perhaps be worried about the possible legal complications if he should return to America to claim his property; and so on. Once again, I believe, they would soon find themselves thinking of him and treating him as the same person as the dead Princetonian. Once again the factors inclining us to say that the one who died and the one who appeared are the same person would outweigh the factors inclining us to say that they are different people. Once again we should have to extend our usage of "the same person" to cover this new case.

Third picture: My third supposal is that the replica, complete with memory, etc., appears, not in Australia, but as a resurrection replica in a different world altogether, a resurrection world inhabited by resurrected persons. This world occupies its own space, distinct from the space with which we are now familiar.[13] That is to say, an object in the resurrection world is not situated at any distance or in any direction from an object in our present world, although each object in either world is spatially related to each other object in the same world.

Mr. X, then, dies. A Mr. X replica, complete with the set of memory traces which Mr. X had at the last moment before his death, comes into existence. It is composed of other material than physical matter, and is located in a resurrection world which does not stand in any

spatial relationship with the physical world. Let us leave out of consideration St. Paul's hint that the resurrection body may be as unlike the physical body as is a full grain of wheat from the wheat seed, and consider the simpler picture in which the resurrection body has the same shape as the physical body.[14]

In these circumstances, how does Mr. X know that he has been resurrected or recreated? He remembers dying; or rather he remembers being on what he took to be his death-bed, and becoming progressively weaker until, presumably, he lost consciousness. But how does he know that (to put it Irishly) his "dying" proved fatal; and that he did not, after losing consciousness, begin to recover strength, and has now simply waked up?

The picture is readily enough elaborated to answer this question. Mr. X meets and recognizes a number of relatives and friends and historical personages whom he knows to have died; and from the fact of their presence, and also from their testimony that he has only just now appeared in their world, he is convinced that he has died. Evidences of this kind could mount up to the point at which they are quite as strong as the evidence which, in pictures one and two, convince the individual in question that he has been miraculously translated to Australia. Resurrected persons would be individually no more in doubt about their own identity than we are now, and would be able to identify one another in the same kinds of ways, and with a like degree of assurance, as we do now.

If it be granted that resurrected persons might be able to arrive at a rationally founded conviction that their existence is *post-mortem*, how could they know that the world in which they find themselves is in a different space from that in which their physical bodies were? How could such a one know that he is not in a like situation with the person in picture number two, who dies in America

---

[13] On this possibility, *see* Anthony Quinton, "Spaces and Times," *Philosophy*, XXXVII, No. 140 (April, 1962).

[14] As would seem to be assumed, for example, by Irenaeus (*Adversus Haereses*, Bk. II, Ch. 34, Sec. 1).

and appears as a full-blooded replica in Australia, leaving his corpse in the U.S.A. —except that now the replica is situated, not in Australia, but on a planet of some other star?

It is of course conceivable that the space of the resurrection world should have properties which are manifestly incompatible with its being a region of physical space. But on the other hand, it is not of the essence of the notion of a resurrection world that its space should have properties different from those of physical space. And supposing it not to have different properties, it is not evident that a resurrected individual could learn from any direct observations that he was not on a planet of some sun which is at so great a distance from our own sun that the stellar scenery visible from it is quite unlike that which we can now see. The grounds that a resurrected person would have for believing that he is in a different space from physical space (supposing there to be no discernible difference in spatial properties) would be the same as the grounds that any of us may have now for believing this concerning resurrected individuals. These grounds are indirect and consist in all those considerations (*e.g.*, Luke 16:26) which lead most of those who consider the question to reject as absurd the possibility of, for example, radio communication or rocket travel between earth and heaven.

V

In the present context my only concern is to claim that this doctrine of the divine creation of bodies, composed of a material other than that of physical matter, which bodies are endowed with sufficient correspondence of characteristics with our present bodies, and sufficient continuity of memory with our present consciousness, for us to speak of the same person being raised up again to life in a new environment, is not self-contradictory. If, then, it cannot be ruled out *ab initio* as meaningless, we may go on to consider whether and how it is related to the possible verification of Christian theism.

So far I have argued that a survival prediction such as is contained in the *corpus* of Christian belief is in principle subject to future verification. But this does not take the argument by any means as far as it must go if it is to succeed. For survival, simply as such, would not serve to verify theism. It would not necessarily be a state of affairs which is manifestly incompatible with the nonexistence of God. It might be taken just as a surprising natural fact. The atheist, in his resurrection body, and able to remember his life on earth, might say that the universe has turned out to be more complex, and perhaps more to be approved of, than he had realized. But the mere fact of survival, with a new body in a new environment, would not demonstrate to him that there is a God. It is fully compatible with the notion of survival that the life to come be, so far as the theistic problem is concerned, essentially a continuation of the present life, and religiously no less ambiguous. And in this event, survival after bodily death would not in the least constitute a final verification of theistic faith.

I shall not spend time in trying to draw a picture of a resurrection existence which would merely prolong the religious ambiguity of our present life. The important question, for our purpose, is not whether one can conceive of after-life experiences which would *not* verify theism (and in point of fact one can fairly easily conceive them), but whether one can conceive of after-life experiences which *would* serve to verify theism.

I think that we can. In trying to do so I shall not appeal to the traditional doctrine, which figures especially in Catholic and mystical theology, of the Beatific Vision of God. The difficulty presented by this doctrine is not so much that of deciding whether there are grounds for believing it, as of deciding what it means. I shall not, however, elaborate this difficulty, but pass directly to the investigation of a different and, as it seems to me, more intelligible possibility. This is the possibility not of a direct vision of God, whatever that might mean, but of a *situation* which points unambiguously to the existence of a loving God. This would be a situation which, so far as its religious significance is concerned, contrasts in a certain important respect with our present situation. Our present situation is one which in some ways seems to confirm and in other ways to contradict the truth of theism. Some events around us suggest the presence of an unseen benevolent intelligence and others suggest that no such intelligence is at work. Our situation is religiously ambiguous. But in order for us to be aware of this fact we must already have some idea, however vague, of what it would be for our situation to be not ambiguous, but on the contrary wholly evidential of God. I therefore want to try to make clearer this presupposed concept of a religiously unambiguous situation.

There are, I suggest, two possible developments of our experience such that, if they occurred in conjunction with one another (whether in this life or in another life to come), they would assure us beyond rational doubt of the reality of God, as conceived in the Christian faith. These are, *first*, an experience of the fulfillment of God's purpose for ourselves, as this has been disclosed in the Christian revelation; in conjunction, *second*, with an experience of communion with God as he has revealed himself in the person of Christ.

The divine purpose for human lfie, as this is depicted in the New Testament documents, is the bringing of the human person, in society with his fellows, to enjoy a certain valuable quality of personal life, the content of which is given in the character of Christ—which quality of life (*i.e.* life in relationship with God, described in the Fourth Gospel as eternal life) is said to be the proper destiny of human nature and the source of man's final self-fulfillment and happiness. The verification situation with regard to such a fulfillment is asymmetrical. On the one hand, so long as the divine purpose remains unfulfilled, we cannot know that it never will be fulfilled in the future; hence no final falsification is possible of the claim that this fulfillment will occur —unless, of course, the prediction contains a specific time clause which, in Christian teaching, it does not. But on the other hand, if and when the divine purpose *is* fulfilled in our own experience, we must be able to recognize and rejoice in that fulfillment. For the fulfillment would not be for us the promised fulfillment without our own conscious participation in it.

It is important to note that one can say this much without being cognizant in advance of the concrete form which such fulfillment will take. The before-and-after situation is analogous to that of a small child looking forward to adult life and then, having grown to adulthood, looking back upon childhood. The child possesses and can use correctly in various contexts the concept of "being grown-up," although he does not know, concretely, what it is like to be grown-up. But when he reaches adulthood he is nevertheless able to know that he has reached it; he is able to recognize the experience of living a grown-up life even though he did not know in advance just what to expect. For his understanding of adult maturity grows as he himself matures. Something similar may be supposed to happen in the case of the fulfillment of the divine purpose for human life. That fulfillment may be as far removed from our present condition as is mature adulthood from the mind of a little child; nevertheless, we possess already a comparatively vague notion of this final fulfillment, and as we move towards it our concept will itself become more adequate; and if and when we finally reach that fulfillment, the problem of recognizing it will have disappeared in the process.

The other feature that must, I suggest, be present in a state of affairs that would verify theism, is that the fulfillment of God's purpose be apprehended *as* the fulfillment of God's purpose and not simply as a natural state of affairs. To this end it must be accompanied by an experience of communion with God as he has made himself known to men in Christ.

The specifically Christian clause, "as he has made himself known to men in Christ," is essential, for it provides a solution to the problem of recognition in the awareness of God. Several writers have pointed out the logical difficulty involved in any claim to have encountered God.[15] How could one know that it was *God* whom one had encountered? God is described in Christian theology in terms of various absolute qualities, such as omnipotence, omnipresence, perfect goodness, infinite love, etc., which cannot as such be observed by us, as can their finite analogues, limited power, local presence, finite goodness, and human love. One can recognize that a being whom one "encounters" has a given finite degree of power, but how does one recognize that he has *un*limited power? How does one observe that an encountered being is *omni*present? How does one perceive that his goodness and love, which one can perhaps see to exceed any human goodness and love, are actually infinite? Such qualities cannot be given in human experience. One might claim, then, to have encountered a Being whom one presumes, or trusts, or hopes to be God; but one cannot claim to have encountered a Being whom one recognized to be the infinite, almighty, eternal Creator.

This difficulty is met in Christianity by the doctrine of the Incarnation—although this was not among the considerations which led to the formulation of that doctrine. The idea of incarnation provides answers to the two related questions: "How do we know that God has certain absolute qualities which, by their very nature, transcend human experience?" and "How can there be an eschatological verification of theism which is based upon a recognition of the presence of God in his Kingdom?"

In Christianity God is known as "the God and Father of our Lord Jesus Christ."[16] God is the Being about whom

Jesus taught; the Being in relation to whom Jesus lived, and into a relationship with whom he brought his disciples; the Being whose *agape* [self-giving love] toward men was seen on earth in the life of Jesus. In short, God is the transcendent Creator who has revealed himself in Christ. Now Jesus' teaching about the Father is a part of that self-disclosure, and it is from this teaching (together with that of the prophets who preceded him) that the Christian knowledge of God's transcendent being is derived. Only God himself knows his own infinite nature; and our human belief about that nature is based upon his self-revelation to men in Christ. As Karl Barth expresses it, "Jesus Christ is the knowability of God."[17] Our beliefs about God's infinite being are not capable of observational verification, being beyond the scope of human experience, but they are susceptible of indirect verification by the removal of rational doubt concerning the authority of Christ. An experience of the reign of the Son in the Kingdom of the Father would confirm that authority, and therewith, indirectly, the validity of Jesus' teaching concerning the character of God in his infinite transcendent nature.

The further question as to how an eschatological experience of the Kingdom of God could be known to be such has already been answered by implication. It is God's union with man in Christ that makes possible man's recognition of the fulfillment of God's purpose for man as being indeed the fulfillment of *God's* purpose for him. The presence of Christ in his Kingdom marks this as being beyond doubt the Kingdom of the God and Father of the Lord Jesus Christ.

It is true that even the experience of the realization of the promised Kingdom of God, with Christ reigning as Lord of the New Aeon, would not constitute a logical certification of his claims nor, accordingly, of the reality of God. But this will not seem remarkable to any philosopher in the empiricist tradition,

[15] For example, H. W. Hepburn, *Christianity and Paradox*, 1958, pp. 56f.

[16] II Cor. 11:31.

[17] *Church Dogmatics*, Vol. II, Pt. I, p. 150.

who knows that it is only a confusion to demand that a factual proposition be an analytic truth. A set of expectations based upon faith in the historic Jesus as the incarnation of God, and in his teaching as being divinely authoritative, could be so fully confirmed in *post-mortem* experience as to leave no grounds for rational doubt as to the validity of that faith.

VI

There remains of course the problem (which falls to the New Testament scholar rather than to the philosopher) whether Christian tradition, and in particular the New Trestament, provides a sufficiently authentic "picture" of the mind and character of Christ to make such recognition possible. I cannot here attempt to enter into the vast field of Biblical criticism, and shall confine myself to the logical point, which only emphasizes the importance of the historical question, that a verification of theism made possible by the Incarnation is dependent upon the Christian's having a genuine contact with the person of Christ, even though this is mediated through the life and tradition of the Church.

One further point remains to be considered. When we ask the question, "*To whom* is theism verified?" one is initially inclined to assume that the answer must be, "To everyone." We are inclined to assume that, as in my parable of the journey, the believer must be confirmed in his belief, and the unbeliever converted from his unbelief. But this assumption is neither demanded by the nature of verification nor by any means unequivocally supported by our Christian sources.

We have already noted that a verifiable prediction may be conditional. "There is a table in the next room" entails conditional predictions of the form: if someone goes into the next room he will see, etc. But no one is compelled to go into the next room. Now it may be that the predictions concerning human experience which are entailed by the proposition that God exists are conditional predictions and that no one is compelled to fulfill those conditions. Indeed we stress in much of our theology that the manner of the divine self-disclosure to men is such that our human status as free and responsible beings is respected, and an awareness of God is never forced upon us. It may then be a condition of *post-mortem* verification that we be already in some degree conscious of God by an uncompelled response to his modes of revelation in this world. It may be that such a voluntary consciousness of God is an essential element in the fulfillment of the divine purpose for human nature, so that the verification of theism which consists in an experience of the final fulfillment of that purpose can only be experienced by those who have already entered upon an awareness of God by the religious mode of apperception which we call faith.

If this be so, it has the consequence that only the theistic believer can find the vindication of his belief. This circumstance would not of course set any restriction upon who can become a believer, but it would involve that while theistic faith can be verified—found by one who holds it to be beyond rational doubt—yet it cannot be proved to the nonbeliever. Such an asymmetry would connect with that strand of New Testament teaching which speaks of a division of mankind even in the world to come.

Having noted this possibility I will only express my personal opinion that the logic of the New Testament as a whole, though admittedly not always its explicit content, leads to a belief in ultimate universal salvation. However, my concern here is not to seek to establish the religious facts, but rather to establish that there are such things as religious facts, and in particular that the existence or nonexistence of the God of the New Testament is a matter of fact, and claims as such eventual experiential verification.

Bibliography

PHILOSOPHY OF RELIGION

Abernathy, G. and Langford, T. *Philosophy of Religion*. 2d ed. New York: The Macmillan Company, 1968.

Alston, William. *Religious Belief and Philosophical Thought*. New York: Harcourt, Brace and World, Inc., 1963.

Baillie, John. *Our Knowledge of God*. New York: Charles Scribner's Sons, 1939.

Bevan, E. *Symbolism and Belief*. Boston: Beacon Press, 1957.

Cahn, Stephen. *Philosophy of Religion*. New York: Harper and Row, Publishers, 1970.

Campbell, C. A. *Selfhood and Godhood*. London: George Allen and Unwin Ltd., 1957.

Carnell, E. J. *Christian Commitment*. New York: The Macmillan Company, 1962.

Cullmann, Oscar. *Immortality of the Soul or Resurrection of the Body*. London: Epworth Press, 1958.

Farrar, A. *Finite and Infinite*. London: Dacre Press, 1943.

————. *The Glass of Vision*. London: Dacre Press, 1948.

Ferre, F. *Logic, Language and God*. New York: Harper and Row, Publishers, 1961.

Flew, A. *God and Philosophy*. New York: Harcourt, Brace and World, Inc., 1966.

Frank, E. *Philosophical Understanding and Religious Truth*. New York: Oxford University Press, Inc., 1945.

Hick, John. *Classical and Contemporary Readings in the Philosophy of Religion*. 2d ed. Englewood Cliffs, N.J.: Prentice-Hall, Inc., 1970.

————. *Faith and Knowledge*. 2d ed. Ithaca, N.Y.: Cornell University Press, 1966.

————, ed. *Faith and the Philosophers*. New York: St. Martin's Press, Inc., 1964.

————. *Philosophy of Religion*. Englewood Cliffs, N.J.: Prentice-Hall, Inc., 1963.

Hook, S., ed. *Religious Experience and Truth*. London: Oliver and Boyd Ltd., 1962.

James, William. *Essays on Faith and Morals*. New York: The World Publishing Company, 1962.

————. *The Varieties of Religious Experience*. New York: The New American Library, Inc., 1958.

————. *The Will To Believe*. New York: Dover Publishers, Inc., 1956.

Kant, Immanuel. *Religion Within the Limits of Reason Alone*. New York: Harper and Row, Publishers, 1960.

Lewis, C. S. *Mere Christianity*. New York: The Macmillan Company, 1956.

————. *Miracles*. New York: The Macmillan Company, 1955.

————. *Screwtape Letters*. London: William Collins Sons and Company, 1943.

Lewis, H. D. *Our Experience of God*. London: George Allen and Unwin Ltd., 1959.

MacGregor, G. and Robb, J. *Readings in Religious Philosophy*. Boston: Houghton Mifflin Company, 1963.

Martin, C. B. *Religious Belief*. Ithaca, N.Y.: Cornell University Press, 1959.

Mavrodes, G. *Belief in God*. New York: Random House, Inc., 1970.

———— and Hackett, S. *Problems and Perspectives in the Philosophy of Religion*. Boston: Allyn and Bacon, Inc., 1967.

McIntyre, A. C. *Metaphysical Beliefs*. London: SCM Press Ltd., 1957.

Mitchell, Basil. *Faith and Logic*. London: George Allen and Unwin Ltd., 1957.

Niebuhr, H. R. *The Meaning of Revelation*. New York: The Macmillan Company, 1941.

Niebuhr, R. *The Nature and Destiny of Man*. New York: Charles Scribner's Sons, 1941.

Pike, Nelson. *God and Timelessness*. New York: Schocken Books, Inc., 1970.

Plantinga, Alvin, ed. *Faith and Philosophy*. Grand Rapids, Mich.: Eerdmans Publishing Company, 1964.

————. *God and Other Minds*. Ithaca, N.Y.: Cornell University Press, 1967.

Ramsey, Ian, ed. *The Prospect for Metaphysics*. New York: Philosophical Library, Inc., 1961.

————. *Religious Language*. New York: The Macmillan Company, 1963.

Smart, Ninian. *Philosophers and Religious Truth.* London: SCM Press Ltd., 1964.

————. *Reasons and Faiths.* London: Routledge and Kegan Paul Ltd., 1958.

Smith, John. *Experience and God.* New York: Oxford University Press, Inc., 1968.

Stace, W. T. *Time and Eternity.* Princeton, N.J.: Princeton University Press, 1952.

Taylor, A. E. *The Faith of a Moralist.* New York: The Macmillan Company, 1932.

Temple, William. *Nature, Man and God.* New York: The Macmillan Company, 1956.

von Hugel, Baron. *Essays and Addresses.* 2 vols. London: J. M. Dent and Sons Ltd., 1921.

Yandell, Keith. *Basic Issues in the Philosophy of Religion.* Boston: Allyn and Bacon, Inc., 1971.

————. *God, Man and Religion.* New York: McGraw-Hill Book Company, forthcoming.